Cross to the Star

Jesse Joseph Engel

To my friends & Becca

Jesse Joseph Engel

Copyright © Jesse Joseph Engel 2019

Disclaimer

This is a work of nonfiction. No names have been changed, no characters invented, no events fabricated. The conversations in the book come from the author's recollections, though they are not written to represent word-for-word transcripts. Instead, the author has retold them in a way that evokes the feeling and meaning what was said and in all instances, the essence of the dialogue is accurate.

Quote from "The Ancient Hebrew Lexicon of the Bible; Pages 11-13" With permission from the Author Jeff A. Benner of Ancient Hebrew Thought.

Quotes and references by name and permission: The Authorized Version or King James Version (KJV), 1611, 1769. Outside of the United Kingdom, the KJV is in the public domain. Within the United Kingdom, the rights to the KJV are vested in the crown.

Quotes and references by name and permission: Complete Jewish Bible, an English version by David H. Stern, Published by Jewish New Testament Publications:

Messianic Jewish Publishers
6120 Day Long Lane
Clarksville, MD 21029

ISBN: 9781099388897

Copyright © 2019 by Jesse Joseph Engel

Acknowledgements

I truly want to give a special thank you to Jeff A. Benner who gave me permission to use his apt description of the use of Greek, Hebrew to the English language in "Chapter 15 – Greek via Hebrew." It is with a strong recommendation that you read his book "Ancient Hebrew Lexicon of the Bible" and subtitled "Hebrew Letters, Words and Root Defined within Their Ancient Cultural Context." As an Author I extend my gratitude to use this information in my book "Cross to the Star".

Also, my friend David Zimmerman took the time on my first draft to give me his input and hard work weeding through the draft. His suggestions and ideas led me to a rewrite of this book. His encouragement helped me to shape the next draft for the reader's enjoyment.

I extend my gratitude to Rabbi Reuel Dillion of Synagogue Chavurat HaMashiach of Spokane Valley, Washington; for sharing Shabbat & Moedim Service Introduction in Chapter 19. If you are in the area please stop in and enjoy the fellowship as I do, with my family of Messianic Believers.

Readers Response

We all believe in something higher in one way or another. At some point we have all had questions or don't quite understand something and after reading and rereading it's still not clear. So we seek out an answer from a pastor or someone we trust and guess what, every answer is different and causes more confusion. This was me!

I wanted to know the "why" and I wanted to understand His Word better. I often thought, "This can't be this difficult, it's not a secret code!" Jesse's new book, Cross to the Star, has the "why". Great news for me as his book hits all the more important topics and several of my questions. The one thing to realize when reading and studying Cross to the Star is you have references and not an opinion. Fact is where my walk started to take a turn for the better. I enjoy opinion but I choose to challenge it for fact. Jesse has provided fact and the basis for further challenge and study.

Get his new book and begin again in your walk with all the topics you might have questions on and the guidance of God's Word to help you understand.

Scott Freeman

This profound journey brings home a thought-provoking understanding that will validate your faith. And yet, puts in place a path that may not be that familiar to some. Combined with basic teaching and biblical history that is very well explained through scripture, God's word comes to life. And a brother's testimony that reveals trials and testing that would make anyone of us stronger in the faith and brought near to God. Shalom

David Zimmerman

The Author of this book has a great knowledge and spirit of the Bible. How his spirit brought him up from all the trial he faced. God is great His love is never ending. A great read for all of us who read it. May we learn to love God like He loved us, as your loving friend.

Sue Love.

Contents

Disclaimer 2

Acknowledgements 3

Readers Response 4

Dedication 8

Introduction 10

Chapter 1 - Born Again.. 12

Chapter 2 – Sin 19

Chapter 3 – Faith 30

Chapter 4 – Grace... 40

Chapter 5 – Salvation.. 43

Chapter 6 – Works... 49

Chapter 7- Baptism 52

Chapter 8 - Who Killed Jesus 57

Chapter 9 - Anti-Semitism....................................... 63

Chapter 10 – The Way 67

Chapter 11 - Legalism 76

Chapter 12 - The Law.. 81

Chapter 13 - Loving God 84

Chapter 14 – Sabbath (Shabbat)............................. 88

Chapter 15 - Greek via Hebrew 93

Chapter 16 – Yeshua... 97

Chapter 17 - First Messianic Believers 103

Chapter 18 - The Believer...................................... 114

   The Early Messianic Gentile Church 119

   The Messianic believers and Christian Church History ... 121

   Messianic Judaism Today.. 122

Chapter 19 - Messianic Synagogue 127

Chapter 20 – Greatest Commandment 131

Chapter 21 – Author's Journey 135

    The Darkness 135

    Love of God 139

    War 144

    Broken 152

    The Cross, Born Again 160

    Dreams 172

    Spirit of Wisdom 180

    Spirit of Understanding 188

    Spirit of Counsel 196

    Spirit of Strength 202

    Spirit of Knowledge 208

    Fear of God 218

    Living in the Spirit 228

    Troubles 233

    Joy 246

    Conviction 252

    Abandoned 266

    Fallen 275

    Returning Home 285

    Sarah 293

Dedication

This book is dedicated to the one who is seeking the truth about God and His Holy Word the Bible.

But seek ye first the kingdom of God, and his righteousness; and all these things shall be added unto you. (Matthew 6:33 KJV)

Then to the Born-again believers' who have been seeking the truth in the Scriptures. Who have been confronted with excuses for why the church is teaching, and doctrines do not match up with the Bible. I too have been left wanting an answer to how they can teach these doctrines made of men and not holding fast to the teachings of God.

But in vain they do worship me, teaching for doctrines the commandments of men.
(Matthew 15:9 KJV)

We all must take heed to the warning that is given in both the commonly referred to Old Testament and New Testament.

Ye shall not add unto the word which I command you, neither shall ye diminish ought from it, that ye may keep the commandments of the LORD your God which I command you. (Deuteronomy 4:2 KJV)

And if any man shall take away from the words of the book of this prophecy, God shall take away his part out of the book of life, and out of the holy city, and from the things which are written in this book. (Revelation 22:19 KJV)

This book is dedicated first and foremost to our Lord and God; Our Redeemer and Saviour Yeshua the Messiah. It is only by Him., We can do anything in this world or the world to come. He is everything to us; I was lost in life and a sinner with my pride, the adversary did not need to intervene; all the damage and sin in my life was my choice. Yeshua found his way into my heart, and the light of truth set me free from the bondage of sin. It is this life he gave me with the trials and troubles that made me secure. It is my prayer that you too fall in love with Gods' Holy Word.

"And ye shall know the truth, and the truth shall make you free." (John 8:32 KJV)

Lastly, to thank my wife Sarah for understanding the passion I have for the Scriptures; while I write this book, her support has meant a great deal to me. Proverbs 31:10-12 *"Who can find a capable wife? Her value is far beyond that of pearls. Her husband trusts her from his heart, and she will prove a great asset to him. She works to bring him good, not harm, all the days of her life."*

Introduction

For to me to live is Messiah, and to die is gain.

(Philippians 1:21)

The arrangement of this book is rather simplistic and to the point. Each chapter is arranged according to questions that I faced on my journey in the past. It is my hopes it can be used as a quick guide for the reader to use on their journey. Its order does not determine the importance of each chapter by any means; but it is my prayers that it will be a help on your journey to our desired destination.

The most important question I ask others can you present the Gospel of the Good News from the commonly referred to as the Old Testament? With emphases that the disciples of Jesus the Messiah (Yeshua his Jewish name), taught from the Old Testament. Yeshua quoted Deuteronomy more than any other Books of the Old Testament, which is the last book of the Torah. Note, that the Torah is the first five books of the Old Testament, which the Christian community refers to as the Pentitude.

About fifty percent of the New Testament is quotes and paraphrases' from the Old Testament. Keep in mind at that time the New Testament had not been canonized and written for over a century. Yeshua had died and risen, and his Disciples were all dead by the time it was canonized as scripture.

"All scripture is given by inspiration of God, and is profitable for doctrine, for reproof, for correction, for instruction in righteousness: That the man of God may be perfect, throughly furnished unto all good works."

(2 Timothy 3:16-17 KJV)

The word Torah means "Teaching or Instruction" it is most unfortunate that most Christian Bibles refer to it as the Law. God loves us and has given us instruction on how to live. Yeshua taught from these instructions and the Disciples turned the world on its ear with these instructions. Think for a moment can you present the Good News of the Gospel using the Torah? Something to think about as you take this journey from the "Cross to the Star."

As we go through chapter by chapter, these things that cause doubt and trouble deep within my soul. This research along my journey has built faith, hope, and direction overtime which gave me a strong foundation of God's Word. God says what he means and means what he says. God has a burning desire to have a personal relationship with every one of His children. So now, let us take this journey together, thus sharing some of these things, which I have discovered that may help your journey. When we arrive at the end of the book I will give my story and journey which I am still engaged in today; knowing God is with me in His Love, and most of all that I love Him, and His instructions for Life.

Chapter 1 - Born Again

"Yes, indeed," Yeshua answered him, "I tell you that unless a person is born again from above, he cannot see the Kingdom of God." (John 3:3 CJB)

Every journey has a starting point, but not all who start on a journey arrive at their chosen destination. If you are not prepared for the journey and have the right supplies to undertake this journey it could lead to a disastrous climax.

This journey you will need the Bible *(Basic Instructions Before Leaving Earth)* then follow the instructions on how to reach your destination. In the pages of this book gives the Basics to guide you on your journey to truth, the way and the life.

John 14:6 Yeshua said, *"I AM the Way; and the Truth and the Life; no one comes to the Father except through me.*

Getting to the heart of what it is to be born again. We need to read how Yeshua the Messiah explained this to a Pharisees, named Nicodemus, a ruler of the Jews. The story is found in John Chapter three. I have *paraphrased the scriptures to get to the point, but you need to do some research for yourself and test everything.

John 3: 1-2 *Nicodemus came to Yeshua by night, and said unto him, Rabbi, we know that thou art a teacher come from God: for no man can do these miracles that you do, except God be with him.*

When we undertake a journey it is very helpful to have a map and a compass. The following scriptures are here for your benefit to keep you on course to your destination.

Reference: John 19:38-42 - After Yeshua was crucified, Nicodemus and Joseph of Arimathaea, being a disciple of

Yeshua, but secretly for fear of the Jews, met with Pilate that he might give them permission to take the body of Yeshua. Pilate gave them permission then they took the body of Yeshua, and wrapped it in linen cloth with the spices, as the manner of the Jews. There in the garden this sepulcher had never been used; it was there they laid the body of Yeshua. It was getting late in the day not yet the evening, and Jewish preparation day was coming that evening. They hurried and did what they could then left.

1. Nicodemus secret meeting with Yeshua in John chapter three, we see later that Nicodemus may have made the journey to be born again.
2. John 7:52 A meeting of the religious order of the Jews, Nicodemus gives a rebuttal which was not well received. This conversation is interesting because of the lack of knowledge of Yeshua. It appears they were unaware that Yeshua was born in Bethlehem but, only knew he came from; "...out of Galilee ariseth no prophet."
3. Matthew 27:57 Joseph of Arimathaea a rich man became a disciple of Yeshua.
4. Mark15:43 Joseph of Arimathaea, an honorable counsellor, went in boldly unto Pilate, asking for the body of Yeshua.
5. John 19:38 Joseph of Arimathaea, being a disciple of Jesus, but secretly for fear of the Jews, asked Pilate for the body of Yeshua.

Later these side notes will be helpful as you continue on this journey. Touching a dead body and what the Torah says:

Numbers 9:6-10 "And *there were certain men, who were defiled by the dead body of a man, that they could not keep the Passover on that day: and they came before Moses and before Aaron on that day: And those men said unto him, We are defiled by the dead body of a man: wherefore are we kept back, that we may not offer an offering of the LORD in his appointed season among the children of Israel? And Moses said unto them, Stand still, and I will hear what the LORD will command concerning you.*

And the LORD Spake unto Moses, saying, Speak unto the children of Israel, saying, if any man of you or of your posterity shall be unclean by reason of a dead body, or be in a journey afar off, yet he shall keep the Passover unto the LORD.

Jewish time for a day – For that is how the Torah describes it in:

Genesis 1:5 "God called the light Day, and the darkness he called Night. So there was evening, and there was morning, one day."

The day begins with the onset of night by the morning. According to Jewish teachers, night and morning begin with sunset and sunrise respectively.

We now continue with the conversation between Yeshua and Nicodemus.* John 3: 3-9

Yes, indeed," Yeshua answered him, "I tell you that unless a person is born again from above, he cannot see the Kingdom of God."

Nicodemus replied, how can a man be born when he is old? Can he enter the second time into his mother's womb, and be born?

Yeshua's reply I say unto thee, except a man is born of water and of the Spirit; he cannot enter into the kingdom of God. That which is born of the flesh is flesh; and that which is born of the Spirit is spirit. Marvel not that I said unto you, that you must be born again. The wind blows where it wants to, and you hear its sound, but you don't know where it comes from or where it's going. That's how it is with everyone who has been born from the Spirit."

Nicodemus answered and said unto him, how can these things be?

Yeshua explained what it is to be born again, and it seems to be made quite simple and let's keep it that way. First we are born from our mothers when the water breaks forth then we arrive born of the flesh. Seems straight forward, to be born of the Spirit is to receive the Spirit of God into your life.

Being born of the flesh has its problems:

Job 15:14 "What is man, that he should be clean? And he which is born of a woman, that he should be righteous?"

Romans 7:5 "For when we were in the flesh, the motions of sins, which were by the law, did work in our members to bring forth fruit unto death."

The solution is to be born of the Spirit or to be born again. King David a man after Gods own heart said:

Psalms 51:10-12 *"Create in me a clean heart, O God; and renew a right spirit within me. Cast me not away from thy presence; and take not thy Holy Spirit from me. Restore unto me the joy of thy salvation; and uphold me with thy free spirit."*

1 Peter 1:3-5 *"Blessed be the God and Father of our Messiah Yeshua, which according to his abundant mercy hath (begotten us again) born again unto a lively hope by the resurrection of the Messiah Yeshua from the dead, To an inheritance incorruptible, and undefiled, and that fadeth not away, reserved in heaven for you, Who are kept by the power of God through faith unto salvation ready to be revealed in the last time."*

Suggest that you read 1 Peter 1:3-12 to understand the full thought and context of this scripture.

New heart – being born again of the Spirit, it is not a new idea it has been foretold by the prophets as shown in the following scriptures:

Ezekiel 18:31 *"Cast away from you all your transgressions, whereby ye have transgressed; and make you a new heart and a new spirit: for why will ye die, O house of Israel?"*

Ezekiel 36:26 *"A new heart also will I give you, and a new spirit will I put within you: and I will take away the stony heart out of your flesh, and I will give you an heart of flesh."*

We continue the discussion as Yeshua challenges Nicodemus says in:

 * John 3:10-15 *Yeshua answered him, "You hold the office of teacher in Yisra'el (Israel), and you don't know this? Yes, indeed! I tell you that what we speak about, we know; and what we give evidence of, we have seen; but you people don't accept our evidence! If you people don't believe me when I tell you about the things of the world, how will you believe me when I tell you about the things of heaven? No one has gone up into heaven; there is only the one who has come down from heaven, the Son of Man. Just as Moshe lifted up the serpent in the desert, so must the Son of Man be lifted up; so that everyone who trusts in him may have eternal life."*

Yeshua knowing Nicodemus's heart appeals to his position and status in Israel. Then Yeshua reveals an age old mystery to Nicodemus which had been an object of many discussions of the Jewish leaders and Rabbis over the years. This mystery was related to the serpent of brass Moses made reference in *Numbers 21:4-9 *"Then they traveled from Mount Hor on the road toward the Sea of Suf (Red Sea) in order to go around the land of Edom; but the people's tempers grew short because of the detour. The people spoke* *against God and against Moshe: "Why did you bring us up out of Egypt? To die in the desert? There's no real food, there's no water, and we're sick of this miserable stuff we're eating!" In response, Adonai (the word Adonai - LORD is often used instead of the proper name of God) sent poisonous snakes among the people; they bit the people, and many of Isra'el's people died. The people came to Moshe and said; "We sinned by speaking against Adonai and against you. Pray to Adonai that he rid us of these snakes." Moshe prayed for the people, and Adonai answered Moshe: "Make a poisonous snake and put it on a pole. When anyone who has been bitten sees it, he will live." Moshe made a bronze snake and put it on the pole; if a snake had bitten someone, then, when he looked toward the bronze snake, he stayed alive."*

The story opens the eyes of Nicodemus being a teacher and a student of the Torah this made a world of since. Unfortunate for us in western society we tend to read over this, not understanding the Jewish background and historic story of the children of Israel in the desert after leaving Egypt.

The point of the story is that after the children of Israel complained to Moses. Adonai (Used in the place of God's Holy Name) in this story which simply means LORD – Master. God sent poisonous snakes to bite the complaining people who are sinning against God's appointed deliverer Moses who led the people out of Egypt.

This is most important for us today. That all people of all Nations who sin against God not following the deliverer our Saviour from Sin (covered in future chapters). Man has been bitten by his old nature which is sinful and the serpent of old Satan leads us off the path of our journey in the desert.

Our Saviour Yeshua the Messiah took our sin upon himself and he was place on a cross, dies then rose again from the dead. This is the picture of Moses placing the bronze serpent on the pole and when the people looked upon it they were saved from the serpent's poison which is sin.

Taking a closer look at these scriptures in John 3:14-19; Yeshua explains the importance of why we must be born again, and what that means:

John 3:14-19 *"And as Moses lifted up the serpent in the wilderness, even so must the Son of man be lifted up; that whosoever believeth may in him have eternal life. For God so loved the world, that he gave his only begotten Son, that whosoever believeth on him should not perish, but have eternal life. For God sent not the Son into the world to judge the world; but that the world should be saved through him. He that believeth on him is not judged: he that believeth not hath been judged already, because he hath not believed on the name of the only begotten Son of God. And this is the judgment, that the light is come into the world, and men loved the darkness rather than the light; for their works were evil."*

It is imperative that we know we must be born again. But, this is only the first step on the journey to our destination. There will be mountains to climb and valleys to cross. Along the way there will be many obstacle's which we will be faced. Just how we handle these obstacles determines if our heart is focused on our devotion and most of all our commitment to God.

Chapter 2 – Sin

My people are destroyed for lack of knowledge: because thou hast rejected knowledge, I will also reject thee, that thou shalt be no priest to me: seeing thou hast forgotten the (teachings – Instructions) law of thy God, I will also forget thy children. (Hosea 4:6)

What is sin and how does it affect my life? This question must be resolved to continue on our journey to the desired destination. Having instructions, map and a compass is a good thing. Not having the knowledge to use them we can get lost. The understanding of what sin is and how to use this knowledge to navigate without getting lost, this is paramount in our journey. To make this journey we will encounter many obstacles. The first obstacle which takes many forms is sin.

Sin, what is sin? Let's see what the instruction manual for life has to say:

(Genesis 4:7) *"If you are doing what is good, shouldn't you hold your head high? And if you don't do what is good, sin is crouching at the door; it wants you, but you can rule over it."*

(James 1:13-15) *"No one being tempted should say, "I am being tempted by God." For God cannot be tempted by evil, and God himself tempts no one. Rather, each person is being tempted whenever he is being dragged off and enticed by the bait of his own desire. Then, having conceived, the desire gives birth to sin; and when sin is fully grown, it gives birth to death."*

(James 4:17) *"So then, anyone who knows the right thing to do and fails to do it is committing a sin.*

The word sin has been in use for thousands of years it is vitiated state of human nature in which the self is estranged from God. If we continue in sin it leads to death which is not the desired destination of our journey.

Sin or the sinful nature of man has a hold on our lives. This is why Yeshua said *"I tell you that unless a person is born again from above, he cannot see the Kingdom of God."*

Sin originated through disobedience to Gods instructions on how Adam and Eve were to conduct themselves in the garden. Later on as we see that sin began to grow in the next generation when Cain killed Able out of anger.

The condition of mankind has not improved over time; it has become worse in the many ways man has found to disobey God and openly defy God, even to the point to say there is no God. The justification for this is if there is no God then I can do what I want and there is no penalty. I find this liked to a man who says I do not believe in gravity ,and walks off a ten story building to prove this law of gravity has no power over him, The results, Death!

(Romans 5:12) *"Here is how it works: it was through one individual that sin entered the world, and through sin, death; and in this way death passed through to the whole human race, inasmuch as everyone sinned."*

As we continue on our journey we must identify temptations of sin that leads us off the desired path to our destination? If we can identify the pitfalls of sin then we can avoid these dangerous detours leading to the wrong destination. It is clear at this point to be born again is the first step on our journey to the desired destination.

(James 1:12) *"How blessed is the man who perseveres through temptation! For after he has passed the test, he will receive as his crown the Life which God has promised to those who love him."*

(Romans 3:23) "For all have sinned, and come short of the glory of God;"

Knowing that this condition of sin has infected all mankind, we must investigate where sin first entered the lives of mankind. Look to the Instruction Manual of life, the Bible we will find the answers to avoid this obstacle in our path on this journey. I encourage you to read Chapter Three of Genesis to further your knowledge of this subject. Using the Bible I will break down the strategy that the enemy (The Adversary – Satan) has been using effectively on man since that time, in the garden, were sin entered the lives of all mankind. As I *paraphrase the scriptures in Genesis 3:1-6, I encourage you to test everything and dig deeper into the Word of God.

* Genesis 3:1 *"Now the serpent (The Adversary) was very clever more than any wild animal which (The true Name of God is used here in Hebrew), God, had made. He said to the woman, "Did God really say, 'You are not to eat from any tree in the garden'?"*

1. Doubting the instructions of God is a real temptation. This should always be a red flag that there is danger ahead in our journey. This mine field you are about to enter is full of dangers that the Adversary has placed in your path, beware.

* Genesis 3:2-3 *"The woman said to the serpent (the Adversary), "We may eat from the fruit of the trees of the garden, but the fruit of the tree in the middle of the garden God said, 'You are neither to eat from it nor touch it, or you will die.' "*

At this point it appears that the woman indeed knew that they were not to eat of the tree and the punishment was death. The instructions were in her head but the understanding was not in her heart. Which leaves her open to the temptation.

*Genesis 3:4-5 *The serpent (the Adversary) reply, "It is not true that you will surely die; because God knows that on the day you eat from it, your eyes will be opened, and you will be like God, knowing good and evil."*

Now the doubt and the possibilities that God was wrong and the serpent (the Adversary) might be right leads to her into the mine field of doubt. This is a dangerous area, be warned, follow the Word of God it leads to Life.

*Proverbs 3:18 "She (the Word of God, His Instruction) is a tree of life to them that lay hold upon her (the Word of God, His Instruction): and happy is every one that retaineth her.

*Genesis 3:6 *the woman looked at the tree and though it was good for food, that it had a pleasing appearance and that the tree was desirable for making one wise, she took some of its fruit and ate. She also gave some to her husband, who was with her; and he ate.*

Let us break this down so we can identify Temptation before it becomes a sin. The Adversary the enemy uses this strategy from the very beginning of mankind on this earth and it has been deadly.

1. Doubting Gods instructions and thus thinking we are smarter than God. We take matters into our own hands.
2. We tend to dwell on the Idea until the desire is more important than God.
3. *Then Sin is born* when we give in to our own desires, which have become more important than obeying Gods instructions.

To fight off this temptation we must resist our own ideas of what is right and wrong.

*Proverbs 16:25 *There is a way that seems right to a man, but this leads to the ways of death.*

To identify the mine field of doubt that leads to destruction, Gods instructions are vital to our journey.

(Proverbs 3:5-8) *"Trust in the LORD with all thine heart; and lean not unto thine own understanding. In all thy ways acknowledge him, and he shall direct thy paths. Be not wise in thine own eyes: fear the LORD, and depart from evil. It shall be health to thy navel, and marrow to thy bones."*

We can now see how very important it is to read and understand the instructions that God has for us to follow, that we will complete our journey to the desired destination. The Bible (Basic Instructions Before Leaving Earth) is the instructions for Life. I find it interesting that the word "Law "used in most Bibles is a very poor translation. The word is "Torah" which means "Instruction or Teaching" in Hebrew and the meaning has been lost due to a Greek and a Western mind set. Over a period of time the idea that Torah means law has developed and has soured mother's milk, more this in the chapters ahead.

*Matthew 22:36-40 "Rabbi, (asking Yeshua referring to him as teacher) which of the mitzvot (Commandment) in the Torah (Teaching – Instructions) is the most important? Yeshua's reply, " 'you are to love Adonai (Referring to the proper name of God), your God with all your heart, with all your soul and with all your strength.' This is the greatest and most important mitzvah (commandment). And the second is similar to it, 'You are to love your neighbor as yourself.' All of the Torah (teachings –instructions) along with the Prophets is dependent on these two mitzvot (commandments)."

Yeshua's has summarized for us how to follow Gods Commandments. We can see that it starts with the condition of the heart (mind). What we dwell on or meditate on is very important to being obedient to God.

The word picture in Psalms 1:1-6 demonstrates this very idea, it shows us how to follow Gods instructions of the mind.

*Psalms 1:1-3 *blessed is the man that walks not in the counsel of the ungodly, or stands in the way of sinners, or sits on the seat of the scornful. But his delight is in the law (instructions) of the LORD; and in his law (Instructions) doth he meditate day and night. And he shall be like a tree planted by the rivers of water, that brings forth his fruit in his season; his leaf also shall not wither; and whatsoever he does shall prosper.*

But in contrast the person who does not take Gods word into his life is expounded on in *Psalms 1:4-6 *the ungodly are not so: but are like the chaff which the wind drifts away. Therefore the ungodly shall not stand in the judgment, or sinners in the congregation of the righteous. For the LORD knoweth the way of the righteous: but the way of the ungodly shall perish (Death).*

The next item Yeshua expounded on is to Love God with all our soul. The Soul is who we are, the very depths of our very existence. The soul is outwardly demonstrated in what we do and how we do it.

*Galatians 5:24-25 *"And they that are the Messiah's have crucified the flesh with the affections and lusts. If we live in the Spirit, let us also walk in the Spirit."*

The final but not the least of these is strength. This is the key to our journey to have victory in the path that leads us on our journey to our true destination.

Psalms 140:7 *"O GOD the Lord, the strength of my salvation, thou hast covered my head in the day of battle."*

The spiritual battle as well as the troubles and trials of this world are real. In Ephesians 6:10-18 uses a word picture of putting on Armour which comes from God. In the scriptures it describes the spiritual war and battles we are faced with daily. We must apply the Armour to defend ourselves from the Adversary and the darkness of the spiritual realm.

Ephesians 6:10-18 *"Finally, my brethren, be strong in the Lord, and in the power of his might. Put on the whole armour of God that ye may be able to stand against the wiles of the devil. For we wrestle not against flesh and blood, but against principalities, against powers, against the rulers of the darkness of this world, against spiritual wickedness in high places. Wherefore take unto you the whole armour of God that ye may be able to withstand in the evil day, and having done all, to stand. Stand therefore, having your loins girt about with truth, and having on the breastplate of righteousness; And your feet shod with the preparation of the gospel of peace; Above all, taking the shield of faith, wherewith ye shall be able to quench all the fiery darts of the wicked. And take the helmet of salvation, and the sword of the Spirit, which is the word of God: Praying always with all prayer and supplication in the Spirit, and watching thereunto with all perseverance and supplication for all saints;"*

Suggest you read the Book of Ephesians to become more equip with God's Word to proceed on the journey. The more we know about God's Word it will build your defenses for this spiritual battle we are all in. The war is raging right now for the Souls of all mankind.

Listed here are the items covered in Ephesians 6:10-18 which we need to understand and become experts in using each one. The armour is not complete without one of the items, we must use them all. We must also understand that this fight does not include people (Humans). But, the battle is *against principalities, against powers, against the rulers of the darkness of this world, against spiritual wickedness in high places. Wherefore take unto you the whole armour of*

God that ye may be able to withstand in the evil day, and having done all, to stand.

- **Truth**, it is the belt that holds the armour together. Psalms 33:4 *"For the word of the LORD is right; and all his works are done in truth."* We can rely on God and His Holy Word. Titus 1:2*"In hope of eternal life, which God, that cannot lie, promised before the world began;"* I encourage you to dig into the Scriptures seeking the truth and how it is so important to our journey. To grasp the thing we must meditate and dwell on is truth. In this scripture we see the truths we are to meditate on. Philippians 4:8-9 *"Finally, brethren, whatsoever things are true, whatsoever things are honest, whatsoever things are just, whatsoever things are pure, whatsoever things are lovely, whatsoever things are of good report; if there be any virtue, and if there be any praise, think on these things. Those things, which ye have both learned, and received, and heard, and seen in me, do: and the God of peace shall be with you."*
- **Righteousness** which is our breastplate that protects our heart (Mind). The battle is fought in the battleground of our minds. Therefore we must understand what is written in *2 Corinthians 10:3-6 *for though we walk in the flesh, we do not war after the flesh (against people): (For the weapons of our warfare are not carnal (not of this world), but mighty through God to the pulling down of strong holds ;) Casting down imaginations, and every high thing that is against God's Word which is itself against the knowledge of God, and bringing into captivity every thought to the obedience of Messiah; and having in a readiness to revenge (stop) all disobedience, when your obedience is full to overflowing in victory.*

- **Peace** – This is the very foundation of which we stand firm. This item is likened unto shoes that protect us as we walk along on our journey. For anyone who has taken a long hiking trip will confirm how important is to have good walking shoes. The Gospel which is the good news we received when we became born again. Romans 10:15 *"And how shall they preach, except they be sent? As it is written, how beautiful are the feet of them that preach the gospel of peace, and bring glad tidings of good things!"* This Peace is so powerful it is hard to fully express it, the Hebrew word Shalom is described in the following scripture to give you some idea of what Shalom (Peace) is: *Philippians 4:7 *And the peace of God, which passeth all understanding, shall keep your hearts and minds through Yeshua the Messiah.* We can share this peace with others on how God has enabled us to have victory over sin. Our testimony of how we live our lives and trust God for everything will speak volumes to people around us.
- **Faith** – Our shield to fight off the flaming arrows of the enemy (The adversary and the fallen ones who follow him). The very next chapter we will cover this topic more in depth. This scripture in Hebrews 11:1 gives an apt description of faith. *"Now faith is the substance of things hoped for, the evidence of things not seen."*
- **Salvation** – Which is likened to the helmet of the Armour, Which protects our head were reason, thinking and action takes place. In a future Chapter of this book, we will take a more in depth look at Salvation. This scripture in Psalms 18:2-3 gives an insightful word picture of Salvation: *"The LORD (Gods True Name) is my rock, and my fortress, and my deliverer; my God, my strength, in whom I will trust; my buckler, and the horn of my salvation, and*

my high tower. I will call upon the LORD (Gods True Name), who is worthy to be praised: so shall I be saved from mine enemies."* In this Psalm it depicts the warfare and the importance of our personal relationship with God. Being born again is a life style that is pleasing to God.

- **Word of God (The Bible) -** which is our sword of the Spirit, when we are born again we now are the Temple of God who dwelling in us. 1 Corinthians 6:19-20 *or don't you know that your body is a temple for the (Holy Spirit) Ruach HaKodesh who lives inside you, whom you received from God? The fact is, you don't belong to yourselves; for you were bought at a price. So use your bodies to glorify God.* When Yeshua died on the Cross, which was the price God paid for us. Yeshua said in *John 15:12-14 *this is my commandment, that you love one another, as I have loved you. Greater love hath no man than this, which a man laid down his life for his friends. You are my friends, if you do whatsoever I command you.* Being born again and through our obedience we demonstrate our love to Yeshua. When we apply this truth to our lives Yeshua now calls us His friend that is a powerful statement.

- **Prayer -** and supplication in the Spirit. On our journey we want to keep in contact with our commander and chief, better said our God in Heaven and of Earth. This process to some seems very difficult. Once we realize that prayer is a means of bearing out our heart to God and sharing with him Thanksgiving, praise and our daily needs. He loves to hear from His children. There is nothing too hard for God. When we are in trouble we know how to pray like David in *Psalms 86:6-7 *Give ear, O LORD, unto my prayer; and attend to the voice of my supplications. In the day of my trouble I will call upon thee: for you will answer me.* God is always ready to hear our prayer of praise and thanksgiving. Psalms 69:30 *"I will praise the name of God with a song, and will magnify him with thanksgiving."* When do we pray? Ephesians 6:18 "Praying always with all prayer and supplication in the Spirit, and watching thereunto with all perseverance and supplication for all saints;" This subject of Prayer I recommend you dig into the Word of God and find the treasure that is in the pages of your Bible; while you take this journey.

Sin is like a ball and chain that holds us captive thus preventing us from making progress on our journey. Using the Armour of God will help you to make progress on this life long journey to our desired destination.

Luke 4:18 " Yeshua read these word in the Synagogue, this scripture in his home town of Nazareth, from the book of the prophet Isaiah: also reference in Luke 4:18-21 *"The Spirit of the Lord is upon me, because he hath anointed me to preach the gospel to the poor; he hath sent me to heal the brokenhearted, to preach deliverance to the captives, and recovering of sight to the blind, to set at liberty them that are bruised, To preach the acceptable year of the Lord."*

And he Yeshua closed the book, and he gave it again to the minister, and sat down. And the eyes of all them that were in the synagogue were fastened on him. And he began to say unto them, *"This day is this scripture fulfilled in your ears."* Yeshua has broken the chains of sin and we are set free!

Chapter 3 – Faith
Now faith is the substance of things hoped for, the evidence of things not seen.

(Hebrews 11:1 KJV)

We are making head way to prepare for our journey. Taking any journey it is wise to count the cost. Preparing for a journey in a dangerous world we live in we need to be prepared for the battles, pitfalls and mine fields that lay ahead of us. We can avoid some but not all of these dangers on our journey. When we are prepared for the journey we have a peace of mind that we will arrive at our desire destination, in a word we have "Faith" that we will complete the journey.

Yeshua said we need to prepare before building a tower, or in our case taking a journey. We will need a good (foundation) plan to accomplish the journey.

*(Luke 14:28) For *which of you, intending to build a tower, sitteth not down first, and counting the cost, whether he have sufficient to finish it?*

The great chapter of faith in the Bible is found in Hebrews Chapter Eleven. The example of these Peoples of Faith should encourage you to grow in your love and trust in God to guide and protect you on your journey to your desired destination. Also, it would be wise to study each one of these people and their stories in the Bible, which are found in what Christians call the Pentitude (First Five Books of the Bible) or the Hebrew Torah. Reading the Genesis, Exodus, Leviticus, Numbers and Deuteronomy will give you a very strong foundation of Gods instructions to mankind also an understanding of Faith.

Hebrews 11:1-3 *"Now faith is the substance of things hoped for, the evidence of things not seen. For by it the elders obtained a good report. Through faith we understand that the worlds were framed by the word of God, so that things which are seen were not made of things which do appear."*

God has made all things seen and unseen. On our journey keep this in mind that God is the creator and author of our lives. He is not surprised at what we are faced with and has made provisions for our journey. Just like what he has done for all mankind from the very beginning of Creation.

John 1:2-3 *"The same was in the beginning with God. All things were made by him; and without him was not anything made that was made."*

Let's take a look at the People of faith and righteousness in their walk with God:

Hebrews 11:4 *"By faith Abel offered unto God a more excellent sacrifice than Cain, by which he obtained witness that he was righteous, God testifying of his gifts: and by it he being dead yet speaketh."*

We can see in this verse that God approved of Abel's offering. Abel was the first generation born to mankind and he was found righteous before God. God is giving Abel a good report, that Abel is a righteous man and God accepted the gifts from Abel. This scripture goes on and tells how God and Abel spoke to one another even after his death. This should give us great comfort knowing when we leave this life, to life everlasting we will be face to face with our Creator a mighty living God.

*Mark 12:24-27 *"And Yeshua answering said unto them, do ye not therefore err, because ye know not the scriptures, neither the power of God? For when they shall rise from the dead, they neither marry, nor are given in marriage; but are as the angels which are in heaven. And as touching the dead, that they rise: have ye not read in the book of Moses, how in the bush God spake unto him, saying, I am the God of Abraham, and the God of Isaac, and the God of Jacob? He is not* the God of the dead, but the God of the living: ye therefore do greatly err."

Enoch was the seventh generation from Adam:

Hebrews 11:5-6 *"By faith Enoch was translated that he should not see death; and was not found, because God had translated him: for before his translation he had this testimony, that he pleased God. But without faith it is impossible to please him: for he that cometh to God must believe that he is, and that he is a rewarder of them that diligently seek him."*

Enoch when you read his story in Genesis he took a walk with God, and they went to God's house and remained there. It appears Enoch did not die, read his story, truly a man of faith. God is the God of the living not the dead.

Genesis 5:22-24 *"And Enoch walked with God after he begat Methuselah three hundred years, and begat sons and daughters: And all the days of Enoch were three hundred sixty and five years: And Enoch walked with God: and he was not; for God took him."*

God watches over his people of faith and righteousness, we can take this to heart. Noah his testimony is also, a man of faith which God protected and started a renewed human race.

Hebrews11:7 *"By faith Noah, being warned of God of things not seen as yet, moved with fear, prepared an ark to the saving of his house; by the which he condemned the world, and became heir of the righteousness which is by faith."*

Most of us know that Noah made an Ark to save his family and the animals that God chose to be saved from the flood. Think about this, Noah was a great man of Faith he builds this Ark and it took a hundred years. Noah I believe was one of the most tenacious men of faith.

Genesis 7:5-6 *"And Noah did according unto all that the LORD commanded him. And Noah was six hundred years old when the flood of waters was upon the earth."*

Abram, later called Abraham left on a journey to land that God has promised him. Knowing and believing that he would someday dwell with his Creator, in a home that God had prepared for him. We will see in future verses in Hebrews 11:14-19 more about Abraham and his faith.

Hebrews 11:7-10 *"By faith Abraham, when he was called to go out into a place which he should after receive for an inheritance, obeyed; and he went out, not knowing whither he went. By faith he sojourned in the land of promise, as in a strange country, dwelling in tabernacles with Isaac and Jacob, the heirs with him of the same promise: For he looked for a city which hath foundations, whose builder and maker is God."*

John 14:1-3 Yeshua said *"Don't let yourselves be disturbed. Trust in God and trust in me. In my Father's house are many places to live. If there weren't, I would have told you; because I am going there to prepare a place for you. Since I am going and preparing a place for you, I will return to take you with me; so that where I am, you may be also."*

Sarai, Sarah demonstrated her faith through a miracle of child birth, even though she was well over the age to bear a child. She believed God and would be faithful believing the promise that God had made that through her an heir would be born to Abraham. And she would be a mother of many nations.

Hebrews 11:11-12 *"Through faith also Sarah herself received strength to conceive seed, and was delivered of a child when she was past age, because she judged him faithful who had promised. Therefore sprang there even of one, and him as good as dead, so many as the stars of the sky in multitude, and as the sand which is by the sea shore innumerable."*

Genesis 17:15-16 *"And God said unto Abraham, As for Sarai thy wife, thou shalt not call her name Sarai, but Sarah shall her name be. And I will bless her, and give thee a son also of her: yea, I will bless her, and she shall be a mother of nations; kings of people shall be of her."*

The point is made in Hebrews 11:13 all of these people of faith during their life time did not always received all that was promised. Still, they knew there would be a time in the future that God would complete the promise.

Hebrews 11:13-14 *"These all died in faith, not having received the promises, but having seen them afar off, and were persuaded of them, and embraced them, and confessed that they were strangers and pilgrims on the earth. For they that say such things declare plainly that they seek a country. And truly, if they had been mindful of that country from whence they came out, they might have had opportunity to have returned. But now they desire a better country, that is, an heavenly: wherefore God is not ashamed to be called their God: for he hath prepared for them a city."*

Abraham and his story of him taking Isaac to be sacrificed unto God has been told over and over. This story bears much study. Isaac was not a little boy, but a grown man and could have overpowered his father Abraham from making him a sacrifice to God. Isaac trusted his father and in obedience even if it meant to die. We can see faith that is like Yeshua obedience to die and be raised from the dead. This is a great foreshadow of Yeshua willing to die out of obedience to His father in heaven.

Hebrews 11:17-19 *"By faith Abraham, when he was tried, offered up Isaac: and he that had received the promises offered up his only begotten son, Of whom it was said, That in*

Isaac shall thy seed be called: Accounting that God was able to raise him up, even from the dead; from whence also he received him in a figure."

Abraham sons were both blessed: Hebrews 11:20 "By faith Isaac blessed Jacob and Esau concerning things to come." They both became a great nation as promised.

Continuing with Jacob he adopted Joseph's sons as his own sons. They now became part of the tribes of Israel with an inheritance.

Hebrews 11:21 *"By faith Jacob, when he was a dying, blessed both the sons of Joseph; and worshipped, leaning upon the top of his staff."*

*Genesis 48:3-6 "And Jacob said unto Joseph, God Almighty appeared unto me at Luz in the land of Canaan, and blessed me, And said unto me, Behold, I will make thee fruitful, and multiply thee, and I will make of thee a multitude of people; and will give this land to thy seed after thee for an everlasting possession. And now thy two sons, Ephraim and Manasseh, which were born unto thee in the land of Egypt before I came unto thee into Egypt, are mine; as Reuben and Simeon, they shall be mine. And thy issue, which you were born to you after them, shall be mine, and shall be called after the name of their brethren in their inheritance."

Before Joseph did he commanded his brethren when they left Egypt to take his body to be buried in the Promised Land.

Hebrews 11:22 *"By faith Joseph, when he died, made mention of the departing of the children of Israel; and gave commandment concerning his bones."*

Genesis 50:22-26 *"And Joseph dwelt in Egypt, he, and his father's house: and Joseph lived an hundred and ten years.*

And Joseph saw Ephraim's children of the third generation: the children also of Machir the son of Manasseh were brought up upon Joseph's knees. And Joseph said unto his brethren, I die: and God will surely visit you, and bring you out of this land unto the land which he sware to Abraham, to Isaac, and to Jacob. And Joseph took an oath of the children of Israel, saying, God will surely visit you, and ye shall carry up my bones from hence. So Joseph died, being an hundred and ten years old: and they embalmed him, and he was put in a coffin in Egypt."

*Exodus 13:19 *"And Moses took the bones of Joseph with him: for he had straightly sworn the children of Israel, saying, God will surely visit you; and you shall carry up my bones away in a hurry with you."*

Moses, his parents having faith, saved Moses for being killed. God in His divine plan used this opportunity to use Moses as a Deliverer of the people of Israel from slavery in Egypt.

Hebrews 11:23 *"By faith Moses, when he was born, was hid three months of his parents, because they saw he was a proper child; and they were not afraid of the king's commandment."*

Moses was then used by God and protected in Pharaohs house hold. It was there he was raised by the Pharaohs daughter. Moses mother was his wet-nurse till the time he was weaned. Moses made a choice to be loyal to Israel and God. God used him in an amazing way. Reading the Books of Exodus, Numbers and Deuteronomy will strengthen your faith for the journey. As you learn what Moses and the Children of Israel went through before and after leaving Egypt will give you great insight to what God has planned for his children today. Moses relationship with God is one we should all understand.

*Hebrews 11:24-29 *"By faith Moses, when he was come to years, refused to be called the son of Pharaoh's daughter; Choosing rather to suffer affliction with the people of God, than to enjoy the pleasures of sin for a season; Esteeming the reproach of Messiahs greater riches than the treasures in Egypt: for he had respect unto the recompence of the reward. By faith he forsook Egypt, not fearing the wrath of the king: for he endured, as seeing him who is invisible. Through faith he kept the Passover, and the sprinkling of blood, lest he that destroyed the firstborn should touch them. By faith they passed through the Red sea as by dry land: which the Egyptians assaying to do were drowned."*

Moses was the deliverer that brought the people out of slavery (bondage), Yeshua is the Messiah that Moses spoke of, who would come and deliverer the people from the bondage of sin. The Passover is a fore shadow of the coming Messiah. It is by the blood of Yeshua we are Passover from death to everlasting life.

*Deuteronomy 18:15-17 *The LORD (The proper Name of God) Our God will raise up a Prophet from Israel, of thy brethren, he will be like me; listen to Him; According to all that you desire of the LORD thy God in Horeb in the day of the assembly, saying, Let me not hear again the voice of the LORD my God, neither let me see this great fire any more, that I die not. And the LORD said unto me, they have wellspoken that which they have spoken.*

John 5:46 Yeshua said "For had ye believed Moses, ye would have believed me: for he wrote of me."

Acts 7:37 *"This is that Moses, which said unto the children of Israel, A prophet shall the Lord your God raise up unto you of your brethren, like unto me; him shall ye hear."*

Joshua and the people of Israel now enter into the Promised Land. Nearly forty years wandering in the desert is over since they crossed over from Egypt are now crossing over to the Land that has been promised. The story of the two spies that were sent to reconnoiter Jericho was hidden by Rahab, who later in history she is one of Yeshua's Ancestors. Here we can find this story in the book of Joshua, a must read to further your understanding of faith and (Grace which we will cover in the next Chapter).

Hebrews 11:30-31 "By faith the walls of Jericho fell down, after they were compassed about seven days. By faith the harlot Rahab perished not with them that believed not, when she had received the spies with peace."

Joshua 2:1 *"And Joshua the son of Nun sent out of Shittim two men to spy secretly, saying, Go view the land, even Jericho. And they went, and came into a harlot's house, named Rahab, and lodged there."*

Joshua 6:25 *"And Joshua saved Rahab the harlot alive, and her father's household, and all that she had; and she dwelleth in Israel even unto this day; because she hid the messengers, which Joshua sent to spy out Jericho."*

The List goes on of great people of the Bible demonstrating great faith and righteousness which led to Salvation, which we will cover in a future chapter. The books of Judges and Samuel hold more stories of Faith and commitment such as the Book of Ruth and Daniel. This faith has given the strength needed to go through troubles, torment and even death with the knowledge that their last breath on earth would lead them to the next breath in heaven for their reward and treasures are waiting for them.

Hebrews 11:32-40 *"And what shall I more say? for the time would fail me to tell of Gedeon, and of Barak, and of Samson, and of Jephthae; of David also, and Samuel, and of the prophets: Who through faith subdued kingdoms, wrought righteousness, obtained promises, stopped the mouths of lions, Quenched the violence of fire, escaped the edge of the sword, out of weakness were made strong, waxed valiant in fight, turned to flight the armies of the aliens. Women received their dead raised to life again: and others were tortured, not accepting deliverance; that they might obtain a better resurrection: And others had trial of cruel mockings and scourgings, yea, moreover of bonds and imprisonment: They were stoned, they were sawn asunder, were tempted, were slain with the sword: they wandered about in sheepskins and goatskins; being destitute, afflicted, tormented; (Of whom the world was not worthy:) they wandered in deserts, and in mountains, and in dens and caves of the earth. And these all, having obtained a good report through faith, received not the promise: God having provided some better thing for us, that they without us should not be made perfect."*

Moving on to the next part of our journey is Grace and we will see how being born again and knowing the dangers of sin that can hold us back or detour us from our journey to the wrong destination. But by faith we gain strength and endurance to continue on our journey and remain on course to our final destination.

Chapter 4 – Grace

Genesis 6:8

"But Noah found grace in the eyes of the LORD."

Through the many years I spent in Christian Church, for the most part I was taught that grace was only found in the New Testament. Over the years I have heard many preachers, pastors and men who meant well, and truly believed grace was only demonstrated in the New Testament. This could not be farther from the truth. In the King James Bible it is in 38 verses where people of faith found grace (Favor in the sight of God) and some asked for grace.

The Hebrew word חן (Grace) found in the Strongs it is translated using several other words in English in the following manner: grace (38x), favour (26x), gracious (2x), pleasant (1x), precious (1x), well-favored (with H2896) (1x). Which brings the total to 69 times it is used in the Old Testament. This word appears 131 times in the New Testament, which nearly half are referring to Scriptures in the Old Testament.

Then what is grace? The Merriam – Webster Dictionary gives this definition:

Unmerited divine assistance given to humans for their regeneration or sanctification; a virtue coming from God; a state of sanctification enjoyed through divine assistance.

By definition grace is a gift from God.

John 1:14 *"And the Word was made flesh, and dwelt among us, (and we beheld his glory, the glory as of the only begotten of the Father,) full of grace and truth."*

John 1:17 *"For the law (teaching – instructions) was given by Moses, but grace and truth came by Yeshua the Messiah."*

Ephesians 2:8-9 *"For by grace are ye saved through faith; and that not of yourselves: it is the gift of God: Not of works, lest any man should boast."*

Grace is a gift from God that we do not deserve, which has been imparted to us from Yeshua's obedience unto death. Yeshua paid the price for our sins on the cross, so we are bought with the price of the perfect demonstration of love that was accomplished through Yeshua's death, resurrection and ascension to the right hand of the Father in heaven.

No one can work their way into heaven, if man could there would be a contest of who is the best and pride would destroy them as it did Satan.

Isaiah 14:11-12 *"Your (Satan – Lucifer) pride has been brought down to Sh'ol with the music of your lyres, under you a mattress of maggots, over you a blanket of worms. How did you come to fall from the heavens, morning star, son of the dawn? How did you come to be cut to the ground, conqueror of nations?"*

*Proverbs 16:18-19 *Pride goeth before destruction and a haughty spirit before a fall. Better it is to be of a humble spirit with the lowly, than to divide the spoil with the proud.*

Grace was set in place that pride would not be an issue, but grace is a free gift only God gives this gift to His children. The subject of works will be addressed in a future chapter of this book.

Grace what does it look like?

For Noah it was a saving grace from God that saved him and his family from the judgement and destruction of all life on earth by means of a flood. Moses received grace from God.

Jacob found grace from his brother Esau. Joseph found grace from Pharaoh and became the second in power over all of Egypt. Ruth found grace from Boaz, the ancestor of David and Yeshua. Esther found grace from the King; this grace saved the Nation the Jewish people from being destroyed. David the King received grace. The Old Testament in whole demonstrates God's grace to his people and people whom joined with Israel. The Hebrew (TaNaKh) which is the Old Testament is loaded with acts of grace from God and others showing grace. The New Testament demonstrates grace through the Messiah Yeshua and his disciples.

Grace can be demonstrated acts of mercy (grace imparts to one person or persons), But, Devine Grace that leads to everlasting life, only comes from God.

*1 Peter 5:6-11 *humble yourselves therefore under the mighty hand of God, that he may exalt you in due time: Casting all your cares upon him; for God cares for you. Be sober, be vigilant; because your adversary the devil, as a roaring lion, walketh about, seeking whom he may devour: Whom resist stedfast in the faith, knowing that the same afflictions are accomplished in your brethren that are in the world. But the God of all grace, who hath called us unto his eternal glory by Yeshua the Messiah, after that ye have suffered a while, make you perfect, stable, strengthen, settle you. To him be glory and dominion for ever and ever. Amen.*

As the journey begins, we now have our equipment for the journey and our provisions in our packs. We know we will not be alone on this journey. But, it is up to each one of us to do our part, and trust God to do his part. What a wonderful plan, to have the creator of all things by our sides as we embark on the journey, traveling to our desired destination.

Chapter 5 – Salvation

Then said Yeshua unto his disciples, If any man will come after me, let him deny himself, and take up his cross, and follow me.

Matthew 16:24

The scripture in Matthew 16:24 must have been a shock when the disciples heard it. Death by means of the cross was a very cruel and torturous means of punishment instituted by the Romans during the time of Yeshua. This word picture if made into a poster or campaign for signing on as one of the team would not gain many volunteers. But, it did not leave any doubt that if you became a disciple of Yeshua it was going to be a time of hardship.

Yeshua continued in Matthew 16:25 and says "For whosoever will save his life shall lose it: and whosoever will lose his life for my sake shall find it. For what is a man profited, if he shall gain the whole world, and lose his own soul? Or what shall a man give in exchange for his soul? For the Son of man shall come in the glory of his Father with his angels; and then he shall reward every man according to his works."

WOW! Yeshua has laid it out, if you give up this life, you will have everlasting life. The he lays out the importance of Salvation. Even if we gain the whole world, and give up our soul, where does that leave you? And every man will be reward for his works? (This will be covered in the next chapter.)

Life here and now is of lesser importance and is temporary. But everlasting life with Yeshua is the goal, it is our preferred destination. Now we have instruction and a map for our journey. We need to learn to use our spiritual compass to guide us to our destination. This next scripture some it up how our compass should work.

Philippians 1:21 "For to me, life is the Messiah, and death is gain."

Yes the Messiah is breaking the trail for us to follow he is our perfect example.

GPS (Gods Perfect Salvation) better than any compass and will help you get around the obstacles in life's journey.

Salvation is a hot topic!

Let's take a moment and think about this.

First of all Yeshua and His disciples were Jewish. During the time of Yeshua and his disciples the scriptures that were available was the Old Testament (Referred to by Christians) the Hebrew TaNaKh which contained the Torah, Prophets and the Writings.

Yeshua gives a stern warning which He placed great importance on the Old Testament (TaNaKh) in Matthew 5:17-20 *"Don't think that I have come to abolish the Torah or the Prophets. I have come not to abolish but to complete. Yes indeed! I tell you that until heaven and earth pass away, not so much as a Yod or a Stroke will pass from the Torah; not until everything that must happen have happened. So whoever disobeys the least of these mitzvot (commandments) and teaches others to do so will be called the least in the Kingdom of Heaven. But whoever obeys them and so teaches will be called great in the Kingdom of Heaven. For I tell you that unless your righteousness is far greater than that of the Torah-teachers and Pharisees, you will certainly not enter the Kingdom of Heaven!"*

In the New Testament Paul (Sha'ul) wrote to Timothy these words:

2 Timothy 3:16-17 *"All scripture is given by inspiration of God, and is profitable for doctrine, for reproof, for correction, for instruction in righteousness: That the man of God may be perfect, throughly furnished unto all good works."*

The above scriptures should leave little doubt that the Bible from Genesis to Revelation are the Word of God. (The next chapter we will look at works), But at this time we will focus on salvation.

In the King James Version (KJV) Salvation is used 164 times from Genesis to Revelation. The first time it is used is in Genesis 49:18 *"I have waited for thy salvation, O LORD."* In this chapter Jacob is blessing his children before he dies. Jacob (Israel) between the blessing of Dan then Gad Jacob interjects this statement before continuing the blessings to his children. The route word for Salvation is Yeshua which later in history is the name of the Messiah. In English versions of the Bible the Messiahs name is Jesus.

The Bible has two categories of Salvation:

1. National Salvation
2. Personal Salvation

We will focus on personal Salvation and what this entails and how to apply it to our lives. The foundation of Salvation that most everyone is familiar is found in Ephesians 2:8-9 *"For by grace are ye saved through faith; and that not of yourselves: it is the gift of God: Not of works, lest any man should boast."*

We see that to be saved (Salvation) it is the gift of God. It is grace (Unmerited favor) and through faith that this gift of salvation is given to us as a gift from God. Below is the steps we see in this verse that leads to salvation:

1. Grace (Unmerited favor) is not given to us because who we are (Sinners), but who God is in our lives, it is a personal relationship living according to God's Will, Plan and Purpose.
2. Faith (This is an act or acts of righteousness) our obedience to God's Word because we love HIM.
3. Salvation (Not based on works – more on this in the next chapter) in short you cannot buy or work your way into heaven. We must not think that once we believe and just say a prayer we are saved. Without a full commitment to allow God to work in your life you will be as lost as you first started. This is like saying you have fire insurance, but you haven't purchased it yet. Then the house burns down and then you decide to buy insurance and expect them to cover your loss. You will be very disappointed.

Yeshua gives an example of this very idea and explains it in Matthew 25:31-40, this shows us by what means we can reach the desired destination of our journey.

"When the Son of man shall come in his glory, and all the holy angels with him, then shall he sit upon the throne of his glory: And before him shall be gathered all nations: and he shall separate them one from another, as a shepherd divideth his sheep from the goats: And he shall set the sheep on his right hand, but the goats on the left. Then shall the King say unto them on his right hand, Come, ye blessed of my Father, inherit the kingdom prepared for you from the foundation of the world:

For I was an hungred, and ye gave me meat: I was thirsty, and ye gave me drink: I was a stranger, and ye took me in: Naked, and ye clothed me: I was sick, and ye visited me: I was in prison, and ye came unto me. Then shall the righteous answer him, saying, Lord, when saw we thee an hungred, and fed thee? or thirsty, and gave thee drink?

When saw we thee a stranger, and took thee in? or naked, and clothed thee? Or when saw we thee sick, or in prison, and came unto thee?

And the King shall answer and say unto them, Verily I say unto you, Inasmuch as ye have done it unto one of the least of these my brethren, ye have done it unto me.

Yeshua is showing the motivation and acts of righteousness that are accounted to them as righteousness, that leads to that personal relationship with God that they have received the gift of grace which is salvation.

Reading Matthew 25:41-46 the contrast of them who did not demonstrate their faith through obedience, this is not the destination which we desire to arrive.

Then shall he say also unto them on the left hand, Depart from me, ye cursed, into everlasting fire, prepared for the devil and his angels: For I was an hungred, and ye gave me no meat: I was thirsty, and ye gave me no drink: I was a stranger, and ye took me not in: naked, and ye clothed me not: sick, and in prison, and ye visited me not.

Then shall they also answer him, saying, Lord, when saw we thee an hungred, or athirst, or a stranger, or naked, or sick, or in prison, and did not minister unto thee?

Then shall he answer them, saying, verily I say unto you, Inasmuch as ye did it not to one of the least of these, ye did it not to me.

And these shall go away into everlasting punishment: but the righteous into life eternal.

As we have read in (Chapter Three Faith), we review the chapter of faith in Hebrews eleven demonstrating what faith is to righteousness. Summed up in this verse: (Hebrews 11:1 KJV) *"Now faith is the substance of things hoped for, the evidence of things not seen."*

To understand what Gods part is and what our part is it is imperative we understand what it is to be truly born again, how faith and grace leads us to a righteous life to receive the gift of Salvation. It is our personal relationship of love that we find ourselves born again of the Spirit of God, then by faith and obedience our righteousness shines to our Father God and he imparts Grace to us unto salvation. All these things work together to the glory and purposes of Gods will for each of us as we undertake this journey to our desired destination.

"He also shall be my salvation: for an hypocrite shall not come before him." (Job 13:16)

"But I have trusted in thy mercy; my heart shall rejoice in thy salvation. I will sing unto the LORD, because he hath dealt bountifully with me." (Psalms 13:5-6)

Chapter 6 – Works

For the Son of man shall come in the glory of his Father with his angels; and then he shall reward every man according to his works.

(Matthew 16:27)

This step of the journey we will find many stumbling blocks of stone that has been place in our way to trip us up due to doctrines and misleading teaching on this subject of works. Using our instructions the Word of God, then making sure we know what His Word says about this subject will free us up from stumbling over these blocks of stone that may trip us up. Once we can clearly see the problem, then we can avoid falling on our face on this journey.

Psalms 17:4-5 *"Concerning the works of men, by the word of thy lips I have kept me from the paths of the destroyer. Hold up my goings in thy paths, that my footsteps slip not."*

God will keep us from stumbling as we take this journey while we do the works he has placed before us. He will guide our path that the destroyer (Adversary) will not stumble us on the path of righteous living.

2 Timothy 3:17 *"That the man of God may be perfect, throughly furnished unto all good works."*

God has a plan and purpose for each of us as individuals; it is this personal relationship that we demonstrate our love to God through our obedience to his will. One might say what does that look like? The following verses may give you some insight on just what it is to show our love to God through obedience. (More on this subject in a future chapter).

John 14:15 *"If ye love me, keep my commandments."*

John 14:21 *"He that hath my commandments, and keepeth them, he it is that loveth me: and he that loveth me shall be loved of my Father, and I will love him, and will manifest myself to him."*

We can see from the scriptures above that to show our love to God obedience is the mechanism in which we can show our love to Almighty God. (More on this subject in a future chapter loving God).

*Titus 3:5-7 *" Not by works of righteousness which we have done, but according to his mercy he saved us, by the washing of regeneration, and renewing of the Holy Ghost; Which he shed on us abundantly through Yeshua the Messiah our Saviour; That being justified by his grace, we should be made heirs according to the hope of eternal life."*

We need not throw the baby out with the bath water. Showing our love to God through obedience by doing acts of righteousness does not produce salvation. But, not doing the will of God and being disobedient produces the judgement of God. For if we reject God he will reject us. It is through our loving relationship with God that produces works unto righteousness. We have read of the many godly people in the Hebrews chapter eleven, through their faith produced righteousness unto Salvation. I encourage you to review this chapter on faith to keep this fresh in your mind.

Psalms 28:4-5 *"Pay them back for their deeds, as befits their evil acts; repay them for what they have done, give them what they deserve. For they don't understand the deeds of Adonai (Gods proper Name) or what he has done. He will break them down; he will not build them up."*

*Matthew 16:24-27 *" Then said Yeshua unto his disciples, If any man will come after me, let him deny himself, and take up his cross, and follow me. For whosoever will save his life* shall lose it: and whosoever will lose his life for my sake shall find it. For what is a man profited, if he shall gain the whole world, and lose his own soul? Or what shall a man give in exchange for his soul? For the Son of man shall come in the glory of his Father with his angels; and then he shall reward every man according to his works."

Works of righteousness are placed before us when we become born again. These will empower us to keep on the path that leads to our desired destination.

Psalms 1:1-3 *"Blessed is the man that walketh not in the counsel of the ungodly, nor standeth in the way of sinners, nor sitteth in the seat of the scornful. But his delight is in the law (Instructions –Teachings) of the LORD; and in his law doth he meditate day and night. And he shall be like a tree planted by the rivers of water, that bringeth forth his fruit in his season; his leaf also shall not wither; and whatsoever he doeth shall prosper."*

Chapter 7 - Baptism

"Yeshua came and talked with them. He said, "All authority in heaven and on earth has been given to me. Therefore, go and make people from all nations into talmidim (Disciples), immersing them into the reality of the Father, the Son and the Ruach HaKodesh (Holy Spirt), and teaching them to obey everything that I have commanded you. And remember! I will be with you always, yes, even until the end of the age."

(Matthew 28:18-20 CJB)

This part of our journey we find in the scripture above which commonly referred to as the Great Commission. Yeshua the Messiah commands us to (Immerse) Baptize others in to the reality of the Father, Son and Holy Spirit. We are to teach others how to obey the commandments (Instructions) in the Torah. Knowing Yeshua is with us always.

Once you have been born again this will be an important step of faith and obedience to show your love to God by being baptized. This is not a great suggestion but the great commission!

History of Baptism- The Background

The tvilah is the act of immersion in natural sourced water (Living or Running Water such as a stream or River), This is referred to as a mikvah In the TaNaKh, or the Old Testament in the Bible. Other Jewish texts; immersion in water for ritual purification was established for restoration to a condition of "ritual purity" in specific circumstances.

For example, The Children of Israel who according to the Law of Moses (Instructions –Teachings) became ritually defiled by contact with a corpse had to use the mikvah before being allowed to participate in the Holy Temple.

Numbers 9:6-10 "And there were certain men, who were defiled by the dead body of a man, that they could not keep the Passover on that day: and they came before Moses and before Aaron on that day: And those men said unto him, We are defiled by the dead body of a man: wherefore are we kept back, that we may not offer an offering of the LORD in his appointed season among the children of Israel? And Moses said unto them, Stand still, and I will hear what the LORD will command concerning you. And the LORD Spake unto Moses, saying, Speak unto the children of Israel, saying, if any man of you or of your posterity shall be unclean by reason of a dead body, or be in a journey afar off, yet he shall keep the Passover unto the LORD."

Mikvah or immersion is required for converts to Judaism as part of their conversion

The background of baptism can be traced to Old Testament times. Genesis first book of the Bible symbolically eight people were saved from the great flood of God's judgment. As God washed away the deeds of sinful man and raised all who he spared were in the ark up to start a new life on earth.

Peter pointed out that the water of the flood:

1 Peter 3:18-22 *"For the Messiah himself died for sins, once and for all, a righteous person on behalf of unrighteous people, so that he might bring you to God. He was put to death in the flesh but brought to life by the Spirit; and in this form he went and made a proclamation to the imprisoned spirits, to those who were disobedient long ago, in the days of Noach, when God waited patiently during the building of the ark, in*

which a few people; to be specific, eight; were delivered by means of water. This also prefigures what delivers us now, the water of immersion, which is not the removal of dirt from the body, but one's pledge to keep a good conscience toward God, through the resurrection of Yeshua the Messiah. He has gone into heaven and is at the right hand of God, with angels, authorities and powers subject to him. "

Old Testament prophets such as Isaiah, Ezekiel, and David likewise used water as an external symbol for internal cleansing:

Isaiah 1:16-17 *"Wash you, make you clean; put away the evil of your doings from before mine eyes; cease to do evil; Learn to do well; seek judgment, relieve the oppressed, judge the fatherless, plead for the widow."*

Ezekiel 36:24-26 *"For I will take you from among the nations, gather you from all the countries, and return you to your own soil. Then I will sprinkle clean water on you, and you will be clean; I will cleanse you from all your uncleanness and from all your idols. I will give you a new heart and put a new spirit inside you; I will take the stony heart out of your flesh and give you a heart of flesh."*

Psalms 51:3-9 *"God, in your grace, have mercy on me; in your great compassion, blot out my crimes. Wash me completely from my guilt, and cleanse me from my sin. For I know my crimes, my sin confronts me all the time. Against you, you only, have I sinned and done what is evil from your perspective; so that you are right in accusing me and justified in passing sentence. True, I was born guilty, was a sinner from the moment my mother conceived me. Still, you want truth in the inner person; so make me know wisdom in my inmost heart. Sprinkle me with hyssop, and I will be clean; wash me, and I will be whiter than snow."*

History of Baptism-John the Baptist

(John the Baptist) Yochanan the Immerser was the greatest of the prophets according to Yeshua. John baptized Yeshua in the Yarden (Jordan), he was ushering in the Messianic fulfillment of TaNaKh (Old Testament) prophecy.

Matthew 11:11-13 Yeshua said *"Verily I say unto you, among them that are born of women there hath not risen a greater than John the Baptist: notwithstanding he that is least in the kingdom of heaven is greater than he. And from the days of John the Baptist until now the kingdom of heaven suffereth violence, and the violent take it by force. For all the prophets and the law (Instructions – Teachings) prophesied until John."*

Mikvah (baptism) is a representation of the atoning blood of Yeshua the Messiah, which demonstrated His obedience and love to the father even unto death, then later as He was raised from the dead to Life.

Behind the symbolism of baptism, were being immersed in water (Living or Running Water such as a stream or River). When we are under the water we are making the statement that in death of the old nature, we rise up clean in the new nature of being born again.

John 4:*10 " Yeshua answered her, "If you knew God's gift, that is, who it is saying to you, 'Give me a drink of water,' then you would have asked him; and he would have given you living water."*

John 7:*37-39 "Now on the last day of the festival, (the great day of the feast) Hoshana Rabbah, Yeshua stood and cried out, "If anyone is thirsty, let him keep coming to me and drinking! Whoever puts his trust in me, as the Scripture says, rivers of living water will flow from his inmost being!" (Now he said this about the Spirit, whom those who trusted in him were to receive later; the Spirit had not yet been given, because Yeshua had not yet been glorified.)"*

We continue our journey we can now see how being born again is important. We must remain vigilant knowing that there is a mine field we must get through in this world known as sin. We must take every thought into captivity. We can accomplish this by putting on the whole armor of God. We must remind ourselves that this war – spiritual battles are not against people but of the Adversary and powers of darkness. We must use each part of the Armour not forgetting one:

Truth, righteousness, the gospel of good news, faith, salvation, the Word of God, and be praying always for one another. These are all vital items we must take with us on our journey to our desired destination.

Chapter 8 - Who Killed Jesus

"Therefore doth my Father love me, because I lay down my life, that I might take it again. No man taketh it from me, but I lay it down of myself. I have power to lay it down, and I have power to take it again. This commandment have I received of my Father."

John 10:17-18

This part of the journey we want to take a long hard look at who really killed Yeshua. Through the history of the church this has caused the deaths of many a Christians, Hebrew (Jewish People) and Messianic Believers. (More on this subject next chapter "Anti-Semitism").

We do not have to go far to find the answer to this question, but let's see where some take the wrong fork in the road on their journey and why they believe a lie that the Adversary has place in the church to place division and hate.

John 19:10-11 "So Pilate said to him, "You refuse to speak to me? Don't you understand that it is in my power either to set you free or to have you executed on the stake?"

Yeshua answered, "You would have no power over me if it hadn't been given to you from above; this is why the one who handed me over to you is guilty of a greater sin."

This is where the debate begins. Who was it that delivered Yeshua to be killed? Which of the following:

1. Judas
2. The Jews
3. Romans

There are more choices I am sure but let's look at Judas first.

*Matthew 26:14-16 *"Then one of the Twelve, the one called Judas Iscariot (Y'hudah from K'riot), went to chief priests (the head cohanim) and said, "What are you willing to give me if I turn Yeshua over to you?" They counted out thirty silver coins and gave them to Y'hudah. From then on he looked for a good opportunity to betray him."*

Matthew 26:23-25 *"He answered, "The one who dips his matzah in the dish with me is the one who will betray me. The Son of Man will die just as the Tanakh says he will; but woe to that man by whom the Son of Man is betrayed! It would have been better for him had he never been born!"*

Y'hudah (Y'hudah from K'riot), the one who was betraying him, then asked, *"Surely, Rabbi, you don't mean me?"*

Yeshua answered, *"The words are yours."*

Judas did indeed betray Yeshua, but did he kill Yeshua?

*John 19:11b *"...why the one who handed me over to you is guilty of a greater sin."*

Yeshua did not say that Judas killed him, but betrayed (handed over) Yeshua.

Next on our list are the Jews:

*Matthew 26:57 *"And they that had laid hold on Yeshua led him away to Caiaphas the high priest, where the scribes and the elders were assembled."*

*Matthew 27:1-2 *"When the morning was come, all the chief priests and elders of the people took counsel against Yeshua to put him to death: And when they had bound him, they led him away, and delivered him to Pontius Pilate the governor."*

Historically at that time only the Roman government had authority to exercise capital punishment. This is why they took him to Pontius Pilate the governor who has the authority to condemn Yeshua to death.

*John 18:31-32" *Then said Pilate unto them, Take ye him, and judge him according to your law. The Jews therefore said unto him, It is not lawful for us to put any man to death: That the saying of Yeshua might be fulfilled, which he spake, signifying what death he should die."*

*Matthew 27:24-26 " When Pilate saw that he was accomplishing nothing, but rather that a riot was starting, he took water, washed his hands in front of the crowd, and said, *"My hands are clean of this man's blood; it's your responsibility."*

All the people answered, *"His blood is on us and on our children!"*

Then he released to them Bar-Abba; but Yeshua, after having Yeshua whipped, he handed over to be executed on a stake.

The Jewish people placed a curse on themselves, which from that time in history and to the present have been call the "Messiah Killers." As we can see from scripture the Jews did not kill him.

Next on our list did the Romans kill Yeshua?

*John 18:33-37: Then Pilate entered into the judgment hall again, and called Yeshua, and said unto him, "Art thou the King of the Jews?"

Yeshua answered him, did someone tell you this thing or did you think of it yourself?

Pilate answered, "Am I a Jew? Your own nation and the chief priests have brought you here to me: what do you say that you are accused of?

Jesus answered, My kingdom is not of this world: if my kingdom were of this world, then would my servants fight, that I should not be delivered to the Jews: but now is my kingdom not from here.

Pilate said unto him, Art thou a king then?

Jesus answered; it is as you said I am a king. To this end was I born, and for this cause I came into this world, that I should bear witness unto the truth. Every one that is of the truth hears my voice.

*John 19:10-12: Then saith Pilate unto Yeshua, why do you remain quiet? Do you not understand I have power to crucify you, and have power to release you?

Yeshua answered, you have no power over me, except it was given to you from above: therefore he that delivered me to you has the greater sin.

And from that time Pilate sought to release him: but the Jews cried out, saying, If thou let this man go, thou art not Caesar's friend: whosoever maketh himself a king speaketh against Caesar.

Clearly Yeshua did not say that Pilot or the authority he represents has the power to kill him. Then who was the one who killed Yeshua?

John 15:9-17 *"Just as my Father has loved me, I too have loved you; so stay in my love. If you keep my commands, you will stay in my love; just as I have kept my Father's commands and stay in his love. I have said this to you so that my joy may be in you, and your joy be complete. "This is my command: that you keep on loving each other just as I have loved you. No one has greater love than a person who lays down his life for his friends. You are my friends, if you do what I command you. I no longer call you slaves, because a slave doesn't know what his master is about; but I have called you friends, because everything I have heard from my Father I have made known to you. You did not choose me, I chose you; and I have commissioned you to go and bear fruit, fruit that will last; so that whatever you ask from the Father in my name he may give you. This is what I command you: keep loving each other!"*

John 10:17-18 *"Yeshua said "Therefore doth my Father love me, because I lay down my life, that I might take it again. No man taketh it from me, but I lay it down of myself. I have power to lay it down, and I have power to take it again. This commandment have I received of my Father."*

Yes, Yeshua willingly died on the cross a horrible and traumatic death for our sins. It was love that held him to the cross. He loved us so much that he gave up his life so we can have everlasting life. No one killed Yeshua, but our sins placed him on that cross. We all have sinned and all sin leads to death.

Note: (Adonai is used in the place of Gods' Holy proper Name.)

Yeshua completed this prophecy in Isaiah:

*Isaiah 53:1-12 *"Who believes our report? To whom is the arm of (Gods true name is used here) Adonai revealed? For before him he grew up like a young plant, like a root out of dry ground. He was not well-formed or especially handsome; we saw him, but his appearance did not attract us.*

People despised and avoided him, a man of pains, well acquainted with illness. Like someone from whom people turn their faces, he was despised; we did not value him.

In fact, it was our diseases he bore, our pains from which he suffered; yet we regarded him as punished, stricken and afflicted by God.

But he was wounded because of our crimes, crushed because of our sins; the disciplining that makes us whole fell on him, and by his bruises [: and in fellowship with him] we are healed. We all, like sheep, went astray; we turned, each one, to his own way; yet Adonai laid on him the guilt of all of us.

Though mistreated, he was submissive; he did not open his mouth. Like a lamb led to be slaughtered, like a sheep silent before its shearers, he did not open his mouth. After forcible arrest and sentencing, he was taken away; and none of his generation protested his being cut off from the land of the living for the crimes of my people, who deserved the punishment themselves. He was given a grave among the wicked; in his death he was with a rich man.

Although he had done no violence and had said nothing deceptive, yet it pleased Adonai to crush him with illness, to see if he would present himself as a guilt offering. If he does, he will see his offspring; and he will prolong his days; and at his hand Adonai's desire will be accomplished.

After this ordeal, he will see satisfaction. "By his knowing [pain and sacrifice], my righteous servant makes many righteous; it is for their sins that he suffers. Therefore I will assign him a share with the great, he will divide the spoil with the mighty, for having exposed himself to death and being counted among the sinners, while actually bearing the sin of many and interceding for the offenders."

This selfless Act of Love, Yeshua gives no blame for his death. But, it was all the sins of all people in history and future generations that Yeshua died, Love... what a great and awesome saving love.

Chapter 9 - Anti-Semitism

Then answered all the people, and said, His blood be on us, and on our children.

(Matthew 27:25)

The verse of scripture in Matthew 27:25 these very words used against the Jewish people and millions have died because of this very self-proclaimed curse and very prophetic verse in scripture. The past two-millenniums the Christian Church have used this very scripture; professing the Jews were Messiah-Killers and the church in German word Judenhass (Jew-haters). The Idea seems pre-judgmental and vulgar. However, to use the word antisemitism seemed more acceptable and scientific on the view of Darwinism.

Friedrich Wilhelm Adolph Marr was a German agitator and publicist, who popularized the term "antisemitism." On the other hand, it does seem likely that Marr influenced by Ernst Haeckel, a professor who popularized the notion of Social Darwinism among Germany's educated classes.

Despite his influence, Marr's ideas not immediately adopted by German nationalists. The Pan-German League, founded in 1891, allowed for the membership of Jews, the provision they are fully assimilated into German culture. It was only in 1912, eight years after Marr's death, that the League declared racism as an underlying principle. Nevertheless, Marr was a significant link in the evolving chain of German racism that erupted into genocide during the Nazi era.

Satan will use humanity to destroy humankind; we must remember that our battle and the spiritual battles we face each day are not with humanity.

(Ephesians 6:12) *"For we wrestle not against flesh and blood, but against principalities, against powers, against the rulers of the darkness of this world, against spiritual wickedness in high places."*

Looking at history, we can see that the people of Israel have faced with absolute utter destruction from principalities behind kingdoms and nations. Satan and his fallen once and darkness of this world are doing all they can to destroy Israel so the Messiah could not Redeem Israel and the Nations.

Reading the Tanakh (Old Testament) Satan and his fallen ones and the darkness of this world planned genocide for Israel and its peoples. Just a few examples, Pharaoh killing the male babies, later chasing down Israel into the desert to destroy them at the Red Sea were God intervened. The people crossed over on dry land, and Pharaoh and his army destroyed. The Book of Esther shows a plot of genocide was planned to destroy the Jewish people.

History itself we see the dehumanization of the Jewish people through the world. The real accomplishments of the Jewish people have been looked at as threat to others and not a gift. It is this mindset that has caused the deaths of millions of God's Chosen people Israel.

Because God chose Israel as his people and had given them the Instruction and Teaching to live as righteous people, the Chosen people have fallen from Gods ways to their own. Thus, Millions suffered from their sinful acts. Some examples are Israel taken into captivity by Assyria; later Juda was taken into captivity in Babylon.

Only proves that sin leads to death, but through the Messiah comes life.

The problem is real because the spiritual war for the souls of humanity is real. The Messiah was not murdered by any peoples or nation, let alone the Jewish people.

John 10:17-18 *"Yeshua said "Therefore doth my Father love me, because I lay down my life, that I might take it again. No man taketh it from me, but I lay it down of myself. I have power to lay it down, and I have power to take it again. This commandment have I received of my Father."*

Yeshua the Messiah came first as the suffering servant "Yeshua Ben Yosef" and will return as "Yeshua Ben David" a conquering King of kings setting up his Kingdom on earth.

The battle belongs to the HaShem (Referring to God's Holy Name), but we have our part to do as we continue on our journey to our desired destination. Living a life pleasing to HaShem we can make a difference in this world and the world to come.

Knowing that the enemy has a plan to destroy Israel and the Nations it is no surprise. He (HaSatan) wants to take as many as he can with him to judgment.

Revelation 12:7-9 *"And there was war in heaven: Michael and his angels fought against the dragon; and the dragon fought and his angels, and prevailed not; neither was their place found any more in heaven. And the great dragon was cast out, that old serpent, called the Devil, and Satan, which deceives the whole world: he was cast out into the earth, and his angels were cast out with him."*

Revelation 12:12 *"Therefore rejoice, ye heavens, and ye that dwell in them. Woe to the inhabiters of the earth and of the sea! For the devil is come down unto you, having great wrath, because he knoweth that he hath but a short time."*

On this journey we are undertaking we must understand this life and what we see, touch, hear, feel, taste are just temporary. The world to come is forever and ever. We must stand ready and prepared on this journey for the trick and the tactics of the Adversary and the workers of darkness.

The enemy of humankind has taken every lawful act he can play against humans. It is God Himself that restrains and prevents utter destruction (genocide) of Israel. Moreover, the Nations of the world, God has a plan; it is His perfect plan that he has made before the foundation of the world. We must follow the Instructions –Teachings which is in the Torah.

Following the instruction will help us from falling down the cliff, or leaving the path that leads us to our desired destination.

Psalms 119:105-106: נ NUN. *"Thy word is a lamp unto my feet, and a light unto my path. I have sworn, and I will perform it, that I will keep thy righteous judgments."*

Chapter 10 – The Way

"But this I do admit to you: I worship the God of our fathers in accordance with the Way (which they call a sect). I continue to believe everything that accords with the Torah and everything written in the Prophets. (Acts 24:14)

The Pharisees also the Sadducees referred to the followers of Yeshua a sect called "The Way". Along our journey we will find that the followers of Yeshua the Messiah had a rough road ahead.

Luke made the statement in Act 24:14 that those who followed Yeshua were referred to as "The Way." Luke made it clear that he was a Torah observant Jew and followed the Writings and the Prophets (TaNaKh which is referred to by Christians today as the Old Testament). This very important point the Messianic Believers who are born-again believers are on the same journey as we are.

The first century believers spreading the word to an uninformed and unbelieving world about the Messiah had died, risen from the dead and now at the right hand of the Father. The Good News they carried with them was the Messiah is coming back and be ready.

Before Yeshua the Messiah ascended into heaven he gave the disciples this command, which the Christians today call the Great Commission. This is not by any means the great suggestion! We who are this journey have been commanded by our Messiah to do the following as it is written:

Matthew 28:16-20 "So the eleven talmidim (disciples) went to the hill in the Galil (Galilee) where Yeshua had told them to go. When they saw him, they prostrated themselves before him; but some hesitated. Yeshua came and talked with them. He said, 'All authority in heaven and on earth has been given to me. Therefore, go and make people from all nations into talmidim (disciples), immersing them into the reality of the Father, the Son and the Ruach HaKodesh (Holy Spirit), and teaching them to obey everything that I have commanded you. And remember! I will be with you always, yes, even until the end of the age.'"

A very important note here is that the New Testament had not been written and it would be close to a hundred years before the letters of Sha'ul (Paul) and the other Disciples (Apostles) writings would be canonized (Tested) and placed together making the New Testament as we know it today. It was the TaNaKh the Old Testament which they shared with the Jewish world and the Gentiles that the Messiah has come and will return.

The prophets revealed two opposing characteristics of the Messiah; the first is the suffering servant (Mashiach ben Yosef) an example is found in Isaiah 53:1-12:

"Who believes our report? To whom is the arm of *Adonai (substituting the proper and Holy Name of God), revealed? For before him he grew up like a young plant, like a root out of dry ground. He was not well-formed or especially handsome; we saw him, but his appearance did not attract us. People despised and avoided him, a man of pains, well acquainted with illness. Like someone from whom people turn their faces, he was despised; we did not value him. In fact, it was our diseases he bore, our pains from which he suffered; yet we regarded him as punished, stricken and afflicted by God. But he was wounded because of our crimes, crushed because of our sins; the disciplining that makes us whole fell on him, and by his bruises and in fellowship with him we are healed. We all, like sheep, went astray; we turned, each one, to his own way; yet Adonai laid on him the guilt of all of us. Though mistreated, he was submissive; he did not open his mouth. Like a lamb led to be slaughtered, like a sheep silent

*before its shearers, he did not open his mouth. After forcible arrest and sentencing, he was taken away; and none of his generation protested his being cut off from the land of the living for the crimes of my people, who deserved the punishment themselves. He was given a grave among the wicked; in his death he was with a rich man. Although he had done no violence and had said nothing deceptive, yet it pleased *Adonai to crush him with illness, to see if he would present himself as a guilt offering. If he does, he will see his offspring; and he will prolong his days; and at his hand *Adonai's desire will be accomplished. After this ordeal, he will see satisfaction. "By his knowing pain and sacrifice, my righteous servant makes many righteous; it is for their sins that he suffers. Therefore I will assign him a share with the great; he will divide the spoil with the mighty, for having exposed himself to death and being counted among the sinners, while actually bearing the sin of many and interceding for the offenders."*

The above scripture is an apt description of Yeshua the Messiah the suffering servant (Mashiach ben Yosef).

The second characteristic of the Messiah (Mashiach ben David) the conquering king who will set up His Kingdom in the last days, which you can see in Zechariah 14:1-9:

*"Look, a day is coming for *Adonai (substituting the proper and Holy Name of God) when your plunder, Jerusalem (Yerushalayim), will be divided right there within you. "For I will gather all the nations against Jerusalem (Yerushalayim) for war. The city will be taken, the houses will be rifled, the women will be raped, and half the city will go into exile; but the rest of the people will not be cut off from the city."*

*Then *Adonai will go out and fight against those nations, fighting as on a day of battle. On that day his feet will stand on the Mount of Olives, which lies to the east of Jerusalem (Yerushalayim); and the Mount of Olives will be split in half* *from east to west, to make a huge valley. Half of the mountain will move toward the north, and half of it toward the south. You will flee to the valley in the mountains, for the valley in the mountains will reach to Atzel (Azal). You will flee, just as you fled before the earthquake in the days of `Uziyah (Uzziah) king of Y'hudah (Judah). Then *Adonai my God will come to you with all the holy ones. On that day, there will be neither bright light nor thick darkness; and one day, known to *Adonai, will be neither day nor night, although by evening there will be light. On that day, fresh water will flow out from Yerushalayim, half toward the eastern sea and half toward the western sea, both summer and winter. Then *Adonai will be king over the whole world. On that day Adonai will be the only one, and his name will be the one name (One - Echad).*

The People and both the Pharisees and Sadducees were looking for a deliver a leader to make Israel free from the Roman Empire and rule over them. There hope and sights were not looking for a suffering servant like Joseph. It was Joseph who saved Israel from the great famine on the earth and brought the people of Israel to Egypt to live. This historic story is recorded in Genesis starting in chapter 37-50.

To better understand who the Messiah is and why he is referred to as (Mashiach ben Yosef) studying and then comparing this to Yeshua and His ministry will be an eye opening experience.

When Yeshua came and taught his disciples, he completed a picture of himself painted in the pages (Scrolls of the Torah). When we having a preconceived idea and hold that as the lens of truth, we to can be miss led or lose our way on this journey. In order to complete our journey to the desired destination we must look at the Bible a fresh as if it was our first time. A close mind can lock out the truth, but an open mind seeks the truth and tests every word. On our journey with prayer and testing the Word of God with the

Word of God will give us a heading to complete our journey.

As the suffering servant (Mashiach ben Yosef) there are many places in scripture that stand out, such as Psalms 22:1-31 A psalm of David:

"My God! My God! Why have you abandoned me?"

Why so far from helping me, so far from my anguished cries? My God, by day I call to you, but you don't answer; likewise at night, but I get no relief. Nevertheless, you are holy, enthroned on the praises of Israel. In you our ancestors put their trust; they trusted, and you rescued them. They cried to you and escaped; they trusted in you and were not disappointed. But I am a worm, not a man, scorned by everyone, despised by the people. All who see me jeer at me; they sneer and shake their heads:

"He committed himself to *Adonai (substituting the proper and Holy Name of God), so let him rescue him! Let him set him free if he takes such delight in him!"

But you are the one who took me from the womb; you made me trust when I was on my mother's breasts. Since my birth I've been thrown on you; you are my God from my mother's womb. Don't stay far from me, for trouble is near; and there is no one to help. Many bulls surround me; wild bulls of Bashan close in on me. They open their mouths wide against me, like ravening, roaring lions. I am poured out like water; all my bones are out of joint; my heart has become like wax; it melts inside me; my mouth is as dry as a fragment of a pot, my tongue sticks to my palate; you lay me down in the dust of death. Dogs are all around me, a pack of villains closes in on me like a lion at my hands and feet. "They pierced my hands and feet." I can count every one of my bones, while they gaze at me and gloat. They divide my garments among themselves; for my clothing they throw dice. But you, Adonai, *don't stay far away! My strength, come quickly to help me! Rescue me from the sword, my life from the power of the dogs. Save me from the lion's mouth! You have answered me from the wild bulls' horns. I will proclaim your name to my kinsmen; right there in the assembly I will praise you: "You who fear *Adonai, praise him! All descendants of Ya`akov (Jacob), glorify him! All descendants of Israel stand in awe of him! For he has not despised or abhorred the poverty of the poor; he did not hide his face from him but listened to his cry. "Because of you I give praise in the great assembly; I will fulfill my vows in the sight of those who fear him. The poor will eat and be satisfied; those who seek *Adonai will praise him; your hearts will enjoy life forever. All the ends of the earth will remember and turn to *Adonai; all the clans of the nations will worship in your presence. For the kingdom belongs to *Adonai, and he rules the nations. All who prosper on the earth will eat and worship; all who go down to the dust will kneel before him, including him who can't keep himself alive. A descendant will serve him; the next generation will be told of *Adonai. They will come and proclaim his righteousness to a people yet unborn, that he is the one who did it.*

The preconception that the Messiah was going to be a military leader, this idea was well in the forefront of the religious Jewish leaders at the time of Yeshua. Overlooking that the Messiah would first demonstrate himself as the suffering servant as Mashiach ben Yosef. They saw themselves as one suffering and the coming Messiah would rid them of the Roman's and all would be right.

On our journey we need to watch out that we do not get caught up in the news of the day; thinking this has happened then Messiah is coming back now. Yes looking forward to Yeshua's return is a wonderful thought. But, what are we supposed to be doing till he returns?

Yeshua gave us many examples of this one of these can be found in *Matthew 24:42-45:

"Watch therefore: for you know not what hour your Lord doth come. But know this that if the good man of the house had known in what watch the thief would come, he would have watched, and would not have suffered his house to be broken up. Therefore are you also ready: for in such an hour as you think not the Son of man cometh. Who then is a faithful and wise servant, whom his lord hath made ruler over his household, to give them meat in due season?"

Our journey is to look ahead and keep our bearings to the desired destination. As historical and biblical records have shown, the disciples did in fact go out as they were commanded. They too had on their hearts and urgency to share the Gospel to the World taking the message far and wide to the nations. Their first concern was not for their own welfare but... *"Making people from all nations into talmidim (disciples), immersing them into the reality of the Father, the Son and the Ruach HaKodesh (Holy Spirit), and teaching them to obey everything that I have commanded you. And remember! I will be with you always, yes, even until the end of the age.'"*

In a future chapter (The believer's) we will cover more about the disciples and others that took the Great Commission to heart and to the Nations of the World.

On my journey to the desired destination I have found in the New Testament (Brit Hadashah) the Christian versions call the believers Christians. It was not so, till the early fourth century when the Bible was translated from Greek to Latin this terminology was established. There is a underlining agenda at that time to take the Jewishness out of the Bible. To establish a Christian religion based on the Greek mind set. This will be covered in a future chapter (Greek via Hebrew).

An example a scripture that have been changed that could lead one off the path of our journey; So that it now appears that the Messianic Believers are now called Christians. Comparing the KJV to the CJB:

Acts 11:26 KJV: *"And when he had found him, he brought him unto Antioch. And it came to pass, that a whole year they assembled themselves with the church, and taught much people. And the disciples were called (Christians) first in Antioch."*

Acts 11:26 CJB: *"And when he found him, he brought him to Antioch. They met with the congregation there for a whole year and taught a sizeable crowd. Also it was in Antioch that the talmidim (disciples) for the first time were called ("Messianic.")*

In the King James Version the word used in Greek is Χριστός (G5547) which means "Christian, a follower of Messiah"

In the Hebrew the word is משיחיים which means Messianic a believer who believes the Messiah has come and will return again.

This subtle change from Hebrew to Greek has caused much confusion close to, two thousand years of history. Keep this in mind as history progress you hear little about the Messianic believers. History has placed a division between the Jew and Christians, both overlooking the Messianic believers who believe that the Messiah has come and will come again. This confusion has come from the Adversary, beware and test all things.

Yeshua said this of the Adversary and the Religious leaders in John 8:44:

"You are of your father the devil (Adversary), and the lusts of your father you will do. He was a murderer from the begin-

ning, and abode not in the truth, because there is no truth in him. When he speaketh a lie, he speaketh of his own: for he is a liar, and the father of it."

On our journey you will find many hidden treasures which will encourage you and give you strength to continue to our desired destination.

*Zephaniah 3:8-9 *"Therefore wait you upon me, saith the *LORD (substituting the proper and Holy Name of God), until the day that I rise up to the prey: for my determination is to gather the nations, that I may assemble the kingdoms, to pour upon them mine indignation, even all my fierce anger: for all the earth shall be devoured with the fire of my jealousy. For then will I turn to the people a pure language, that they may all call upon the name of the LORD, to serve him with one consent."*

Chapter 11 - Legalism

"Howbeit in vain do they worship me, teaching for doctrines the commandments of men."

Mark 7:7

Continuing our journey we will come across this stumbling block of Legalism. To some it may not look like a big thing, but we must keep our feet on the path to our desired destination. To do this we must know how to identify this stumbling block so we can go around it safely. As you will discover it could appear the pot is calling the kettle black, but is that the case?

This definition of Legalism, in Christian theology, is the act of putting the law above the gospel. This establishes requirements for salvation beyond the fact of Grace (covered in a previous chapter) that repentance, obedience; works according to the law is out of date.

This is what Yeshua has to say about the subject of legalism:

Matthew 5:17-20 *"Think not that I am come to destroy the law, or the prophets: I am not come to destroy, but to fulfil (complete). For verily I say unto you, till heaven and earth pass, one jot or one tittle shall in no wise pass from the law, till all be fulfilled(completed). Whosoever therefore shall break one of these least commandments, and shall teach men so, he shall be called the least in the kingdom of heaven: but whosoever shall do and teach them, the same shall be called great in the kingdom of heaven. For I say unto you, that except your righteousness shall exceed the righteousness of the scribes and Pharisees, ye shall in no case enter into the kingdom of heaven."*

Have you, as a Believer, ever been accused of legalism? That word is often used in the Christian subculture incorrectly. For example, some people might call someone a legalist because they view him as narrow-minded. But the term legalism does not refer to narrow-mindedness. In reality, legalism manifests itself in many subtle ways.

First off legalism involves nonrepresentational application of the law of God from its original context. Some people seem to be preoccupied in the Believers life when they are obeying rules and regulations, and many conceive of Christianity or Messianic Believers as being a series of do's and don'ts, cold and deadly set of moral and spiritual principles. That's one form of legalism, where one is concerned merely with the keeping of God's law as a means to Salvation.

God certainly cares about us being obedient to His commandments; this is how we demonstrate our love to Him. Yeshua explained this in John 15:9-14:

"Just as my Father has loved me, I too have loved you; so stay in my love. If you keep my commands, you will stay in my love; just as I have kept my Father's commands and stay in his love. I have said this to you so that my joy may be in you, and your joy is complete. "This is my command: that you keep on loving each other just as I have loved you. No one has greater love than a person who lays down his life for his friends. You are my friends, if you do what I command you."

This selfless act of love for us on the cross was perfectly demonstrated by Yeshua with His love for us.

John 3:16-21: *"For God so loved the world, that he gave his only begotten Son, that whosoever believeth in him should not perish, but have everlasting life. For God sent not his Son into the world to condemn the world; but that the world through him might be saved. He that believeth on him is not condemned: but he that believeth not is condemned already, because he hath not believed in the name of the only begotten Son of God. And this is the condemnation, that light is come into the world, and men loved darkness rather than light, because their deeds were evil. For every one that doeth evil hateth the light, neither cometh to the light, lest his deeds should be reproved. But he that doeth truth cometh to the light that his deeds may be made manifest, that they are wrought in God."*

On our journey we have found that Gods love is the very act of grace. We can demonstrate our love to God in (Obedience is covered in future chapters and Loving God). This act of saving grace has set us apart from the world, which is Good News. Our part of Gods Loving plan is to serve Him with a pure motive of love.

Mark 12:28-31 *"And one of the scribes came, and having heard them reasoning together, and perceiving that he had answered them well, asked him, which is the first commandment of all?"*

And Yeshua answered him, *"The first of all the commandments is, Hear, O Israel; The Lord our God is one Lord: And thou shalt love the Lord thy God with all thy heart, and with all thy soul, and with all thy mind, and with all thy strength: this is the first commandment. And the second is like, namely this, Thou shalt love thy neighbour as thyself. There is none other commandment greater than these."*

God gave the Ten Commandments in the context of the covenant with gracious act of redeeming His people out of slavery in Egypt. God entered into a loving, personal relationship with Israel. It was only after taking his people out of Egypt, that grace-based relationship was established. Then God began to define the specific laws - instructions that are pleasing to Him that would guide his people to live a righteous life.

To understand the second type of legalism, there's no love, joy, life, or passion. It's a mechanical form of law-keeping call externalism. Believing you can work your way to heaven. The legalist focuses only on obeying bare rules, destroying the broader context of God's Love, Redemption and Grace in which devoid the purpose of the Law. This form of legalism removes the letter of the law not observing the spirit of the law, which is love. This obedience is a self-righteous act that violates the spirit of the law of love. There's only a slight distinction between this form of legalism and the one previously mentioned.

The third type of legalism adds to God's law, then treating them as divine. It is the most common and deadly form of legalism.

Yeshua rebuked the Pharisees at this very point, saying in Matthew 15:7-9:

"You hypocrites! Yesha`yahu (Isaiah) was right when he prophesied about you, *'These people honor me with their lips, but their hearts are far away from me. Their worship of me is useless, because they teach man-made rules as if they were doctrines.'* "

We have no right to heap up restrictions on people where God himself has no stated restriction. The gospel calls men to repentance, holiness, and righteousness. Because of this, the world finds the gospel offensive, a list of do's and don'ts.

Yeshua said in Matthew 11:28-30:

"Come unto me, all of you that labour and are heavy laden and I will give you rest. Take my yoke upon you, and learn of me; for I am meek and lowly in heart: and ye shall find rest unto your souls. For my yoke is easy, and my burden is light."

On our journey we know that we must not add to or take away from God's instruction –teachings in the law, Deuteronomy 4:2:

"You shall not add unto the word which I command you, neither shall ye diminish ought from it, that you may keep the commandments of the LORD your God which I command you."

Psalms 19:7-8: *"The law of the LORD is perfect, converting the soul: the testimony of the LORD is sure, making wise the simple. The statutes of the LORD are right, rejoicing the heart: the commandment of the LORD is pure, enlightening the eyes."*

As we continue our journey knowing that what God has said, is what God means, It becomes clear the direction which we must take our journey and arrive at our preferred destination. The next chapter we will cover more on the Law, and how wonderful it is to know the Law/Torah simply means (Instructions – Teaching).

Chapter 12 - The Law

Blessed is the man that walketh not in the counsel of the ungodly, nor standeth in the way of sinners, nor sitteth in the seat of the scornful. But his delight is in the law of the LORD; and in his law
(Instructions – teachings) doth he meditate day and night.
(Psalms 1:1-2)

This part of our journey we see the instructions and teachings that God has set before us to guide us on our journey to our desired destination. We must place these instructions into our mind so that we do not forget them. Reading the instructions and taking the time to study the instructions they become second nature to you as you continue on your journey. Knowing and understanding these instructions will give you strength, direction and confidence that you will arrive at your destination.

תּוֹרָה tôwrâh, to-raw'; or תּוֹרָה tôrâh; from Strong's H3384; a precept or statute, especially the Decalogue or Pentateuch:—law (law, direction, *instruction*).

The reference to where we find the law is located in the Pentateuch or what the Hebrew refers to as the Torah. But that is the location, the meaning of the word Torah is (Instruction – teachings).

The examples of the law (Instructions – teachings) come to life through the life and ministry of Yeshua the Messiah in the apostolic writings, which the Christian refer to as the New Testament. The Messianic Believers refer to these as the בְּרִית חֲדָשָׁה (B'rit Hadashah). It includes the four Gospels, the Acts of the Apostles, twenty-one epistles by St. Paul and others, and the book of Revelation.

The failure to separate the Torah as the location in the scriptures; thus calling it the Law has over the centuries gave way to the true meaning in Hebrew as (Instructions – Teachings) has cause many problems of false doctrines in the western mind set and the church.

Yeshua said in Matthew 5:17-20:

"Think not that I am come to destroy the law (Torah), or the prophets: I am not come to destroy, but to fulfil (Complete). For verily I say unto you, till heaven and earth pass, one jot or one tittle shall in no wise pass from the law, till all be fulfilled (Completed). Whosoever therefore shall break one of these least commandments, and shall teach men so, he shall be called the least in the kingdom of heaven: but whosoever shall do and teach them, the same shall be called great in the kingdom of heaven. For I say unto you, that except your righteousness shall exceed the righteousness of the scribes and Pharisees, ye shall in no case enter into the kingdom of heaven."

Yeshua came to be an example in instruction and teaching the fullness of the Torah. He did not do away with it. The proof is in the passage. As long as there is a heaven and earth the law (Torah) is in effect.

All the instructions on how to live a righteous life can be found in what the Christians call the Old Testament, the Hebrew refer to it as the TaNaKh. This is a Hebrew acronym for Torah (Pentateuch), Nevi'im (The Prophets), and Kethuvim (The writings).

The Messianic Hebrew Bible is the same as the Christian Bible, but the books may be in a different order:

Tanakh	B'rit Hadashah
TORAH – Instructions –	Gospels and
The five Books of Moses	Emissaries
Genesis – B'reshit בראשית	Matthew – Mattityahu מתי
Exodus – Sh'mot שמות	Mark - מרקוס
Leviticus – Vayikra ויקרא	Luke - לוקא
Numbers – B'midbar במדבר	John –Yochanan יוחנן

Deuteronomy - D'varim - דברים   Acts of the Shlichim - פרכסיס דשליחא

Nevi'im – The Proph   The Major Testimonies
Joshua – Y'hoshua– יהושע   Hebrews - עבריא דלות
Judges – Shof'tim – שן   James – Ya'akov - יעקב
1 Samuel – Shmuel Alef - א שמואל   Jude – Yehudah - יהודה
2 Samuel – Shmuel Bet – ב שמואל   1 Peter – 1 Kefa - פטרוס א
1 Kings – M'lakim Alef – א מלכים   2 Peter – 2 Kefa - פטרוס ב
2 Kings – M'lakim Bet – ב מלכים   Romans – Rahomena - רהומנא
Isaiah – Yesha'yahu – ישעיה   1 Corinthians – 1 Karamita - קרמיתא א
Jeremiah – Yirmeyahu – ירמיה   2 Corinthians – 2 Karamita - קרמיתא ב
Ezekiel – Yechezk'el – יחזקאל
Hosea – Hoshea – הושע

                                    The Ten – Epistles - Letters
Joel – Yo'el – יואל   Galatians – Galatea - גלתיא
Amos – Amos – עמוס   Ephesians – Apsia - אפסיא
Obadiah – Ovadyah – עבדיה   Philippians – Phillipsie - פיליפסיא
Jonah – Yonah – יונה   Colossians – Colasia - קולס'א
Micah – Mihah – מיכה   1 Thessalonians –
Nahum – Nachum – נחום   1 Datsalunikia - דתסלוניקיא א
Habakkuk – Habakkuk – חבקוק   2 Thessalonians –
Zephaniah – Tz'fanyah – צפניה   2 Datsalunikia – דתסלוניקיא ב
Haggai – Hagai – חגי   1 Timothy –
Zechariah – Z'kharyah – זכריה   1 Datumimus – דטימתאוס א
Malachi – Mal'akhi – מלאכי   2 Timothy –
                                    2 Datumimus - דטימתאוס ב
                                    Titus – Titus - טטוס
                                    Philemon – Philmon - פילמון

                                    The Second Testimony of Yochanan (John)
Kethuvim – The Writings   1 John – 1 Yochanan – וחנן א
Psalms – Tehillim – תהילים   2 John – 2 Yochanan - וחנן ב
Proverbs – Mishlei – משלי   3 John – 3 Yochanan – וחנן ג
Job – Iyov – איוב   Revelation – Vision of the Mes-
siah - חזון ישוע המשיח
Song of Solomon – Shir-HaShirim – אשר השירים
Ruth – Rut – רות
Lamentations – Eikhah – איכה
Ecclesiastes – Kohelet – קהלת
Esther – Ester - אסתר
Daniel – Dani'el – דניאל
Ezra – Ezra – עזרא
Nehemiah – Nehemiah – נחמיה
1 Chronicles – Divrei-HaYamim Alef – דברי הימים א
2 Chronicles – Divrei-HaYamim Bet – דברי הימים ב

Chapter 13 - Loving God

He that hath my commandments, and keepeth them, he it is that loveth me: and he that loveth me shall be loved of my Father, and I will love him, and will manifest myself to him.

(John 14:21)

On our journey we know God loves us, and now we are born-again. How to identify sin to avoid that mine field that could destroy us, knowing that all sin leads to death.

Placing action on our faith, even though we have not seen Yeshua our Messiah and living life according to his instructions and waiting for his soon return. Yeshua said to Thomas in John 20:27-29:

"Then saith he to Thomas, Reach hither thy finger, and behold my hands; and reach hither thy hand, and thrust it into my side: and be not faithless, but believing. And Thomas answered and said unto him, My Lord and my God. Jesus saith unto him, Thomas, because thou hast seen me, thou hast believed: blessed are they that have not seen, and yet have believed."

We can continue our journey with the confidence that it is by grace we have been saved and not of works. But, God has given us works to perform to show our love to Him through obedience.

2 Timothy 3:16-17: *"All scripture is given by inspiration of God, and is profitable for doctrine, for reproof, for correction, for instruction in righteousness: That the man of God may be perfect, throughly furnished unto all good works."*

The desire to show our love and express it to a Holy and Awesome God is demonstrated through our obedience to His instructions and teaching. God loves us, this is a fact and we can love God too. Love is a Verb in the Hebrew language – Action is required to fully express love. Love is not an emotional feeling, but an action demonstrated through obedience to Gods word.

The love relationship is like a husband and wife. Just a few examples: The husband expresses his love to his wife by providing for her needs, protecting her. The wife shows her love by helping her husband with his needs such as preparing a meal, caring for children, and looking her best for her husband.

A problem arises in the relations ships with husband and wife when feelings get in the road of treating each other in love. Love being an action, treating one another like you would yourself. If you're feelings get in the road of doing what is right, that is sin. We covered this in a previous chapter.

"Therefore to him that knoweth to do good and doeth it not, to him it is sin." (James 4:17)

The list above is by no means everything a husband or a wife does for one another, hope you get the Idea. Love is an action of right living, righteousness. The instruction on how to love one another and God are written all through the Bible. The love God had for Adam and Eve was demonstrated by removing them from the garden before they could take of the tree of life and live forever in a sinful nature. God has plans for all of mankind, but not all of mankind is willing to follow along with the plan of Salvation.

We know our salvation is a gift, when you receive a gift, and open it up and take ownership of that gift. Then you apply that gift to your life. But, to place it on the shelf and never open it up, well you know about the gift but, you never took ownership. The gift of grace is like that, you must take owner ship, and loving God is doing just that, taking ownership.

*Psalms 31:23-24 *"O love the LORD, all you his saints (believers): for the LORD preserves the faithful, and plentifully rewards the proud doer. Be of good courage, and he shall strengthen your heart, all you that hope in the LORD."*

*John 15:9-*11* "As the Father hath loved me, so have I loved you: continue you in my love. If ye keep my commandments, ye shall abide in my love; even as I have kept my Father's commandments, and abide in his love. These things have I spoken unto you, that my joy might remain in you, and that your joy might be full."*

The commandment that we keep is found in the Torah, (More in the chapter Greatest Commandment). The instructions that are given in the Torah are not do's and don'ts; they are instructions on how to live life to the fullest. God has given these teachings and instructions because he loves us. We can be disobedient children and try to do things our way. He loves us and he will take us out to the spiritual wood shed and give us the correction we need, this too is because he loves us.

*Proverbs 3:11-12 *"My son, don't despise Adonai's (God's) discipline or resent his reproof; for Adonai corrects those he loves like a father who delights in his son."*

God showed his love in many tangible ways; first off He gave Yeshua to demonstrate this love on the cross. He guides us on our journey to our desired destination which, in some future moment we are reunited with Yeshua. Yeshua will be our King and we will be with our creator forever and ever.

God is making sure that we find our way. It is His desire that we show our love to him by following the Instructions on how to best live life till he calls us home.

*John 14:21-24: Yeshua said *"He that hath my commandments, and keepeth them, he it is that loveth me: and he that loveth me shall be loved of my Father, and I will love him, and will manifest myself to him."*

Judas saith unto him, not Iscariot, Lord, how is it that thou wilt manifesting thyself unto us, and not unto the world?

Yeshua answered and said unto him, "If a man love me, he will keep my words: and my Father will love him, and we will come unto him, and make our abode with him. He that loveth me not keepeth not my sayings: and the word which ye hear is not mine, but the Father's which sent me."

Chapter 14 – Sabbath (Shabbat)

Thus the heavens and the earth were finished, and all the host of them. And on the seventh day God ended his work which he had made; and he rested on the seventh day from all his work which he had made. And God blessed the seventh day, and sanctified it: because that in it he had rested from all his work which God created and made.

(Genesis 2:1-3)

The Sabbath day *"Shabbat"* hasn't ever been changed by God. The fourth commandment of the Ten Commandments reads:

Exodus 20:8-11 *"Remember the sabbath day, to keep it holy. Six days shalt thou labour, and do all thy work: But the seventh day is the sabbath of the LORD thy God: in it thou shalt not do any work, thou, nor thy son, nor thy daughter, thy manservant, nor thy maidservant, nor thy cattle, nor thy stranger that is within thy gates: For in six days the LORD made heaven and earth, the sea, and all that in them is, and rested the seventh day: wherefore the LORD blessed the sabbath day, and hallowed it."*

Yeshua the Messiah taught in the synagogue on the Shabbat (Sabbath):

*Mark 1:21-26 "And they went into Capernaum; and straightway on the Sabbath day he entered into the synagogue, and taught. And they were astonished at his doctrine: for he taught them as one that had authority, and not as the scribes. And there was in their synagogue a man with an unclean spirit; and he cried out, Saying, Let us alone; what have we to do with thee, thou Yeshua of Nazareth? Art thou come to destroy us? I know thee who thou art, the Holy One of God. And Yeshua rebuked him, saying, *"Hold thy peace, and come out of him."* And when the unclean spirit had torn him, and cried with a loud voice, he came out of him."

*Mark 6:2-4 "And when the Sabbath day was come, he (Yeshua) began to teach in the synagogue: and many hearing him were astonished, saying, from whence hath this man these things? And what wisdom is this which is given unto him, that even such mighty works are wrought by his hands? Is not this the carpenter, the son of Mary, the brother of James, and Joses, and of Juda, and Simon? And are not his sisters here with us? And they were offended at him. But Yeshua said unto them, *"A prophet is not without honour, but in his own country, and among his own kin, and in his own house."*

Yeshua's disciples and followers taught on the Sabbath (Shabbat) *Acts 13:42-44:

"And when the Jews were gone out of the synagogue, the Gentiles besought that these words might be preached to them the next Sabbath. Now when the congregation was broken up, many of the Jews and religious proselytes followed Paul and Barnabas: who, speaking to them, persuaded them to continue in the grace of God. And the next Sabbath day came almost the whole city came together to hear the word of God."

So why does the Christian church teach that the day of rest is Sunday? There can be no doubt that Yeshua the Messiah, His disciples, and the first-century Messianic Believers kept Saturday, the seventh-day Sabbath (Shabbat). Yet, today, most of the professing Christian world keeps Sunday, the first day of the week, calling it the Sabbath. Who made this change, and how did it occur?

It has been prophesied in the Bible the Book of Daniel, that Satan will be instrumental in changing the set times and the commandments; the Shabbat is a set time and the fourth commandment.

Daniel 7:25a "He will speak against the Most High and oppress his saints and try to change the set times and the laws."

Historically it has been attributed, Constantine, a Roman Emperor:

The Edict of Constantine; on 3 March 321 A.D., decreed that Sunday (dies Solis) will be observed as the Roman day of rest:

"On the venerable day of the Sun let the magistrates and people residing in cities rest, and let all workshops be closed. In the country however persons engaged in agriculture may freely and lawfully continue their pursuits because it often happens that another day is not suitable for grain-sowing or vine planting; lest by neglecting the proper moment for such operations the bounty of heaven should be lost."

The 4th century, Socrates Scholasticus stated that the Christians of Alexandria and Rome partook of the "mysteries" (the love feast or Eucharist) on the first day of the week (Saturday evening), though they also held worship meetings on Sabbath like almost all other churches.

Later on in 5th century, Sozomen stated that most churches, such as at Constantinople, met both on Sabbath and first day (Saturday evening), but that Rome and Alexandria met only on the first day (Saturday evening) and no longer on Sabbath.

Didache,4 (A.D. 90). Tradition on the Lord's own day (Sunday) because he rose that day, assembles in common to break bread and offer thanks, but first confess your sins so that your sacrifice may be pure."

Ignatius, To the Magnesians, 9:1 (A.D. 110): "If, therefore, those who were brought up in the ancient order of things have come to the possession of a new hope, no longer observing the Sabbath, but living in the observance of the Lord's Day, on which also our life has sprung up again by Him and by His death–whom some deny, by which mystery we have obtained faith, and therefore endure, that we may be found the disciples of Jesus Christ, our only Master."

Clement of Alexandria, Stromata, 6:16 (A.D. 202): "The seventh day, therefore, is proclaimed a rest–abstraction from ills–preparing for the Primal Day,[The Lord's Day] our true rest; which, in truth, is the first creation of light, in which all things are viewed and possessed. From this day the first wisdom and knowledge illuminate us. For the light of truth–a light true, casting no shadow, is the Spirit of God indivisibly divided to all, who are sanctified by faith, holding the place of a luminary, in order to the knowledge of real existences. By following Him, therefore, through our whole life, we become impossible; and this is to rest."

It is man not God that has felt they have more wisdom that that of God to change the Shabbat to Sunday. We must be aware on our journey not to hold to the doctrines and traditions of men.

God has warned us of not changing his commands:

Deuteronomy 4:2: "You shall not add unto the word which I command you, neither shall you diminish ought from it, that you may keep the commandments of the LORD your God which I command you."

* Revelation 22:19: " And if any man shall take away from the words of the book of this prophecy, God shall take away

his part out of the book of life, and out of the holy city, and from the things which are written in this book."

Yeshua said in John 14:15: *"If you love me, keep my commandments."*

The question is should we obey men or God?

Our journey is one which will take us a life time. And God is with us on this journey to our desired destination. We must test everything we hear, read and do; making sure we stay the course on our journey, not to wander of course and find ourselves lost in a mine field of confusion and doubt.

*1 John 4:1-6 *"Dear friends, don't trust every spirit. On the contrary, test the spirits to see whether they are from God; because many false prophets have gone out into the world. Here is how you recognize the Spirit of God: every spirit which acknowledges that Yeshua the Messiah came as a human being is from God, and every spirit which does not acknowledge Yeshua is not from God; in fact, this is the spirit of the Anti-Messiah. You have heard that he is coming. Well, he's here now, in the world already! You, children, are from God and have overcome the false prophets, because he who is in you is greater than he who is in the world. They are from the world; therefore, they speak from the world's viewpoint; and the world listens to them. We are from God. Whoever knows God listens to us; whoever is not from God doesn't listen to us. This is how we distinguish the Spirit of truth from the spirit of error."*

Always refer back to Gods instructions and teaching in the Bible. Testing everything on your journey in this life; so that you do not get lost along the way to our desired destination.

Chapter 15 - Greek via Hebrew

This chapter is copied from "The Ancient Hebrew Lexicon of the Bible; Pages 11-13"

With permission from the Author Jeff A. Benner

Ancient Hebrew Thought

The definition of a word is going to be directly related to the culture in which that word is being used. One word may have different meanings depending on the culture that is using it. In order to place the correct context to a Hebrew word from the Ancient Hebrew language one must first understand Ancient Hebrew thought.

Abstract and Concrete

Greek thought views the world through the mind (abstract thought). Ancient Hebrew thought views the world through the senses (concrete thought).

Concrete thought is the expression of concepts and ideas in ways that can be seen, touched, smelled, tasted or heard. All five senses are used when speaking, hearing, writing and reading the Hebrew language. An example of this can be found in Psalms 1:3; "He is like a *tree* planted by *streams of water*, which yields its *fruit* in season, and whose *leaf* does not *wither*". In this passage the author expresses his thoughts in concrete terms such as; tree, streams of water, fruit and leaf.

Abstract thought is the expression of concepts and ideas in ways that cannot be seen, touched, smelled, tasted or heard. Examples of Abstract thought can be found in Psalms 103:8 "The LORD is *compassionate* and *gracious*,

Slow to *anger,* abounding in *love".* The words compassion, grace, anger and love are all abstract words, ideas that cannot be experienced by the senses. Why do we find these abstract words in passage of concrete thinking Hebrew? Actually, these are abstract English words used to translate to original Hebrew concrete words. The translators often translate this way because the original Hebrew makes no sense when literally translated into English.

Let us take one of the above abstract words to demonstrate the translation from the concrete Hebrew word ◯𝛿 (aph) which literally means "nose), a concrete word. When one is very angry, he begins to breathe hard and the nostrils begin to flare. A Hebrew sees anger as "The flaring of the nose (nostrils)". If the translator literally translated the above passage "Slow to nose", the English reader would not understand.

Appearance and Functional Descriptions

Greek thought describes objects in relation to its appearance, Hebrew thought describes in relation to its function.

A Greek description of a common pencil would be; "it is yellow and about eight inches long". A Hebrew description of the pencil would be related to its function such as "I write words with it". Notice that the Hebrew description uses the verb "write" while Greek description uses the adjective "yellow" and "long". Because of the Hebrew form of functional descriptions, verbs are used much more frequently then adjectives.

To our Greek way of thinking a deer and an oak are to very different objects and we would never describe them in the same way. The Hebrew word for both of these objects is

אֵיִל (ayil) because the functional descriptions of these two objects are identical to the Ancient Hebrew; therefore, the same Hebrew word is used for both.

The Hebraic definition of אֵיִל is "a strong leader". A deer stag is one of the most powerful animals of the forest and is seen as "strong leader" among the other animals of the forest. The wood of an oak tree is very hard compared to other trees and seen as a "strong leader" among the trees of the forest.

Notice the two different translations of Hebrew word

אֵיִל in Psalms 29:9. The NASB and KJV translates it as *"The voice of the LORD makes the deer to calve"* while the NIV translates it as *"The voice of the LORD twist the oaks."* The literal translation of this verse in Hebrew thought would be; *"The voice of the LORD makes the strong leader turn."*

When translating the Hebrew into English, the Greek thinking translator will give a Greek description to the word for the Greek thinking reader, which is why we have two different ways of translating this verse. This same word "Ayil" is also translated as a "Ruler" (a strong leader of men) in 2 Kings 24:15.

Ancient Hebrew will use different Hebrew words for the same thing depending upon its function at the time. For example an ox may be identified as an אֶלֶף (alph) when referring to a lead ox, a שׁוֹר (Shor) when referring to a plow ox, בָּקָר (baqar) when referring to an ox of the field or פַּר (par) when referring to an ox of the threshing floor.

Static and Dynamic

In Modern western language verbs express action (dynamic) while nouns express inanimate (static) objects. In Hebrew all things are in motion (dynamic) including verbs and nouns. In Hebrew sentences the verbs identify the action of an object while nouns identify an object of action. The verb 𐤔𐤋𐤌 (malak) is the "the reign of the king" while the noun 𐤔𐤋𐤌 (melek) is the "the King who reigns". A mountain top is not a static object but the "head lifting up out of the hill." A good example of this action in what appears to be a static passage is the command to "have no other gods before me" (Exodus 20:3). In Hebrew thought this passage is saying "not to bring another one of power in front of my face."

Chapter 16 – Yeshua

She Mary (Mariam) will give birth to a son, and you are to name him Yeshua, (which means 'God saves,' note using Gods proper; name Saves) because he will save his people from their sins."

(Matthew 1:21)

Christians call him Jesus, but his Hebrew name is Yeshua. Continuing on this journey we need to identify who is Messiah. Being born again we have received Gods Spirit which indwells us and guides us on our journey. Building a strong relationship with God our creator and Messiah it is only natural to know more about Him.

*Isaiah 7:14 "Therefore the Lord himself shall give you a sign; Behold, a virgin shall conceive, and bear a son, and shall call his name Immanuel (`Immanu El- God is with us)."

Genesis 1:1-5 *"In the beginning God created the heavens and the earth. The earth was unformed and void, darkness was on the face of the deep, and the Spirit of God hovered over the surface of the water. Then God said, "Let there be light"; and there was light. God saw that the light was good, and God divided the light from the darkness. God called the light Day, and the darkness he called Night. So there was evening, and there was morning, one day."*

John 1:1-5 *"In the beginning was the Word, and the Word was with God, and the Word was God. He was with God in the beginning. All things came to be through him, and without him nothing made had being. In him was life, and the life was the light of mankind. The light shines in the darkness, and the darkness has not suppressed it."*

בְּרֵאשִׁית בָּרָא אֱלֹהִים אֵת הַשָּׁמַיִם וְאֵת הָאָרֶץ׃

The first Hebrew word in Genesis 1:1 is (בְּרֵאשִׁית) re'shiyth which translated means *"in the beginning."* Modern and Ancient Hebrew is written right to left, each letter is represented by a ideogram or pictograph. As demonstrated in the following: ✝ ﬞ ש ﬥ ﬡ ﬡ is the first word in Ancient Hebrew re'shiyth reading the ideogram left to right; house (*tent*), head (*leader*), ox (*strength*), two front teeth like a snake has (*to destroy*), right arm (to work), cross (covenant).

Using these pictographs to form an ideogram we begin to understand its meaning "The *house* of the *leader* who has all *strength;* could mean God who is the first word to be spoken in this first verse. In Hebrew is verb in the beginning, object create and Subject God (Noun with action). The first three pictographs are identifying God.

The next letter is the teeth of a snake (to destroy) the right hand (to work) on a cross (covenant). It appears that *God* knows that *the serpent* is out to *destroy* His *right hand* (covenant) on a cross.

Looks to me that the very first verse in the Hebrew has the foreknowledge of the Messiah the right hand of God to die on the cross, from the very beginning; it is this very thing John was pointing out in John Chapter 1:1-5 which he had saw in the writings of the Hebrew Torah. Showing that the Messiah was God and the Word of God at the creation of all things made by him.

There are seven Hebrew words in the first verse, the second is בָּרָא "bara'" which is to *"create"*. English translation the first two words; *In the beginning create."*

The third, and next word is; אֱלֹהִים *"elohiym"* meaning God. These three words together *"In the beginning create God"* in translation to English *"In the beginning God created."*

There is a rule in Hebrew when using the fourth word; this word which is in the center of the seven words in this verse is אֵת *"'eth"* the Identifier is the word previous which is אֱלֹהִים "elohiym" which means God. The word in Hebrew identifies אֵת "'eth" as God. It is the same as saying in the Greek the Alfa and Omega, or in English A and Z, but in Hebrew it is the Aleph and Tav which is the First and the Last letter of the Hebrew Alphabet, as is A to Z English, and Alfa and Omega in Greek.

*Revelation 1:11 Yeshua said "Saying, I am Alpha (Aleph) and Omega (Tav), the first and the last: and, What you see, write in a book, and send it unto the seven churches which are in Asia; unto Ephesus, and unto Smyrna, and unto Pergamos, and unto Thyatira, and unto Sardis, and unto Philadelphia, and unto Laodicea."

We see Yeshua is the Aleph and the Tav, the first and the last. John has clearly shown us that Yeshua is God.

Deuteronomy 6:4 "Hear, O Israel: The LORD our God is one LORD:"

Deuteronomy 6:4 "Sh'ma, Yisra'el! Adonai Eloheinu, Adonai Echad [Hear, Isra'el! God (using his proper name our God, is one God]

The first verse of the Shema which is to be said three times a day by the children of Israel; the word Echad means "Is One" There is only One God!

God made it simple, He is the only One God and He personally came to this earth fully man and fully God to save us from ourselves.

John 10:17-18 Yeshua said: *"Therefore doth my Father love me, because I lay down my life, that I might take it again. No man taketh it from me, but I lay it down of myself. I have power to lay it down, and I have power to take it again. This commandment have I received of my Father."*

1 John 3:16 Yeshua said: *"The way that we have come to know love is through his having laid down his life for us. And we ought to lay down our lives for the brothers!"*

Knowing Yeshua and how he lived, died and raised from the grave to be seated on the right hand of the Father is paramount to our journey.

*Psalms 16:8-11 *"I have set the LORD always before me: because he is at my right hand, I shall not be moved. Therefore my heart is glad, and my glory rejoiceth: my flesh also shall rest in hope. For thou wilt not leave my soul in hell; neither wilt thou suffer thine Holy One to see corruption. Thou wilt shew me the path of life: in thy presence is fullness of joy; at thy right hand there are pleasures for evermore."*

Psalms 18:36 *"You give me your shield, which is salvation, your right hand holds me up, your humility makes me great."*

Yeshua is the right hand of God in power and in strength, which lived a perfect life without sin. He lived and died for our sins:

John 3:16-*17* *"For God so loved the world that he gave his only and unique Son, so that everyone who trusts in him may have eternal life, instead of being utterly destroyed. For God did not send the Son into the world to judge the world, but rather so that through him, the world might be saved."*

God has a plan which he conceived before the foundation of the earth Psalms 102:25-28:

"In the beginning, you laid the foundations of the earth; heaven is the work of your hands. They will vanish, but you will remain; like clothing, they will all grow old; yes, you will change them like clothing, and they will pass away. But you

remain the same, and your years will never end. The children of your servants will live securely and their descendants be established in your presence."

Hebrews 1:1-14 "God, who at sundry times and in divers manners spake in time past unto the fathers by the prophets, Hath in these last days spoken unto us by his Son, whom he hath appointed heir of all things, by whom also he made the worlds; who being the brightness of his glory, and the express image of his person, and upholding all things by the word of his power, when he had by himself purged our sins, sat down on the right hand of the Majesty on high; Being made so much better than the angels, as he hath by inheritance obtained a more excellent name than they. For unto which of the angels said he at any time, Thou art my Son, this day have I begotten thee? And again, I will be to him a Father, and he shall be to me a Son? And again, when he bringeth in the first begotten into the world, he saith, and let all the angels of God worship him. And of the angels he saith, who maketh his angels spirits, and his ministers a flame of fire. But unto the Son he saith, Thy throne, O God, is for ever and ever: a scepter of righteousness is the scepter of thy kingdom. Thou hast loved righteousness, and hated iniquity; therefore God, even thy God, hath anointed thee with the oil of gladness above thy fellows. And, Thou, Lord, in the beginning hast laid the foundation of the earth; and the heavens are the works of thine hands: They shall perish; but thou remains; and they all shall wax old as doth a garment; And as a vesture shalt thou fold them up, and they shall be changed: but thou art the same, and thy years shall not fail. But to which of the angels said he at any time, Sit on my right hand, until I make thine enemies thy footstool? Are they not all ministering spirits, sent forth to minister for them who shall be heirs of salvation?"

God made a plan to save mankind before he created the foundation of the earth. He knew what it would cost, it was

Love that held him to the cross. Love and obedience even to death for all mankind.

*Zechariah 12:10 *"And I will pour upon the house of David, and upon the inhabitants of Jerusalem, the spirit of grace and of supplications: and they shall look upon me whom they have pierced, and they shall mourn for him, as one mourned for his only son, and shall be in bitterness for him, as one that is in bitterness for his firstborn."*

John 15:9-14 *"As the Father hath loved me, so have I loved you: continue you in my love. If you keep my commandments, you shall abide in my love; even as I have kept my Father's commandments, and abide in his love. These things have I spoken unto you, that my joy might remain in you, and that your joy might be full. This is my commandment, that you love one another, as I have loved you. Greater love hath no man than this that a man lay down his life for his friends. You are my friends, if ye do whatsoever I command you."*

On our journey we see that God has plotted a course for us to follow. Love is demonstrated through obedience to Gods instructions which is our compass heading to our destination. The map he has given us is Yeshua and how he lived, died and has risen to the right had of the father. It is the strength of His right hand that has furnished the means for us to make the journey to our desired destination.

There had been many disciples (Followers of Yeshua the Messiah) who have made the journey. We will look at these Messianic Believers and their journey in the next chapter.

Chapter 17 - First Messianic Believers

"Watch you therefore, and pray always, that ye may be accounted worthy to escape all these things that shall come to pass, and to stand before the Son of man."

(Luke 21:36)

How did the first Messianic believers live and where did they die?

On our journey we will be met with trials, troubles and persecution; do not think this is something strange.

1 Peter 4:12-13:

"Beloved, think it not strange concerning the fiery trial which is to try you, as though some strange thing happened unto you: But rejoice, inasmuch as ye are partakers of Messiahs sufferings; that, when his glory shall be revealed, ye may be glad also with exceeding joy.

Recorded accounts, stories of the disciples of Yeshua, it is safe to say that the apostles took to heart what Yeshua commanded them when he gave them the great commission *Matthew 28:16-20:

"So the eleven talmidim (disciples) went to the hill in the Galil (Galilee) where Yeshua had told them to go. When they saw him, they prostrated themselves before him; but some hesitated. Yeshua came and talked with them. He said, *"All authority in heaven and on earth has been given to me. Therefore, go and make people from all nations into talmidim (disciples), immersing them into the reality of the Father, the Son and the Ruach HaKodesh, and teaching them to obey everything that I have commanded you. And remem-

ber! I will be with you always, yes, even until the end of the age."

Tradition claims they cast lots to determine where each of them would go into the world. The disciples suffered greatly for their faith. Most of these disciples met with violent deaths.

Many wonder how the 12 disciples died, but The New Testament tells of the fate of only two of the apostles:

1. Judas, who betrayed Jesus and then went out and hanged himself (Matthew 27:3-10)
2. James the son of Zebedee, who was executed by Herod about 44 AD (Acts 12:2).

Judas Iscariot: Shortly after the death of Messiah Judas killed himself. According to the Bible he hanged himself, (Matthew 27:5) at Aceldama, on the southern slope of the valley of Hinnom, near Jerusalem, and in the act he fell down a precipice and was dashed into pieces.

James the son of Zebedee, the elder brother of John, and a relative of our Yeshua; for his mother Salome was cousin to Mary (Mariam the mother of Yeshua). Some ten years after the death of Stephen that the second martyrdom took place. Herod Agrippa had been appointed governor of Judea raised a hard persecution against the Messianic believers of the Way. It is a tradition that James, the Son of Zebedee went to India along with Peter. The Apostolic History of Abdias (sixth and seventh centuries) tells a story of James and his interaction with two pagan magicians who eventually confess Yeshua as the Messiah.

A.D. 44, this account given by writer, Clemens Alexandrinus says: "This should not to be overlooked; that, as James was led to the place of martyrdom, his accuser was brought to repent of his conduct by the James the Son of Zebedee with extraordinary courage and faith. The accuser fell down at his feet to request his pardon, professing himself a believer. The accuser now taking a stand that James should not receive the crown of martyrdom alone. The results were they were both beheaded at the same time. James the son of Zebedee: He was put to death by Herod Agrippa I shortly before the day of the Passover, in the year 44 or about 11 years after the death of Messiah. (Acts 12: 1-2).

These disciples martyr cheerfully and resolutely receive that cup, which he had told our Savior he was ready to drink? Timon and Parmenas suffered martyrdom about the same time; the one at Philippi, and the other in Macedonia.

*Matthew 20:20-24 "Then came to Yeshua the mother of Zebedee's children with her sons, worshipping him, and desiring a certain thing of him. And he said unto her, what wilt thou? She saith unto him, Grant that these my two sons may sit, the one on thy right hand, and the other on the left, in thy kingdom. But Yeshua answered and said, you know not what you ask. Are ye able to drink of the cup that I shall drink of, and to be baptized with the baptism that I am baptized with? They say unto him, we are able. And he saith unto them, you shall drink indeed of my cup, and be baptized with the baptism that I am baptized with: but to sit on my right hand, and on my left, is not mine to give, but it shall be given to them for whom it is prepared of my Father. And when the ten heard it, they were moved with indignation against the two brethren."

Stephen before his death gave a speech to his executioners *Acts 7:1-60:

The high priest says to Stephen, "Are these things so?"

Stephen said, "Men, brethren, and fathers, listen; The God of glory appeared unto our father Abraham, when he was in Mesopotamia, before he dwelt in Charran, And said unto him, Get thee out of thy country, and from thy kindred, and come into the land which I shall show you. He left out of the land of the Chaldaeans, and dwelt in Charran: and from there, when his father was dead, he moved into this land, where you now dwell. He gave him no inheritance in it, no, not so much as to set his foot on: yet he promised that he would give it to him for a possession and to his seed after him, now having no child. God spake to him this way that his seed should sojourn in a strange land; that his seed would be placed in bondage then treated evil four hundred years. This nation to whom they shall be in bondage will I judge, said God: and after that shall they come forth, and serve me in this place. God gave him the covenant of circumcision: and so Abraham begat Isaac, and circumcised him the eighth day; and Isaac begat Jacob; and Jacob begat the twelve patriarchs. The patriarchs, moved with envy, sold Joseph into Egypt: but God was with him, and delivered him out of all his afflictions, and gave him favour and wisdom in the sight of Pharaoh King of Egypt; and he made him governor over Egypt and his entire house. Now there came a famine over all the land of Egypt and Chanaan, and great affliction: and our fathers found no sustenance. But when Jacob heard that there was corn in Egypt, he sent out our fathers first. The second time Joseph was made known to his brethren; and Joseph's kindred was made known unto Pharaoh. Then sent Joseph, and called his father Jacob to him, and all his kindred, threescore and fifteen souls. So Jacob went down into Egypt, and died, he, and our fathers, and were carried over into Sychem, and laid in the sepulcher that Abraham bought for a sum of money of the sons of Emmor the father of Sychem. But when the time of the promise drew nigh, which God had sworn to Abraham, the people grew and multiplied in Egypt, till another king arose, which knew not Joseph. The same dealt subtilly with our kindred, and evil entreated our fathers, so that they cast out their young children, to the end they might not live. In which time Moses was born, and was exceeding fair, and nourished up in his father's house three months: And when he was cast out, Pharaoh's daughter took him up, and nourished him for her own son. And Moses was learned in all the wisdom of the Egyptians, and was mighty in words and in deeds. And when he was full forty years old, it came into his heart to visit his brethren the children of Israel. And seeing one of them suffer wrong, he defended him, and avenged him that was oppressed, and smote the Egyptian: For he supposed his brethren would have understood how that God by his hand would deliver them: but they understood not. And the next day he shewed himself unto them as they strove, and would have set them at one again, saying, Sirs, ye are brethren; why do ye wrong one to another? But he that did his neighbour wrong thrust him away, saying, who made thee a ruler and a judge over us? Wilt thou kill me, as thou did the Egyptian Yesterday? Then fled Moses at this saying, and was a stranger in the land of Madian, where he begat two sons. And when forty years were expired, there appeared to him in the wilderness of mount Sina an angel of the Lord in a flame of fire in a bush. When Moses saw it, he wondered at the sight: and as he drew near to behold it, the voice of the Lord came unto him, Saying, I am the God of thy fathers, the God of Abraham, and the God of Isaac, and the God of Jacob. Then Moses trembled, and durst not behold. Then said the Lord to him, Put off thy shoes from thy feet: for the place where you stand is holy ground. I have seen, I have seen the affliction of my people which is in Egypt, and I have heard their groaning, and am come down to deliver them. And now come, I will send thee into Egypt. This Moses whom they refused, saying, Who made thee a ruler and a judge? The same did God send to be a ruler and a deliverer by the hand of the angel which appeared to him in the bush. He brought them out, after that he had shewed wonders and signs in the land of Egypt, and in the Red sea, and in the wilderness forty years. This is that Moses, which said unto the children of Israel, A prophet shall the Lord your God raise up unto you of your brethren, like unto me; him shall You hear. This is he, that was in the tabernacle in the wilderness with the angel which spake to him in the mount Sina, and with our fathers: who received the lively oracles to give unto us: To whom our fathers would not obey, but thrust him from them, and in their hearts turned back again into Egypt, Saying unto Aaron, Make us gods to go before us: for as for this Moses, which brought us out of the land of Egypt, we do not know what has become of him. And they made a calf in those days, and offered sacrifice unto the idol, and rejoiced in the works of their own hands. Then God turned, and gave them up to worship the host of heaven; as it is written in the book of the prophets, O You house of Israel, have you offered to me slain beasts and sacrifices by the space of forty years in the wilderness?) Yea, You took up the tabernacle of Moloch, and the star of your god Remphan, figures which you made to worship them: and I will carry you away beyond Babylon. Our fathers had the tabernacle of witness in the wilderness, as he had appointed, speaking unto Moses, that he should make it according to the fashion that he had seen. Which also our fathers that came after brought in with Yeshua into the possession of the Gentiles, whom God drove out before the face of our fathers, unto the days of David;   Who found favour before God, and desired to find a tabernacle for the God of Jacob. But Solomon built him a house. Howbeit the most High dwelleth not in temples made with hands; as saith the prophet, Heaven is my throne, and earth is my footstool: what house will you build me? Saith the Lord: or what is the place of my rest? Hath not my hand made all these things? You stiff-necked and uncircumcised in heart and ears, you do always resist the Holy Ghost: as your fathers did, so do you. Which of the prophets have not your fathers persecuted? And they have slain them which shewed before of the coming of the Just One; of whom you have been now the betrayers and murderers: Who have received the law by the disposition of angels, and have not kept it.

When they heard these things, they were cut to the heart, and they gnashed on him with their teeth. But he, being full of the Holy Ghost, looked up stedfastly into heaven, and saw the glory of God, and Yeshua standing on the right hand of God, and said, Behold, I see the heavens opened, and the Son of man standing on the right hand of God. Then they cried out with a loud voice, and stopped their ears, and ran upon him with one accord, and cast him out of the city, and stoned him: and the witnesses laid down their clothes at a young man's feet, whose name was Saul (Sha'ul – Paul).

And they stoned Stephen, calling upon God, and saying, Lord Jesus, receive my spirit. And he kneeled down, and cried with a loud voice, Lord; lay not this sin to their charge. And when he had said this, he fell asleep. To such a degree of madness were they excited, that they cast him out of the city and stoned him to death. The time when he suffered is generally supposed to have been at the Passover which succeeded to that of our Lord's crucifixion, and to the era of his ascension, in the following spring.

Upon this a great persecution was raised against all who professed their belief in Messiah: Acts 8:1

And Saul was consenting unto his death. And at that time there was a great persecution against the church which was at Jerusalem; and they were all scattered abroad throughout the regions of Judaea and Samaria, except the apostles.

According to tradition about two thousand suffered martyrdom during the "persecution that arose about Stephen."

Matthew, whose occupation was that of a tax collector, was born at Nazareth. He wrote his gospel in Hebrew, which was afterwards, translated into Greek by James the Less (half-brother of Yeshua). He must have lived many years as an apostle since he was the author of the Gospel of Matthew, which was written at least twenty years after the death of Messiah. Traditional it is believed that he stayed for fifteen years at Jerusalem.

A.D. 60 – Matthew as a missionary to the Persians, Parthians and Medes. The story is that he died a martyr in Ethiopia.

James the Less (His Hebrew name Ya`akov, the half-brother of Yeshua) He was elected to the oversight of the churches of Jerusalem; and was the author of the Epistle ascribed to James. At the age of ninety-four he was beat and stoned by the Jews; and finally had his brains dashed out with a fuller's club.

James son of Alpheus, James it is believed that he was a missionary to Syria. The Jewish historian Josephus reported that he was stoned and then clubbed to death.

Matthias of whom less is known than of most of the other disciples was elected to fill the vacant place of Judas. Tradition has it that he was sent to Syria with Andrew. Later he was executed by burning.

Andrew was the brother of Peter. He preached the gospel to many Asiatic nations; he went to the "land of the man-eaters," in what is now the Soviet Union. Messianic Believers there claim him as the first to bring the gospel to their land. He also preached in Asia Minor, modern-day Turkey, and in Greece, where he is said to have been crucified. He was crucified on a cross, the two ends of which were fixed transversely in the ground. Hence the derivation of the term, St. Andrew's Cross.

Mark was born of Jewish parents of the tribe of Levi. He is supposed to have been converted to Messianic Believer by

Peter. He wrote his Gospel Mark. He was dragged to pieces by the people of Alexandria.

Simon Called Peter by Messiah died 33-34 years after the death of Messiah. According to Smith's Bible Dictionary, there is "satisfactory evidence that he and Paul were the founders of the church at Rome and died in that city. The time and manner of the apostle's martyrdom are less certain.

A.D. 67, 68: Early writers that Peter died at or about the same time with Paul, and in the Neronian persecution. Peter felt himself to be unworthy to be put to death in the same manner as his Master, and was, therefore, at his request, crucified with his head downward."

Paul (his Roman name), the apostle also called Saul (Hebrew Name Sha'ul), after his great travail and unspeakable labors in promoting the Gospel of Messiah, suffered also in this first persecution under Nero. Abdias, declared his execution, Nero sent two of his esquires, Ferega and Parthemius, to bring him word of his execution. Soldiers came and led him out of the city to the place of execution, where Paul, after he prayed then willing laid his neck on the block then was executed with the sword. Ferega and Parthemius came to Paul before he was put to death; asking him to pray for them that they too might believe. Later they were baptized at Paul's sepulcher.

Jude the brother of James was commonly called Thaddeus.

A.D. 72. Jude (Thaddeus): according to tradition Jude taught in Armenia, Syria and Persia where he was martyred. Tradition tells us he was buried in Kara Kalisa in what is now Iran.

Bartholomew preached in several countries in his missionary travels by tradition he traveled to India with Thomas, back to Armenia, and also to Ethiopia and Southern Arabia. Bartholomew had translated the Gospel of Matthew into the language of India. He was beaten and then crucified.

Thomas called Didymus, preached the Gospel in Parthia and India, and was he was executed by pagan priests by being thrust through with a spear.

Luke was the author of the Book of Luke he traveled with Paul through various countries, and is supposed to have been hanged on an olive tree, by the idolatrous priests of Greece.

A.D. 74. Simon the (Zelotes) Zealot, preached the Gospel in Mauritania, Africa, and even in Britain, in which latter country he was crucified, so the story goes while in Persia and was killed after refusing to sacrifice to the sun god.

89 AD to 120 AD - John the "beloved disciple," was brother to James the Great. He was the leader of the church in the Ephesus area and is said to have taken care of Mary the mother of Yeshua in his home. The churches of Smyrna, Pergamos, Sardis, Philadelphia, Laodicea, and Thyatira, were founded by him. From Ephesus he was ordered to be sent to Rome, where he was to be executed in a cauldron of boiling oil, through a miracle John without injury survived the execution. Domitian in fear banished him to the Isle of Patmos, where he later wrote the Book of Revelation. Nerva, the successor of Domitian, set John free and later returned to the mainland. He was the only apostle who escaped a violent death.

About 73 A.D. Barnabas was from Cyprus, but of Jewish descent. It is believed he was martyred but, the story has not been confirmed by history or tradition.

A.D. 54. Philip was born at Bethsaida, in Galilee and was first called by the name of "disciple." He suffered martyrdom at Heliopolis, in Phrygia. He was scourged, thrown into prison, and afterwards crucified. Update: Fox News July 27, 2011, Tomb of the Apostle Phillip is found in Hierapolis.

Judas (not Iscariot) - stoned to death

Sources of information such as the Fox's Book of Martyrs, and Traditions of the early Christian Church and Jewish historians.

Chapter 18 - The Believer

Yeshua said to them, "Come, follow me, and I will make you into fishers for men!"

Mark 1:17)

The first believers were Jewish, most were common hard-working men, fishermen, and a tax collector. Hardly we educated men or of the upper class of Israel. Shavu`ot (Pentecost) in Jerusalem the Holy Spirit (Rach HaKodesh) was poured out on the disciples the believers of the Messiah in Acts 2:1-12:

"The festival of Shavu`ot arrived, and the believers all gathered together in one place. Suddenly there came a sound from the sky like the roar of a violent wind, and it filled the whole house where they were sitting. Then they saw what looked like tongues of fire, which separated and came to rest on each one of them. They were all filled with the Ruach HaKodesh and began to talk in different languages, as the Spirit enabled them to speak. Now there were staying in Yerushalayim religious Jews from every nation under heaven. When they heard this sound, a crowd gathered; they were confused, because each one heard the believers speaking in his own language. Totally amazed, they asked, "How is this possible? Aren't all these people who are speaking from the Galil? How is it that we hear them speaking in our native languages? We are Parthians, Medes, Elamites; residents of Mesopotamia, Y'hudah, Cappadocia, Pontus, Asia, Phrygia, Pamphylia, Egypt, the parts of Libya near Cyrene; visitors from Rome; Jews by birth and proselytes; Jews from Crete and from Arabia. . . ! How is it that we hear them speaking in our own languages about the great things God has done?" Amazed and confused, they all went on asking each other, "What can this mean?"

The very first Messianic congregation was founded in Jerusalem nearly 2,000 years ago when 3,000 people responded to the first gospel sermon that was preached by Peter (Acts 2:14-41). It was a 100 percent Jewish Messianic Believer congregation, now establishing the first Messianic Synagogue of believers; Peter and all of Yeshua and the apostles were Jewish. All the people who responded were Jewish believers. And the person who soon emerged as the leader of the Jerusalem believers was the Jewish half-brother of Yeshua named James (Ya'acov).

These Jewish believers did not build a church with a steeple and an organ. They continued to live as Jews, and they continued to practice the Jewish religion, knowing the Messiah had come and will return again; Thus by their belief they were known as Messianic believers of the sect of The Way.

Paul (his Roman name and Sha'ul his Jewish name) was a trained rabbi committed to the annihilation of the Messianic-believing Jewish sect called "The Way" *and call the Nazarenes*. Later Sha'ul experienced his radical Damascus road conversion (Acts 9:1-9), Sha'ul continued behaving as a Jew and teaching the TaNaKh. Paul (Sha'ul) refers to himself as a Jew, not as a former Jew Acts 22:3"

"I (Sha'ul) am a Jew, born in Tarsus of Cilicia, but brought up in this city and trained at the feet of Gamli'el in every detail of the Torah of our forefathers. I was a zealot for God, as all of you are today."

He (Sha'ul) called himself a Pharisee Acts 23:6:

"But when Paul (Sha'ul) perceived that the one part were Sadducees and the other Pharisees, he cried out in the council, Brethren, I am a Pharisee, a son of Pharisees: touching the hope and resurrection of the dead I am called in question."

Paul (Sha'ul) refers to himself as an Israelite *Romans 11:1:

Paul (Sha'ul) said then, "Has God cast away his people? God forbid. I am an Israelite, of the seed of Abraham, of the tribe of Benjamin."

Paul (Sha'ul) calls himself a Hebrew, 2 Corinthians 11:21-31:

"To my shame, I must admit that we have been too "weak" to do such things! But if anyone dares to boast about something; I'm talking like a fool; I am just as daring. Are they Hebrew-speakers? So am I. Are they of the people of Isra'el? So am I. Are they descendants of Avraham? So am I. Are they servants of the Messiah? (I'm talking like a madman!) I'm a better one! I've worked much harder, been imprisoned more often, suffered more beatings, been near death over and over. Five times I received "forty lashes less one" from the Jews. Three times I was beaten with rods. Once I was stoned. Three times I was shipwrecked. I spent a night and a day in the open sea. In my many travels I have been exposed to danger from rivers, danger from robbers, danger from my own people, danger from Gentiles, danger in the city, danger in the desert, danger at sea, danger from false brothers. I have toiled and endured hardship, often not had enough sleep, been hungry and thirsty, frequently gone without food, been cold and naked. And besides these external matters, there is the daily pressure of my anxious concern for all the congregations. Who is weak without my sharing his weakness? Who falls into sin without my burning inside? If I must boast, I will boast about things that show how weak I am. God the Father of the Lord Yeshua; blessed be he forever; knows that I am not lying!"

Paul (Sha'ul) continued to attend synagogue services on the Sabbath Acts 13:13-14:

"Having set sail from Paphos, Sha'ul and his companions arrived at Perga in Pamphylia. There Yochanan left them and returned to Yerushalayim, but the others went on from Perga to Pisidian Antioch, and on Shabbat they went into the synagogue and sat down."

Also in Acts 14:1-3: "In Iconium the same thing happened; they went into the synagogue and spoke in such a way that a large number of both Jews and Greeks came to trust. But the Jews who would not be persuaded stirred up the Gentiles and poisoned their minds against the brothers. Therefore, Sha'ul and Bar-Nabba remained for a long time, speaking boldly about the Lord, who bore witness to the message about his love and kindness by enabling them to perform signs and miracles."

And in Acts 17:1-4: "After passing through Amphipolis and Apollonia, Sha'ul and Sila came to Thessalonica, where there was a synagogue. According to his usual practice, Sha'ul went in; and on three Shabbats he gave them drashes from the Tanakh, explaining and proving that the Messiah had to suffer and rise again from the dead, and that "this Yeshua whom I am proclaiming to you is the Messiah." Some of the Jews were persuaded and threw in their lot with Sha'ul and Sila, as did a great many of the Greek men who were "God-fearers," and not a few of the leading women.

Paul (Sha'ul) continued to observe the Jewish feast days as one "zealous for the law, Also, when he was accused of teaching Jews to abandon the Law, Paul took some men with him to the Temple to observe the Jewish purification rites: Acts 21:19-26

After greeting them, Sha'ul described in detail each of the things God had done among the Gentiles through his efforts. On hearing it, they praised God; but they also said to him, "You see, brother, how many tens of thousands of believers there are among the Judeans, and they are all zealots for the Torah. Now what they have been told about you is that you are teaching all the Jews living among the Goyim to apostatize from Moshe, telling them not to have a b'rit-milah for their sons and not to follow the traditions. "What, then, is to be done? They will certainly hear that you have come. So do what we tell you. We have four men who are under a vow. Take them with you, be purified with them, and pay the expenses connected with having their heads shaved. Then everyone will know that there is nothing to these rumors which they have heard about you; but that, on the contrary, you yourself stay in line and keep the Torah. "However, in regard to the Goyim who have come to trust in Yeshua, we all joined in writing them a letter with our decision that they should abstain from what had been sacrificed to idols, from blood, from what is strangled and from fornication." The next day Sha'ul took the men, purified himself along with them and entered the Temple to give notice of when the period of purification would be finished and the offering would have to be made for each of them.

Paul (Sha'ul) insisted that Timothy (a Jew) undergo circumcision so that he might be effective in witnessing Yeshua to other Jews in *Acts 16:1-5:

"Then came he to Derbe and Lystra: and, behold, a certain disciple was there, named Timotheus, the son of a certain woman, which was a Jewess, and believed; but his father was a Greek: Which was well reported of by the brethren that were at Lystra and Iconium. Him would Paul have to go forth with him; and took and circumcised him because of the Jews which were in those quarters: for they knew all that his father was a Greek. And as they went through the cities, they delivered them the decrees for to keep, that were ordained of the apostles and elders which were at Jerusalem. And so were the Fellowships (synagogues) established in the faith, and increased in number daily.

The first believers in Yeshua were all Jews who continued to be observant Jews. What set them apart from other Jews was their conviction that they had found the promised Messiah. Paul (Sha'ul) took every opportunity to emphasize that Torah-observance was not a condition of salvation, but to show their love to God.

The Early Messianic Gentile Church

The term "Messianic" was also applied to Gentile believers at the church in Antioch most English Bibles refer to them as Christians, but in fact the Hebrew the term is *Messianic Acts 11:26 in the Complete Jewish Bible: "and when he found him, he brought him to Antioch. They met with the congregation there for a whole year and taught a sizeable crowd. Also it was in Antioch that the talmidim (disciples) for the first time were called "Messianic."*

Messianic believers were referred to as "the Way" Acts 9:2: " and asked him for letters to the synagogues in Dammesek, authorizing him to arrest any people he might find, whether men or women, who belonged to "the Way," and bring them back to Yerushalayim."

They were also referred to as "Nazarenes" which was considered to be a sect of Judaism Acts 24:4-5: "But, in order not to take up too much of your time, I beg your indulgence to give us a brief hearing. We have found this man a pest. He is an agitator among all the Jews throughout the world and a ringleader of the sect of the Natzratim (Nazarenes)."

Over the next 200 years the Messianic believers became increasingly Gentile in membership and nature. Greek thought became dominant over the Hebrew worldview, impacting theology, worship, and church practices. This placed Messianic Jews came under attack from both Jews and Christians.

Although the Jews originally viewed them as a sect of Judaism, they were rejected by the Jewish establishment after the Bar Kochba revolt against the Romans (132-135 AD). When that revolt began, the Messianic Jews supported it, but when Rabbi Akiva declared Bar Kochba to be the Messiah, the Messianic Jews withdrew from the struggle. The result was that after the revolt was crushed, the surviving Jews branded the Messianic as deserters and traitors, and they were thereafter treated as outcasts.

The Gentile converts; an attitude of anti-Semitism was growing. As early 50-117 A.D. as Ignatius of Antioch began teaching that Christians should not partake in Passover meals.

100-106 A.D. Justin Martyr had claiming that the Church had replaced Israel.

155-230 A.D. By the beginning of the 3rd Century, Tertullian and other Church Fathers like Origen were calling the Jews "Messiah killers."

325 A.D. The increasingly hostile attitude of the Church Fathers toward the Messianic believers who had given birth to Christianity came to a head at the Council of Nicea. The council, which was presided over by Emperor Constantine, changed the date of the celebration of the Resurrection so that it would no longer be identified with the Jewish feast of Passover. The council justified its action by stating, "...it is unbecoming beyond measure that on this holiest of festivals [Easter] we should follow the customs of the Jews. Henceforth, let us have nothing in common with this odious people."

341 A.D. The Council of Antioch followed suit when it prohibited Christians from celebrating Passover with Jews.

364 A.D. Council of Laodicea forbade Christians from observing the Jewish Sabbath. The 29th canon adopted by that council stated that "Christians must not Judaize by resting on the Sabbath, but must work on that day." They then commanded all Christians to make the "Lord's Day" their day of rest, and they pronounced an anathema upon any Christians who observed the Sabbath.

The historical record clearly reveals that Messianic Judaism came under attack from both Jews and Christians, and by the 5th Century the Church had become a new religion for the gentile world, it had become anti-Semitic, and dismissing the Jews.

The Messianic believers and Christian Church History

Jewish converts to Christianity often forced to convert or be enslaved, imprisoned or executed for almost 1600 years.

The Christian Church taught "Replacement Theology" that they had replaced Israel. Church leaders argued that God had washed His hands of the Jews when they rejected Jesus. The Church had replaced Israel and had inherited the promises and blessings of the Jews. God had no purpose left for the Jews were now a people without hope, doomed to wander the nations and be persecuted wherever they went.

At the beginning of the Reformation there was hope this attitude might change. Martin Luther was initially very sympathetic to the Jews because he believed their rejection of the Gospel was due to their recognition of the corruption of the Roman Catholic Church. But when they continued to reject the Gospel, Luther turned on them with a vengeance. In 1543 he wrote an anti-Semitic diatribe in which he referred to the Jews as "stupid fools" and "the great vermin of humanity." Having dehumanized and demonized them, Luther then proceeded to call for the burning of their synagogues and houses. He further suggested that their sacred writings be seized, their rabbis be forbidden to teach, their money be confiscated, and they be compelled into forced labor. Later in history Hitler used Martin Luther's writings to justify the genocide of the Jews which is the Holocaust. It is for this reason that to this day, the Holocaust is fixed in Jewish minds as a Christian crime.

During the 19th Century began, there seemed little hope that the Church would ever honor the command of Jesus Acts 1:6-8: *"When they therefore were come together, they asked of him, saying, Lord, wilt thou at this time restore again the kingdom to Israel? And he said unto them, It is not for you to know the times or the seasons, which the Father hath put in his own power. But ye shall receive power, after that the Holy Ghost is come upon you: and ye shall be witnesses unto me both in Jerusalem, and in all Judaea, and in Samaria, and unto the uttermost part of the earth."*

Messianic Judaism Today

Messianic congregations' remnant lay dormant from the world persecutions of the twenty century then a revived movement of Hashem as the prophet foretold in Ezekiel; Israel became a Nation in May 14, 1948; Ezekiel 37:4-14:

"Again he said unto me, Prophesy upon these bones, and say unto them, O ye dry bones, hear the word of the LORD. Thus saith the Lord GOD unto these bones; Behold, I will cause breath to enter into you, and ye shall live: And I will lay sinews upon you, and will bring up flesh upon you, and cover you with skin, and put breath in you, and ye shall live; and ye shall know that I am the LORD. So I prophesied as I was commanded: and as I prophesied, there was a noise, and behold a shaking, and the bones came together, bone to his bone. And when I beheld, lo, the sinews and the flesh came up upon them, and the skin covered them above: but there was no breath in them. Then said he unto me, Prophesy unto the wind, prophesy, son of man, and say to the wind, Thus saith the Lord GOD; Come from the four winds, O breath, and breathe upon these slain, that they may live. So I prophesied as he commanded me, and the breath came into them, and they lived, and stood up upon their feet, an exceeding great army. Then he said unto me, Son of man, these bones are the whole house of Israel: behold, they say, Our bones are dried, and our hope is lost: we are cut off for our parts. Therefore prophesy and say unto them, Thus saith the Lord GOD; Behold, O my people, I will open your graves, and cause you to come up out of your graves, and bring you into the land of Israel. And ye shall know that I am the LORD, when I have opened your graves, O my people, and brought you up out of your graves, And shall put my spirit in you, and ye shall live, and I shall place you in your own land: then shall ye know that I the LORD have spoken it, and performed it, saith the LORD."

But the remnant never destroyed, to be revived in the late 1960's by a remarkable man named Martin Chernoff. Marty, as he was called, was born of Russian immigrant parents in Toronto, Canada in 1920. In 1941 he accepted Yeshua as his Messiah after reading Charles Finney's Revival Lectures. As a new believer, he hit the ground running, convinced that he could "pray down revival" just like Finney.

Marty went to Moody Bible Institute in Chicago and did additional study at Toronto Baptist Seminary. In 1948 he was invited to join the staff of a mission called the Southern Witness to Israel, based in Chattanooga, Tennessee. That same year he experienced the first of three visions that would change his life and ultimately lead to the re-establishment of Messianic Judaism.

The vision was of a vast and endless orchard spread out across the land. The trees were loaded with fruit. The finger of God was stirring the leaves of the trees, and the branches were shaking. Marty interpreted this vision to mean that a great multitude of Jewish people were ready to be saved, and he was to pray for revival.

The next year, while on a speaking tour at the University of Tennessee, Marty met a young woman whom he married later that year. Her name was Joanna. She was a Gentile with a Jewish heart, and she shared Marty's zeal to reach Jews with the good news that Yeshua was their Messiah. They were to become a remarkably effective team of evangelists.

In October of 1970, Marty resigned from the HCAA and incorporated Congregation Beth Messiah in Cincinnati, thus creating the very first Messianic Jewish congregation in the United States.

God is orchestrating a spiritual renewal among Jews worldwide to produce a Jewish first fruits in anticipation of the great harvest of Jewish souls that the Bible says will take place at the end of the Tribulation Zechariah 12:10: "And I will pour upon the house of David, and upon the inhabitants of Jerusalem, the spirit of grace and of supplications: and they shall look upon me whom they have pierced, and they shall mourn for him, as one mourneth for his only son, and shall be in bitterness for him, as one that is in bitterness for his firstborn."

In the 1980's and 1990's the Messianic Congregational Movement continued its rapid growth. It also continued to adopt more Jewish identity. Congregations began to be called synagogues, and the spiritual leaders started using the title of rabbi. Services were shifted from Sunday to the Sabbath. Observance of the Jewish feasts became commonplace.

1975 to the Messianic Jewish Alliance of America, and the American Board of Missions to the Jews became the Chosen People Ministries.

As the 21st Century began, the outlook for Messianic Judaism was optimistic. There were tensions within the movement, as is true of all such movements. There were charismatics and non-charismatics. There were those who were Torah-observant and those who felt that the revival of Jewish identity should not be taken that far. There were those who believed that all Jewish believers should be in Messianic congregations and there were others who felt that church membership was a legitimate and viable alternative.

Ezekiel 37:18-23 *"And when the children of thy people shall speak unto thee, saying, Wilt thou not shew us what thou meanest by these? Say unto them, Thus saith the Lord GOD; Behold, I will take the stick of Joseph, which is in the hand of Ephraim, and the tribes of Israel his fellows, and will put them with him, even with the stick of Judah, and make them one stick, and they shall be one in mine hand. And the sticks whereon thou writest shall be in thine hand before their eyes. And say unto them, Thus saith the Lord GOD; Behold, I will take the children of Israel from among the heathen, whither they be gone, and will gather them on every side, and bring them into their own land: And I will make them one nation in the land upon the mountains of Israel; and one king shall be king to them all: and they shall be no more two nations, neither shall they be divided into two kingdoms any more at all: Neither shall they defile themselves any more with their idols, nor with their detestable things, nor with any of their transgressions: but I will save them out of all their dwelling places, wherein they have sinned, and will cleanse them: so shall they be my people, and I will be their God."*

Chapter 19 - Messianic Synagogue

Continuing faithfully and with singleness of purpose to meet in the Temple courts daily, and breaking bread in their several homes, they shared their food in joy and simplicity of heart, praising God and having the respect of all the people. And day after day the Lord kept adding to them those who were being saved.

(Acts 2:46-47)

This part of my journey has been the most rewarding of all to find a Messianic Synagogue which reflects the first century fellowship as did our Messiah.

Been searching for a Biblically based fellowship for years; Now after all my travels, trials and challenges we all face in life each day; I sat down and started praying and searching on the computer for a Messianic Synagogue. I spotted https://www.messianicspokane.com my wife and I set out to visit the very next Shabbat service.

When we arrived and it was time for the service to start I hear these words which I had been longing for:

Shabbat & Moedim Service Introduction

Shabbat shalom! Welcome to Synagogue Chavurat Ha-Mashiach!

We are a Messianic Jewish synagogue of both Jews and Sojourners pardoned from the penalty of our sin by a legal ransom paid by Yeshua of Natzeret (Nazareth). He is the one and only son of the God of Yisra'el, He is HaMashiach - The Messiah, promised by God's own word. Now free, as both Jews and Sojourners, being grafted into the Olive Tree Of Yisra'el, we have been adopted as legitimate children of the same living God, and together are now His Yisra'el. In freedom, gratitude and unity we seek to learn and live out His Torah (our Father's teachings and instructions for us). Why embrace and teach the Torah if we are free?

We believe that the Torah:

~ convicts us of sin and instructs us in righteousness

~ has shown us the Messiah and teaches us to walk as He walks.

~ shows the true righteousness of God in Messiah Yeshua so that when displayed in our lives,

Yeshua (The Living Torah) will be lifted up and seen by those outside this community and, b'ratzon HaShem (God willing), will be drawn to Him.

We hope that many will be drawn to Him, believe in Him, will have a heart of teshuva (repentance), and receive a brand new life, with no more charge of sin against it! Elohim (God) has seen all of our ways and all of our sin, yet He so loves the world that Messiah Himself paid our penalty for sin with His life. He was without any sin, yet He freely laid down his life to pay for our sin. ..."*for the wages of sin is death*" and that "*there is no forgiveness for sin without the shedding of blood*". Yeshua has been accepted on our behalf by the Father. His love has cancelled our debt...do you believe that?

Three days after His death, HE ROSE FROM THE GRAVE! He was witnessed by many, He ascended to the right hand of the Father, and by that right hand we can and will walk as He walked, as He writes His Torah on our hearts.

We believe God gives His Ruach HaKodesh (Holy Spirit) as a gift to His own. By His Spirit we have a comforter and teacher, enabling our faith and empowering us to do our

Father's will, as taught by His Torah, and displayed by His Messiah.

Yeshua is returning soon! Baruch haba b'shem Adonai! Blessed is He who comes in the name of The Lord! When He does, we need not be ashamed. Be welcome here and find safety and shalom here. Leave the world outside and enjoy this appointed day as an esteemed guest and a citizen among citizens of Yisra'el within the walls of this "embassy".

Join with us, let us celebrate and worship our great God and King!

After attending the service I could see that we were now family, the conversations with my new family in Yeshua was like a dream comes true. We meet on Shabbat Service whereas the liturgy was read, the Torah was read and the whole of scriptures were taught. During the time of worship, there was dancing and now this reminded me of the story when David brought the arc into the city. The music was in my heart and my soul rejoiced as I saw the dancing and the praise of HaShem.

Later we ate together and before we left Birkat Mamazon (The Blessing after the meal). I fell in love with my new family. We pray for one another, we care for one another and we help one another.

When my health had taken a turn for the worst everyone was in prayer for me. I was very concerned a felt that I might die and I wanted all my affairs taken care in advance. A brother their helped me with these details and he even made me a coffin, in the event of my death. Randy took the time and effort to get the information from the Veterans Administration and the specification for a Jewish coffin that would be acceptable; he made arrangement with a funeral home and gave me the information. The results were wonderful, I had everything ready and I spent several hospital stays.

Was discharged from the hospital the evening of Passover and attended, then not more than a week later my oncologist recommends I have three procedures done. Over a period of three months and later two weeks in the hospital, then after six months I began to recover. In short, Prayer and HaShem guiding the hospital staff and doctors.

Now I have a casket in the garage, my health back and this Passover a year later. I know HaShem had the Angel of death Passover me. Thus the product of all this, is this book to give praise to HaShem.

Chapter 20 – Greatest Commandment

And Yeshua answered him, "the first of all the commandments is, Hear, O Israel; The Lord our God is one Lord:"

(Mark 12:29)

As you go through your journey as I have. Knowing what God has in mind for our journey in life he gave us some instructions to follow. Yeshua referred us to the Shema (to listen and act) in Deuteronomy 6:4-9:

"Shema, Yisra'el! Adonai Eloheinu, Adonai Echad [Hear, Isra'el! Adonai our God, Adonai is One]; and you are to love Adonai your God with all your heart, all your being and all your resources. These words, which I am ordering you today, are to be on your heart; and you are to teach them carefully to your children. You are to talk about them when you sit at home, when you are traveling on the road, when you lie down and when you get up. Tie them on your hand as a sign, put them at the front of a headband around your forehead, and write them on the door-frames of your house and on your gates.

To continue the story with Yeshua when he was question about the most important commandment as stated in: Mark 12:28-34

"One of the Torah-teachers came up and heard them engaged in this discussion. Seeing that Yeshua answered them well, he asked him, "Which is the most important mitzvah (Commandment) of them all?"

Yeshua answered, *"The most important is, 'Sh'ma Yisra'el, Adonai Eloheinu, Adonai Echad [Hear, O Isra'el, the Lord our God, the Lord is one], and you are to love Adonai your God* with all your heart, with all your soul, with all your understanding and with all your strength.'

The second is this: 'You are to love your neighbor as yourself.' There is no other mitzvah (Commandment) greater than these."

The Torah-teacher said to him, "Well said, Rabbi; you speak the truth when you say that he is one, and that there is no other besides him; and that loving him with all one's heart, understanding and strength, and loving one's neighbor as oneself, mean more than all the burnt offerings and sacrifices."

When Yeshua saw that he responded sensibly, he said to him, *"You are not far from the Kingdom of God." And after that, no one dared put to him another sh'eilah (any question").*

Yeshua expounded on what it is to love one another in John 13:34-35:

Yeshua said *"I am giving you a new command: that you keep on loving each other. In the same way that I have loved you, you are also to keep on loving each other. Everyone will know that you are my talmidim (disciples) by the fact that you have love for each other."*

At this point of our journey we see that love is the key message sent to us throughout all of scripture. Love is a Verb in Hebrew – this demonstration of love is obedience to God even if it cost us our lives.

John 12:25-26: Yeshua said *"He that loveth his life shall lose it; and he that hateth his life in this world shall keep it unto life eternal. If any man serve me, let him follow me; and where I am, there shall also my servant be: if any man serve me, him will my Father honour."*

What does the LORD (God) require of us Micah 6:8 "He hath shewed thee, O man, what is good; and what doth the LORD require of thee, but to do justly, and to love mercy, and to walk humbly with thy God?"

These are all things we can do because we love HaShem (God) whom we desire to demonstrate our love. Love is the very act of obedience, not to gain anything – such as salvation or piety (pride or position). What we give up in this life and remain humble and just with others speak volumes to our God as love. Love is the motive and the action of living a godly life as God desires of each of us.

At this part of our journey we see being born-again is a life's commitment to serve a loving and caring God. By avoiding sin, keeping the faith in the promises of Yeshua's return. Following God's instructions (Law – Torah) and the whole of scriptures that we have today; these will give us guidance on just how to live.

We know that we have been saved by the Grace of God, through Yeshua. This Salvation we have we rejoice in by showing our love to God through obedience, not simple to follow some rules to show our selves righteous.

The works that we do has been set before us to do as a love offering to God. Building a love relationship with our creator as Yeshua demonstrated in his life as in Ephesians 4:2-7:

"Always be humble, gentle and patient, bearing with one another in love, and making every effort to preserve the unity the Spirit gives through the binding power of shalom (Peace). There is one body and one Spirit, just as when you were called you were called to one hope. And there is one Lord, one trust, one immersion, and one God, the Father of all, who rules over all, works through all and is in all. Each one of us, however, has been given grace to be measured by the Messiah's bounty."

We all go through troubles, trials and persecutions; But to continue in the truth we tend to cause a majority of our own problems. I know if you wish to continue now I will share my journey from darkness and evil of this world. It is my prayer that you find a Biblically based Fellowship that teaches the whole truth, and love of God.

Chapter 21 – Author's Journey

The Darkness

"In their trouble they cried to Adonai, and he rescued them from their distress. He led them from darkness, from death-dark gloom, shattering their chains. Let them give thanks to Adonai for his grace, for his wonders bestowed on humanity!"

(Psalms 107:13-15 CJB)

This is where the journey begins for all of us whether or not we agree; for the darkness comes in various forms. It could be that your career, spouse or just the world, in general, becomes more important than our Creator. Well, that is a problem.

"They have exchanged the truth of God for falsehood, by worshipping and serving created things, rather than the Creator -; praised be he forever. Amen." (Romans 1:25 CJB)

The darkness I faced was ignorance, and the people around me were not much different. My Dad was a hard-working man, but his heart focused on the here and now. His belief was when you die the worms ate you, and that's that.

On the other hand, my mother had gone to the Mormon Church when she was young and hated it, and held to the fact she was agnostic. Both Mom and Dad said when we grow up we can decide for ourselves if we want to go to church or the likes of it.

"Having one's mind controlled by the old nature is death, but having one's mind controlled by the Spirit is life and shalom." (Romans 8:6 CJB)

As I grew up the oldest of four children and the youngest was my sister. My two brothers and I enjoyed working at home. We worked in the garden in the spring till fall, and then we went hunting which was always a great adventure while growing up in Idaho. Sis worked helping mom on her projects and canning in the fall.

Dad would take us boys hunting; this was my favorite time of the year. During the summer we did get a chance to go fishing and swimming. Dad taught all of us how to live off the land. We knew how to read a map, perform first aid to save a life, how to find shelter, water, and food, just about everything we would need to survive and live off the land.

While mom taught us all how to cook, iron, sew, and how to take care of our daily needs; She desired that we would be able to take care of ourselves. We had a home with love and respect for one another. It all sounds good, but where was God in all this?

The ignorance I was faced with was the knowledge of God and His Holy Word. I do not remember one time while growing up that as a family we went to church or said prayers together. The Darkness that filled our lives was the lack of knowledge of God. We were too busy with life that we did not invite the Author of life its self to be a part of our lives.

Remember at the supper table when we all sat together, before eating Dad would say "Grab and growl!" for the most part we lived a good life but, God was not a part of it. That Darkness was heavy on the family.

However, deep inside my heart, I knew there was a God. I remember a time when I was a young teenager working with my Dad. We were putting in a fence line. Dad said to me "Son, you work as hard as any man I know. Here have a cold beer with me." We sat under a shade tree, and the conversation went a little like this. I asked Dad "Do you believe there might be a God?" Dad took a drink of his cold beer and said:" Son when you die, and they put you in the ground, the worms eat you, and that's, that!"

My reply after taking a drink of that cold beer "Dad, look around at all these wonderful trees, mountains and the deer all of nature is saying God made me! I don't think this is all an accident!" Well, I think it upset the apple cart! The look on my Dads face as he said "Well, that's enough talk about that sort. Drink your beer and let's get back to work."

"[For the leader. A psalm of David:] *The heavens declare the glory of God, the dome of the sky speaks the work of his hands."* (Psalms 19:1 CJB)

While I was growing up in the family we attended family gatherings most all the adults avoided me because I would ask so many questions about the family.

There were about two techniques used by the elders of my family when I started to ask questions. One to change the subject, and or leave. The second was to pacify me with a story that seemed real enough at the time.

The fallacy of the first was I would not give up until I had an answer. The second, a believable and repeatable response from two or more of the elders of the family were required to keep me satisfied. I was not happy with the results.

I asked my Dad about the family tree, and all he said was "If you go hunting on our family tree you will probably find someone hanging from it."

Over the years it was a hobby of sorts to solve the mystery of the family tree. I can safely say that there had been six generations in my direct Ancestors on my Dad side, and then on my Moms side were Jack Mormons that did not have a real relationship with God as far as I can tell.

The chances are if something didn't change in my life, that darkness of willful ignorance would soon encompass me just like it had in my family for generations.

Love of God

And it shall come to pass in the last days, saith God, I will pour out of my Spirit upon all flesh: and your sons and your daughters shall prophesy, and your young men shall see visions, and your old men shall dream dreams:

(Acts 2:17)

When I first saw the light of truth, and the Love of God it has been the motiving factor in my life till this day. My family and I were living in Arizona at this time.

At the age of sixteen I received a Bible that belonged to my maternal great-grandfather, The Bible was over 150 years old; it was in mint condition, just like new. I found it odd that it was in such perfect condition. I took it to my bedroom and set it on an apple box that I used for a nightstand. Thinking, Got to get up early in the morning; as I looked over my new treasure; I said to myself "I am going to read this book and see if I can find out anything about God."

"For our rejoicing is this, the testimony of our conscience, that in simplicity and godly sincerity, not with fleshly wisdom, but by the grace of God, we have had our conversation in the world, and more abundantly to you-ward." (2 Corinthians 1:12)

It wasn't long, and I was now in a deep sleep. Next thing I remember, I realized I wasn't asleep at all but wide-awake. I had my backpack on and ready to go camping. My brothers Steven and Harold along with the McDonald Boys were ready to go, waiting for me on the front porch.

We took what was almost a ten-mile hike across the desert and up Soap Creek to the windmill where we always camped. As always, I took the lead. After miles of travel, we reached the fence crossing Soap Creek. Then I held the bottom to wires of the fence down with my foot and the two upper wires up with my hands so the others could go through the fence.

Handing over my backpack to my brother Steven, and then I crawled through the fence. About that time one of the barbs caught on my shirt and scraped my back. Steven unhooked the barbs from my shirt, and it ripped and tore my shirt leaving a remnant on the barb.

Now Clyde took the position on point, as we followed behind. It was a beautiful day, the sun was out, and the flowers were all in bloom, and we could smell the flowers and the heat of the sun on our face and shoulders as we walked on the desert trail.

Noticing we had not seen one rattlesnake today, by this time I would have shot two or three of them and placed them in my game bag. On a beautiful day like this, we always liked to go on what we called the upper trail. It was a very narrow and risky challenge, and that was the point. The path took quite a bit of skill to be able to make it to our destination. The trail was five hundred feet along the steep rocky hillside. From there, we would make our way to the open path on the mesa leading to the foothills of the Bradshaw Mountains. Midway through this narrow passage, the earth started to shake, and rocks began to fall from above my brothers and the Mac Donald boys.

As I watched in anguish, I saw them all falling from the edge of the trail to the bottom of the hill and rocks covering them. My concern was for my brothers and friends, and it appeared to me they were most likely dead from the fall and the rocks covering them.

Then realizing my leg was caught between two large boulders. I could not get free; devastated, now looking up, I see this giant rattlesnake; the snake's head was bigger than my backpack. This colossal giant of a rattlesnake was right in front of me and ready to attack. That moment knowing that this snake was going to kill me; reaching for my rifle, which was a little 22 caliber single shot. Compared to the snake and its size, this may make little difference in my situation. But in a last defiant act of courage, I was going to kill that snake.

I heard what sounded like a loud voice in the sky. The sound of the voice caused me to tremble. Then loud blasts of a horn; at that moment, time stood still. As I aimed at the snake ready to shoot it right between the eyes, then I noticed something. Out of the rocks that fell over my friends and brothers, the stones moved aside, and the boys started rising as if they were never hurt. Beams of light shining through the clouds turn to golden stairs, and my friends and brothers began walking up the stairs. All this was happening in a moment that time had stopped.

Now everything was frozen in time, and I was able to see everything in great detail. Looking up into the sky, I could see many thrones all around one large thrown. The person on the large thrown stepped down out of the sky. He straddled the Bradshaw Mountain Range with one leg on one side and the other on the opposing side. He stood so tall that I couldn't see his face from the clouds, but only the hem of his garment to his belt around his waist was visible. Then I also noticed that there were other people were walking up these beams of light that had turned to stairs.

So now a hand of this colossal giant reached down to pick me up. As the hand clasped around, I felt an overwhelming love and peace, which went way beyond human understanding.

Feeling like I was being taken up at supersonic speed, to the very face of this giant figure of a man. The love that I had experienced, I just wanted to soak up every bit of it;

along with all the knowledge of the entire universe, which was present in this hand. I was like a sponge trying to soak in the love and knowledge and understanding that was pure not tainted by man. It was like I was a small sponge being thrown into the ocean trying to drink it dry but unable to take in all that it wanted. I knew when the hand opened up, and I would see the very face of God. With great anticipation to see my Creator face-to-face was almost more than I could bear. The overwhelming desire for love and peace culminated as the hands started to open.

The alarm clock went off in the next room; it woke me up. Still overwhelmed by the dream, I shook my head and then sat up. WOW! I sat up in bed then turned and put my feet on the floor. It was then I noticed I had massive bruises on my leg. Then I could feel my back hurt. Thinking it might be from the cut I received in my vision. Going to the closet to look at my shirt, and there was a rip in the shirt and a piece missing, just like the dream.

I never remembered having a dream in my life. Thought people who were talking about dreams, it was all fiction. The fact is I had never experienced a dream before at least that I could remember. I found it interesting that it was so real, the colors and smells and now I could see evidence that something unusual had to happen – A Vision.

As time passed, I asked my mom about dreams and visions. She responded and said I have heard that some people have visions, but I never met one. I asked her is there a place I could read in the Bible where it talks about visions. She pointed me to the Book of Revelation, and this was the first book of the Bible I read.

This vision was the first glimpse of light I had experienced. It was the Love I was searching for, that perfect love. How can I experience that love again?

During that summer I did odd jobs for people in the valley area. I would walk up to people doing work outside of their homes. I would ask "Could I help you with this or that?" As I would help them, I would ask if they had any odd jobs they would be willing to pay me to do. When I met a lovely elderly couple they put me to work for a couple of weeks. This elderly couple asks me if I would go to church, so I agreed.

On Sunday early they picked me up at my home. We spent the whole day at church, I heard the speaker say many things we had to do to go to heaven, but nothing about God, love or why. It seemed to me that it was a recruitment program more than a church. I noticed it had little to do with God or his love. So, the next week they asked me to go to church. I said no. Moreover, by the end of the day, they run out of work for me. This was my first encounter with church people and I was not impressed.

The seed of God's love was now planted in my heart; I wanted to know God and the Love he has for me. However, with no one to show me or to teach me I was on my own. In my heart, I knew this was going to be difficult or just how I was going to accomplish my mission.

"And I say unto you, Ask, and it shall be given you; seek, and ye shall find; knock, and it shall be opened unto you. For every one that asketh receiveth; and he that seeketh findeth; and to him that knocketh it shall be opened." (Luke 11:9-10)

War

For we wrestle not against flesh and blood, but against principalities, against powers, against the rulers of the darkness of this world, against spiritual wickedness in high places.

(Ephesians 6:12)

Not much time had passed since my first church experience; I had joined the U.S. Army at the ripe old age of sixteen years and soon to be seventeen. During basic training my acting platoon Sargent had left the Air Force after ten years and joined the army to become a Chaplin. I became his project; he shared a lot about God and some about the Bible. His focus was first, do I believe in God and the second have I ever been baptized.

Story short it was December 1970, snow on the ground at Fort Lewis Washington. He made all the arrangements with the Chaplin to have me baptized inside the Chapel on the base. It was like a small bathtub, and the water was cold. Later, I caught a cold, and it turned into pneumonia.

After basic training, I went to Fort Gordon, Georgia to the United States Southeastern Signal School there for 25 weeks, now seventeen years old. At the end of the course, we received a diploma. Upon graduation, I was waiting for orders for my permanent duty station.

A life-changing message from the Red Cross notifying me that my cousin had died and the funeral scheduled in less than a week. My cousin was nine years older than me; he was like a big brother. Many of my classmates were going to Viet Nam right into a war.

Life has just slapped me in the face. It was so hard for me to think my cousin is gone, leaving a wife and three kids. My love for him was great, and now I was at a loss. Even more, I wanted to know God and hoping that my cousin was in heaven.

The little town in Cambridge, Idaho the service held in the High School Auditorium. The family and my cousin were well known and loved by the community. The auditorium was filled to standing room only. The service was simple, no pastor or man of the cloth spoke; friends spoke of the love and remembrance of the days they spent with my cousin. Behind the curtains was a good friend who played the guitar and sang a song about my cousin, tears filled the auditorium. However, God was never mentioned once during the service. That stuck in my heart with great sorrow. Once again, I had this thought where is God in all of this?

The month before the death of my cousin my Dads uncle had died. Now my cousin's death had shaken my dad because of his dream. My Dad was very concerned about the fact he had a dream about his uncle's death, my cousin's death, and now his brother-in-law's death, my uncle was only five years older than myself, at this time he was alive and well.

Later my Dad shared his dream with me. Then he gave me instructions to warn my uncle. It was our hopes this maybe; just maybe it would not happen if I advise my uncle.

The common thread that my Dad and I have shared is dreams. Dad ever since he was young has had prophetic dreams. After I shared my vision with Dad, he and I had a common thread that held our relationship closer than before. Dad still did not believe in God, but the vision had convinced me that there is a loving God.

Leaving home after receiving my orders, before reporting for duty; I made my way to my uncle's home and visited with him and his family. He had married a beautiful young lady who was a widow, her husband died in Viet Nam. My Uncle married her and adopted her son, and later they had another son. They were a happy family you could feel the love in the home. It was a picture of real happiness.

My uncle was a truck driver, just like my dad's uncle and my cousin. Dads dream reveal to him they would each die in a truck accident within a month of one another. My uncle and I talked a lot as we drove on his truck route. I explained the dream and how it had come to pass with my dad's uncle and my cousin. I asked him to think it over and be careful, maybe find something else to do for a living. I loved my uncle, and he was like a big brother to me, like my cousin.

I reported for duty and was sent to Korea. It was some time later I found out my uncle was killed driving a truck not long after I warned him. Once again, I had this thought where is God in all of this?

Not long after arriving in Korea, two soldiers who outranked me took advantage of me. I was sexually abused. The torment of these men and others were more than I could stand. I learned to become invisible even in plain sight. I avoided all contact with the other soldiers and found a place off the base and lived what the American soldiers called a little hooch. It was an old style Korean home, and I had rented a room.

The abuse I suffered from these soldiers, these were men who had joined the army to leave prison. Most of them had just returned from Viet Nam. These men had spent at least two tours there. They entered the military from prison and were considered lifers. This unit was referred to as a bastard company because of the lifers.

The reason I was assigned to this unit it was my duty to maintain the communications systems for all the aircraft and ground equipment as necessary. I had everything working, and I could lock my communications van, and no one was allowed in my area due to security protocol, it was a restricted area due to the nature of my equipment. It was a haven during duty hours, and I managed to slip out of the base each day due to the help of some Korean soldiers who knew of my abuse.

During my time living in the village, I found a Korean lady who began to stay with me. At the age of seventeen, I fell in love with her and we planned on getting married. She was five years older than me. It did not matter to me I had someone to hold on to and I felt I needed that. The need to feel safe and still, keep my manhood which had been ripped off. Little did I understand that God had a better plan for me? I was even farther from God than when I first began, my life was growing darker.

My fiancée and I made it back to the states. I had to send her ahead of me to my parents' home in Idaho because I had to travel on a military transport. Once I got home, we made arrangements and then we were married. We left for Fort Hood, Texas arrived on time and found a place to stay in the nearby town of Killeen. My wife had met several Korean ladies married to other soldiers. I noticed the Korean connection was growing and she spent much time with her Korean friends.

It was in Texas, and I was twenty years old now when we had our first child. My daughter so beautiful, I'm a dad now and my daughter was now the joy of my life. I relisted in the military, and now the family could return to Korea. We manage to get a beautiful place to live in the City of Uijongbu. I was planning to remain in the Army as a career soldier.

The Korean connection that we left behind in Fort Hood was alive and well in Korea. Things started to fall apart when my company commander notified me that my wife had several ration violations and I was to tell my wife to stop. It didn't end, and I was ordered to receive her ration card, or the punishment with an article 15, a court martial.

Went home to retrieve the ration card, I found her at home with about ten other Korean women counting money out. Back in that time, we used MPC Military Pay Certificates. It was against the Military Orders to have greenbacks. What I saw was the most massive pile of Green Backs, MPC and Korean currency.

My wife and her Korean connection were a Black Market headquarters, and I was beside myself. I was as angry as I barged in, these Korean women scatter like a covey of quail. My wife and I were left, and I demand the ration card, this did not end well. We got into a knock down drag out fight. After the fight I returned to base and turned in the ration card to my commanding officer.

The Korean police came to base with a complaint, and I was placed on house arrest and restricted to base. I had some of my military clothing at home and my Bible that my great-grandfather had given to me. A week later the company commander had the first Sargent drive both of us to my house in the village. When we went in everything was gone even the wallpaper. It was the last time I saw my wife and child for five years.

During this Korean connection, other military husbands faced this dilemma; unlike me they were deeply involved with the Black Market. So the Koreans and many of the soldiers they were upset, I received many threats on my life from both Koreans and Americans. I had upset the balance of economics and enterprise which was a very large illegal operation. To me, I thought doing the right thing would prove to be safe and helpful to the army, wrong too many were involved, and I was now a big problem.

Not too long after my first round of trouble with the black market. I was confronted by several of the soldiers, which led to a fight. I won the fight but lost the battle, received an Article 15 a court marshal and resigned from the army, and for my safety, I was on the next available plane to the states.

Now, headed back to the states leaving my wife and daughter in Korea was devastating to me. However, it was not safe for me in Korea. Many Koreans wanted a piece of me as well as many soldiers who were involved with the Black Market. I found that doing what seems to be right can be very life changing.

Before leaving Korea, I confronted my Battalion Commander on the trumped-up charges and that it wasn't right and he told me to get the hell out of his office. I felt as welcome as a polecat at a wedding. From his response and anger, I thought he too was probably involved in the black market as many of the officers in the Korean connection were.

Returning to the States it was hard to tell the boys from the girls. Long hair, burning the flag was in style, and I was looked down for being in the Army. It was darkness you could almost feel, people were not as friendly as I had remembered. When I left people were waving the flag and being in the service was an honor. Now they burned the flag, and I was an outcast.

Now I was twenty-two years old, and I wanted to start fresh. I was faced with a divorce for abandonment still having no information as to what has happened to my wife and child.

Needed to start a new career, losing out on my first one in the Army I thought it best to get the training I need to become a police officer. I worked for the State Highway Department for about six months. A rumor circulated that I stole a radio out of one of the trucks. The Superintendent confronted me. I told him I did not steal it. Being falsely accused I become outraged. A problem I have had for many decades. So, I quit.

Went to work at a Mill and Molding plant, It was a good job, and I had a second job working at a truck stop at nights. Still trying to get a career I volunteered as a reserve police officer in Fruitland, Idaho. Enjoyed the training time I learned many things and I felt that the time was well spent. Going from the frying pan to the fire I had a girlfriend, and I thought everything was going well. Later I found that she had been spreading rumors about me in the community.

When Police Chief got wind of these rumors, he called me into his office, and he explained that this is becoming a big problem. Well the chief warned me that the Federal Authorities in Texas were going to have me taken in custody and taken to Texas. He showed me a document which said they were investigating my x wife in I still wonder where that came from, and the chief said it would be best if you just disappeared for a while till this scandal blew over. It was the Korean Connection came back to haunt me.

Now things got worse, my dad and I had a few words. He stopped talking to me and did not want to see me. He had overheard a conversation I was having with my little brother. My brother asked me" You are a policeman if I pulled a gun on you would you shoot me" My answer was "I sure would without thinking about it. It would be the right thing to do." Dad didn't hear the whole conversation just that I would shoot my brother. He had nothing to do with me for several years.

Visited my mom on the way out of town, she suggested I see her brother in California and make a fresh start there. In time Dad would come around. So, I sold most all I owned and filled a suitcase with clothes and put it in my 1963 Impala and headed to California just before a big snow storm hit Idaho. Estranged from friends and family, headed to California with Hundred dollars in my pocket; what could go wrong?

"The curse of the LORD is in the house of the wicked: but he blesseth the habitation of the just."

(Proverbs 3:33)

Broken

The sacrifices of God are a broken spirit: a broken and a contrite heart, O God, thou wilt not despise.

(Psalms 51:17)

The trip to California was not without some adventure. I picked up two hitchhikers just outside San Francisco after visiting with a friend of my Dads. The friend was a US Army Nurse who served in Viet Nam; she was working at a hospital in San Francisco. It was a short visit, and I stayed one night then off to see my Uncle in Anaheim California.

The hitchhikers talked with me as we drove down PCH (Pacific Coast Highway) I was about to find out how weird California is. These two guys told me that they were warlocks were going to a witch gathering. They asked to let them off along the way. They asked me if I would like to join them and spend the night. The thought jumped into my head about a story I heard once about the missionaries who were invited for supper with the cannibals, or were they supper?

After leaving them off in the middle of what seemed to me as nowhere it was a pitch-black night, and I was relieved when I let them off, I turned on the radio in the car, and a song came on which had some weird lyrics to the song, as I was driving in a moonless night, Then the song was interrupted with this new alert came on it was midnight. It was a news alert not to pick up hitchhikers also the police were warning about witches were in the area, and there had been some investigations into what seemed to be human sacrifices. The hair on the back of my head stood straight up. I realized God was watching over me. This strange encounter prompted me to be praying, I did not stop praying until I reached my Uncles business in the early morning.

I met my uncle as he was opening up for business. There was a receptions area in the front and an office with a window looking into the Shop which took up the rest of the facility. There were work benches and all sorts of electronic devices at each workbench. Then in the back a small warehouse of electronic parts. Just outside the office were a coffee pot and a radio playing old country western music. And off to the side of this was an extensive library of Electronic books and OEM supplies and Data Sheets on the latest and most significant parts. My uncle gave me the tour, and we sat, and he asked me why I was there and I told him my mother thought it was a good Idea if I stopped in and saw if he had anything for me in the way of work. The receptionist showed up, and my Uncle asked me if I had Breakfast yet. I told him no. He said neither have I lets go eat I'll buy.

We took his truck leaving my car parked in the employee's parking space. When we arrived at what appeared to be a mom and pop diner. We sat down, and my Uncle knew everyone by name, and it seemed that everyone was glad to see him. He flirted with the waitress, and she gave him a big smile and called him honey. We ordered, and it was then my uncle told me I could stay in his shop warehouse loft upstairs. Upstairs in the attic was a bed and a phone I could stay there. I could stay and work around the shop; he would feed me three meals a day. That was the best he could do. If I could help him get some of the projects finished, he might be able to pay me. At the time that sounded pretty good, I would have a place to stay till I could find a job that paid. It would be my job to make sure the shop was cleaned each day. And he would have my work on organizing his R&D Library and also the warehouse of parts.

That was the deal, and over time I arranged everything in the shop and started helping in the office ordering materials and keeping the budget for the company in the black. My uncle found that my abilities as a Technician to make and improve his prototypes; then to manufacture Items for sale were to his advantage. In just a few short months I was running the operation, and my uncle was off selling the new Ideas and demonstrating the prototypes of Items I had made, and my uncle had designed. It wasn't long, and I was developing new products for sale for the company.

During this time I got a paying job and still lived in my uncle's shop and helping him out at the same time. I was saving my money to get my own place. I wasn't in a hurry, and I enjoyed working at the gas station, later becoming the manager. Things were going well with my uncle's business, and I started to make a little money there.

Then as always, Life takes a turn, a friend of my Dads called me at my uncle's office he was in town and wanted to see me. My dad's friend was an insurance salesman from our hometown. He seemed alright I didn't know him like my dad, dad thought of him as a good Christian. He sang in the choir and went to church each Sunday. He had stopped at a gas station not far from the office. He was terrified of the traffic, and could not drive anywhere and was pleading with me to come and get him.

After rescuing him he was so grateful, he asked me where I live, and I told him about the arrangements that I had made with my uncle. He informed me he was going to get a job at an insurance company and he was going to rent an Apartment if I wanted I could move in and pay half the rent. Sounds good to me, so he stayed with me in the shop upstairs for a couple of days, and he had me drive him around, and he made the arrangements for an apartment and got a job as he said.

He asked me if I would like to go to school and get my insurance license. I didn't really want to do that.

I was doing fine working at the gas station and I was the manager now. And I was doing well as an R&D Technician for my uncle. My dad's friend said he had signed me up already, I could go to school and get my license and still keep my jobs. At that time I had this funny feeling something wasn't right.

It wasn't long and that small still voice in my head that warned me that staying with my dad's friend wasn't all that it was cracked up to be. He had used my enrollment into the school to further his career. And once I passed the Insurance school and received my license and was working in the office. Well, he took credit for my sales and the District manager, and my dad's friend had made plans to make him the top salesperson to receive a bonus.

I quit the insurance business, but before I left I warned him never to lie or steal from me again, or I would have a piece of him.

Moved out and found an Apartment for myself. Things were slowing down for my Uncles business. I focused on the service station where I was the manager. Hired a couple of guys to work separate shifts; I was hoping to train someone to be my assistant. I also doubled as the mechanic on duty; it paid good and had the potential means of making it my new career.

Divorced now focusing on work, I hoped this would help me to forget the loss of my wife and child. The last thing I wanted to do is get involved with another relationship. I thought it best to leave it in the past and move on. But, so goes the best plans of mankind.

For thou hast delivered my soul from death: wilt not thou deliver my feet from falling, that I may walk before God in the light of the living? (Psalms 56:13)

Working sixty to eighty hours a week, my employer and his business associate visited me while I was working as the duty mechanic; I had a young man working the gasoline islands. Both my employer and his associate were impressed at the operation. They had just bought another service station, and it was a more extensive operation. They gave me three days off with pay for working hard they also gave me a bonus.

I was ringing up the repairs on a 1957 thunderbird which I completed. The young lady who owned the car, she was about eighteen years old was standing there at the cash register. The employer and his associate gave me ten passbooks to Disneyland. I asked the young lady if she had ever been there. She smiled and said yes, I live very close to Disneyland and I have been there many times. I asked her if she had time I had three days off and I could take her to Breakfast. If she still wanted to go after breakfast after she got to know me, then we would go to Disneyland. She gave me her number and said give her a call to work out the details.

In short, we became terrific friends and later continued to see each other. She was carefree, she dresses like a flower child complete with bellbottom jeans macramé belt, tank top covered with a tie-dyed T-shirt and her long brown hair flowing in the breeze. She was a very good looking young lady and full of life and energy.

As time passed, we made plans to get married. We had been seeing each other for the past year. She was eighteen when we met, now 19 years old. We eloped and got married, and I lived in my apartment. She remained at home to help her mom who was going through a divorce at the time. She was helping her mom make ends meet, and we planned on having a church wedding on her twentieth birthday. Then we would buy a house with my Veterans loan and live together.

Time past and we renewed our vows, and the family did not know we were already married till our fifth wedding anniversary. It was then with all the baggage we both had in our marriage began to cause problems that broke me.

We had bought a house, and her mother came to stay with her brother and a sister. During this time I had just started working at Disneyland as a Union Electrician. I received a call from my Mom and Dad in Idaho, my x-wife left my daughter with them. We went to Idaho and picked her up, and now the house is full.

Now married three years and I had a new career as a Union Electrician at Disneyland, so to be the first Ride Control Technician now in training. As a career, it looked so promising, and we had bought a house using my Veterans Loan, the house was full of family. Helping my wife's family was rewarding and a great challenge at the same time. My daughter who was six years old now was living with us.

My wife's mother got married and moved out leaving her son and daughter with us. The daughter joined the Air Force, and my Mother-In-Law gave me a power of Attorney to take care of her Son who I treated as my own. He had just started High School.

So much was going on and the Idea of going to church was about to become a reality because we felt the need for God to bless us. We felt a need due to the pressures of family and work. My wife lost the first baby, and the emotional loss was far beyond the physical impairment. She went into a deep depression and had to go to counseling. A new age counselor had convinced my wife I was the problem and if she divorced me her life would be better. It was then I suggested we go to church and get counseling from a Pastor, not this New Age counselor who I thought was hitting on my wife.

With my wife's depression, due to the loss of our first child; then her Mom had dumped her son on us to take care of his needs, I became Frustrated, angry and hurt; I tried to do the best I could to hold our readymade family together.

Working about fifty hours a week at Disneyland, I needed to spend more time at home and made arrangements to be on Graveyard from day shift at Disneyland, now I could take care of my wife and the family during the day.

So, now we could go to church, do what is right and learn how to live life. This was our plan, and for the most part, it seemed sound at the time. We were a broken mess, a family put together by broken people. It was then I decided to find a church to attend. We both agreed, and she saw a little church in Riverside where we lived, Hoping to get counseling and help we needed that next Sunday.

Broken and needing help, we hoped to find the answers to what we needed to do. We were both broken. Now twenty-six years old and my wife twenty-three life had hit us hard, and we needed help.

Two are better than one; because they have a good reward for their labour. For if they fall, the one will lift up his fellow: but woe to him that is alone when he falleth; for he hath not another to help him up. Again, if two lie together, then they have heat: but how can one be warm alone? And if one prevail against him, two shall withstand him; and a threefold cord is not quickly broken. (Ecclesiastes 4:9-12)

As I look back to this time of darkness in my life it was my ignorance of who God is and His instructions on how to live. God has given us his Holy Word the Bible to read, study, understand and apply to our lives. When reading through the Bible I have found this phrase," *but every man did that which was right in his own eyes.*"

The heart is deceitful above all things, and desperately wicked: who can know it? I the LORD search the heart, I try the reins, even to give every man according to his ways, and according to the fruit of his doings. (Jeremiah 17:9-10)

The Cross, Born Again

Jesus answered and said unto him, Verily, verily, I say unto thee, except a man be born again, he cannot see the kingdom of God.

(John 3:3)

It was on Sunday, September 2nd, 1979 my wife and her brother and my daughter and I went to church together for the first time. In the newly built building that had just been opened. There were about four to five hundred people in a church building designed for fifteen hundred. The music was lovely and the Pastor came out he had long hair and a beard. I was not impressed, and most of the people there were in their street clothes most of which were hippies, which didn't give me the atmosphere of what I had perceived as a church. Not like the first church experience I had before joining the Army. Learning later in life this was called the Jesus movement.

The Pastor talked about a hole in our hearts that needed to be filled with God. Without this being filled a lot of people choose things like, drugs, sex and things to fill this void. What we needed was the love of God to fill our hearts and lives. We must be born again of the Spirit. He read from John chapter three about a man who came to Jesus at night – and how Jesus told him he needed to be born again. Then he asked for anyone who wanted to be born again to come forward. Then the music played, and the words of the song penetrated my heart:

I have decided to follow Jesus;
No turning back, no turning back.
Tho' none go with me, I still will follow,
No turning back, no turning back.

I have decided to follow Jesus;
No turning back, no turning back.
The cross before me, the world behind me;
No turning back, No turning back.

These words made me realize I was there for a purpose and I went forward and committed my life to serve God from that day ahead.

Later on, that month after church all who wanted to be baptized met up at the lake, I went and so did my wife, and we were baptized together September 23, 1979. It was after our baptism my wife's oldest sister refused to talk with her for the next ten years. They were raised Catholic and what we had done was all wrong!

From that moment when I went forward, I made a promise to God to follow him. I bought my self a new Bible and began to read it from cover to cover. I went to church on a regular basis. As our family grew, we went to church and so did all the children. After five years I had read through the Bible thoroughly. This commitment I made was to God, and I was set entirely on serving Him.

"Hear, O Israel: The LORD our God is one LORD: And thou shalt love the LORD thy God with all thine heart, and with all thy soul, and with all thy might." (Deuteronomy 6:4-5)

As time passed at work, many people had seen a significant change in my life. I was asked by many people at work why. I shared with them what God had done in my life. As time passed many of my friends asked questions about God and the Bible, we started meeting on my lunch break at work, this later became a bible study each day.

One stormy day with lightning was flashing, and the wind was causing a lot of damage at Disneyland. My partner and

I were called to evacuate the skyway ride and manually bring in each cabin with people to safety. We had to hand crank the cable in power went out, and the emergency generator was not working. As we cranked the cable in-betweens each cabin, my partner asked me questions about the Bible. During the evacuation, he wanted what I had in my life and when we had completed the evacuation he wanted me to pray with him, and he too, committing his life to God.

"Therefore if any man is in Messiah, he is a new creature: old things are passed away; behold all things have become new. " (2 Corinthians 5:17)

At home, my brother in law had graduated from High school, and my daughter was in Junior high school. My wife and I had three daughters who were at home. That following year my daughter started High School and my wife wanted to homeschool the other children. God had provided me with a great career at Disneyland, and my wife focused on the homeschooling at home. The Bible and prayer were our focus to teach our children the way God wanted us to live.

But, where there is a blessing, there are the trials and troubles that come from being faithful to God. My daughter was faced with the worldly views of public school and was told she could not bring her Bible to school. I went to the school and managed to straighten that out but, it was a battle none the less.

My daughter was having trouble with her stepmom. The other girls always pointed the finger at her as the troublemaker. Sometimes it was right, but, for the most part, because she was at my side most of the time, there were some hurt feelings.

My brother in law joined the Army and my daughter left for college the attitude of the other girls change toward me. Now working swing shift and they would be asleep when I got home, I got up early so I could spend time with my girls, and give my wife some time to do things she would like to do till I went to work.

Over the years the vision I had as a young teenager seem to fade in my memory. I asked God to help me remember the Love and Joy that I had experienced. But, that did not seem to satisfy my desire to confirm that the vision came from God. So, I had just finished reading once again about a man named Gideon, who said to the Lord God:

And then "Gideon" said unto him "the Lord God," if now I have found grace in thy sight, then shew me a sign that thou told me." (Judges 6:17)

So, after leaving work that night, I prayed: "God, the vision I had that led me this far, was it really from you? Please, if I to have found grace in your sight, the next person I speak to will share his vision which will be like my own."

When I arrived home, everyone was asleep. When I got up in the morning, there was a note on the kitchen table from my wife that she and the kids were going to her mother's house for the day. I ate breakfast and got ready for work after making my lunch for work, and then I thought I would leave a little early. It was a lovely day, and that ended with a loud blast. I had a flat tire on the car. I pulled over and changed it then, continued on to work. I was a little late. On my time card was a note:

We are all going to a retirement party for one of the guys in another department. Meet up with the new guy, who will be working in the Welding Shop, He is installing power to a new welding machine. See you later. *Signed by the Foreman*

I met up with the new guy and introduced myself. He said are you that Bible thumper that I heard about? I smiled and said," That must be me; I am a Christian and love the Lord." His response was God sent "I wonder if you know anything about visions? I had one not too long ago and it so real." The vision he had was so much like my own, I knew this was a confirmation of my prayer to God about my own vision. Don and I remained friends for many years and later in life, I performed his wedding, Don and his family is still serving God to this day.

"Ye shall know them by their fruits. Do men gather grapes of thorns or figs of thistles? Even so, every good tree bringeth forth good fruit; but a corrupt tree bringeth forth evil fruit. "

(Matthew 7:16-17)

It seemed that my children and wife bought into the fuzzy-was-e feels good gospel. What I mean by that if you're saved you're always saved, for the most part, have fire insurance. My wife had a friend over, and she was concerned that she could lose her Salvation, and my wife asked me to show them what the Bible said on the matter. I read the following verses:

"Then said Jesus unto his disciples, If any man will come after me, let him deny himself, and take up his cross, and follow me. For whosoever will save his life shall lose it: and whosoever will lose his life for my sake shall find it." (Matthew 16:24-25)

"In whom ye also trusted, after that ye heard the word of truth, the gospel of your salvation: in whom also after that ye believed, ye were sealed with that Holy Spirit of promise, which is the earnest of our inheritance until the redemption of the purchased possession, unto the praise of his glory." (Ephesians 1:13-14)

I explained that we need to work out our salvation daily by living as Messiah did, and it isn't an easy thing to do. We are sealed if we genuinely believe, and then when Jesus comes back, he will finish the process and redeem us and take us home. Then I read:

"Wherefore, my beloved, as ye have always obeyed, not as in my presence only, but now much more in my absence, work out your own salvation with fear and trembling. For it is God which worketh in you both to will and to do of his good pleasure." (Philippians 2:12-13)

Salvation is something we work on daily in our walk with God; if we turn from God does that qualify us to sin? No! We are a new creation, and we now have to live as children of God. Then I read this:

When the Son of man shall come in his glory, and all the holy angels with him, then shall he sit upon the throne of his glory: And before him shall be gathered all nations: and he shall separate them one from another, as a shepherd divideth his sheep from the goats: And he shall set the sheep on his right hand, but the goats on the left. Then shall the King say unto them on his right hand, Come, ye blessed of my Father, inherit the kingdom prepared for you from the foundation of the world: For I was an hungred, and ye gave me meat: I was thirsty, and ye gave me drink: I was a stranger, and ye took me in: Naked, and ye clothed me: I was sick, and ye visited me: I was in prison, and ye came unto me. Then shall the righteous answer him, saying, Lord, when saw we thee an hungered and fed thee? Or thirsty, and gave thee drink? When saw we thee a stranger, and took thee in? Or naked, and clothed thee? Or when saw we thee sick, or in prison, and came unto thee? And the King shall answer and say unto them, Verily I say unto you, Inasmuch as ye have done it unto one of the least of these my brethren, ye have done it unto me. Then shall he say also unto them on the left hand, Depart from me, ye cursed, into everlasting fire, prepared for the devil and his angels: For I was an hungred, and ye gave me no meat: I was thirsty, and ye gave me no drink: I was a stranger, and ye took me not in: naked, and ye clothed me not: sick, and in prison, and ye visited me not. Then shall they also answer him, saying, Lord, when saw we thee an hungred, or athirst, or a stranger, or naked, or sick, or in prison, and did not minister unto thee? Then shall he answer them, saying, verily I say unto you, Inasmuch as ye did it not to one of the least of these, ye did it not to me. And these shall go away into everlasting punishment: but the righteous into life eternal." (Matthew 25:31-46)

Her friend was happy and left, and my wife was so mad at me, she said I just stumbled a believer she was concerned that she was going to lose her salvation. I said I just read from the Bible and that is what it means. You either believe the Word of God or not and why did you have me talk to your friend anyway; you should have been able to help her yourself?

This was the first sign to me that we did not believe the same. In the following weeks, I asked my wife if we could read and study the Bible together. After some time we did, and she suggested we go to church this Sunday and join a new group they called" Convalescent ministry" We could bring the girls. She told me it is something we can do as a family.

That next Sunday we went to the orientation, and I was very interested, and we signed up for the family. The leader talked with us for some time, and we were assigned a place to meet him. As time passed, we went to this retirement home every Sunday after church. The Leader gave a devotional it was like a mini-church service. The leader played the Guitar, and we all sang some old hymns then we went out and visited with the elderly. The children made so many new friends, and the people loved my daughters, and my wife and I prayed with all who wanted to pray.

Now this was our first taste of ministry and as the family we a seemed to enjoy the time we spent at the retirement home, I could see the anticipation in the children as we left the church to see the old friends they had made.

The leader asked me if I would give a devotional the next Sunday and he was unable to make it for the service. A lady would be joining us to play the piano, and we could sing the hymns. Time passed, and I was asked to continue to give a message or a devotional.

I was willing but, to give out Gods word it was very hard. I did not like to talk in front of a crowd of people. The Services averaged about thirty people. Most retired pastors, Bible teachers, Sunday school teachers, and missionaries. There was this Jewish lady who had been in a concentration camp in Poland. The girls adored her, and my wife treated her as part of our family. She loved to hear the children and looked forward to talking with each one of the children.

One Sunday we went, and we asked where the Jewish lady was after the service. We found out that she had died. My wife and the children were not prepared for this, and they started to cry when another elderly lady came over and comforted them and said "She is in heaven now, with her family she loved so much. We will see her again soon, be happy and full of joy knowing this, we will meet again in heaven. The children and my wife listened, and the lesson was learned. She turned to me and said this Jewish lady heard every word you taught, and I want to thank you for she knows that Jesus is the Messiah. All of us here want to hear more of what you teach each week. As far as I am concerned, you're my pastor and we love you. Sometime later she too passed away, and her grandchildren asked if I would perform the service for her. She had told me before her death to make her funeral a celebration and present the gospel to all who would attend.

Time passes swiftly, and I taught there fourteen years and became one of the leaders of the ministry set up services in over fifteen other retirement homes. My daughters still singing and praying with the elderly, my wife learned to play the guitar, and we held service every Sunday.

The church received a call from the Billy Graham phone ministry, asking for someone to visit an elderly man who was housebound. My wife and I went, and later this started another ministry for disabled shut-ins in our community. We reached out to the church, and some people helped as it was needed to reach out to the people who want a visitor to come and sit with them and share the Word of God. We were asked to help with hospital visitation too, and now we were swamped praying and assisting in these two other ministries. But, God provided the people, and as we disciple them, so they were ready and equipped to help.

Everything was like a dream come true, things were going so well. Maybe too well!

As a leader in ministry, I felt ill equips to answer questions, I had no formal training. Praying now for God to instruct me in his word an opportunity came to join another ministry which their training would last for almost a year. The training was to become a Biblical counselor, to disciple and help people in the church who were having problems. I signed up and later my wife signed up too. We were in different classes at the same time. I was asked why I wanted to take this training and my response was simple "I want to give an answer from the scriptures when people ask me."

"The Lord GOD hath given me the tongue of the learned, that I should know how to speak a word in season to him that is weary: he wakeneth morning by morning, he wakeneth mine ear to hear as the learned." (Isaiah 50:4)

Now, the homework required much reading and study, God had answered my prayer, and I was learning how to give an answer and give hope to the person before they left. Everything I read I tested with the Word of God, which led up to some interesting discussions with the leaders of the ministry and the pastor who oversaw the whole project and training.

The pastor and I became good friends as did the leaders of the ministry. After all the training I was asked to help Counsel in the office during the week. I was on swing shift at work, and so, once or twice a week in the office to counsel.

Then things changed, I left Disneyland and went to work for an electrical company. The last six months at Disneyland I went to 18 funerals. The pressure of new management was enormous on the old timers, and they were dropping like flies. Each one of them was dear friends who had taught me many of the tricks of the trade and the wisdom of these men went beyond that. Most but, not all were brothers in the Lord. The pressure was enormous, and I once again tried to do what was right, but! I became angry and started to find my self-fighting the management. Then after eleven years, I quit, I went to another Union Job.

While working with this company doing some work for a design company who was building an amusement park in Korea. Not, long after that, I was working for them, and I went to Korea for six months.

It was the first time I had been away from my family. I talked with the family on the phone on a weekly basis and wrote home almost every day. The project we work ten hours a day six days a week. I went to a church in Seoul which had just started English speaking bible study. The pastor and his wife became excellent friends. The project that I was working on was called Lottie World. But, promises were made and broken, and I went home and worked for another electrical company to set up clean rooms for the B1 project. This was a great Job, I made a lot of money, and I could continue in the ministry at the church on Saturday and Sunday.

Where ever the job or place, I sought out a place to worship and find believers that were like-minded. It seemed every two years I would find a new place to work with the way the economy and employment was at the time.

No longer, at least it appeared that a person could work for a company for thirty years and get a gold watch and retirement. Over the years I cashed out six retirement funds to keep food on the table and pay for the mortgage on our home.

Now an opportunity to help with a newly formed Messianic congregation, the Rabbi and I had become good friends, and he wanted me to help establish the core group and give and teach biblical counseling. The Rabbi and his wife graduated from Calvary Chapel Bible College. The Rabbi and his wife both Jewish and had left their home in New York after joining up with Jews for Jesus, They had moved to California for a fresh start and formed a Messianic congregation. The biggest problem I found is this:

1. Can Jewish believers become Christians?

2. Should the congregation continue to read the liturgy?

These were the two most significant problems that faced the congregation. But that is only the tip of the iceberg. To expound on all the difficulties encountered there is not room enough to put them in this little book.

After working as the Rabbi's assistant for the last year, my brother in law had passed away from cancer, and I stepped down to care for the family. Trials and troubles were to follow like Dominos one after another.

My brethren, count it all joy when ye fall into divers temptations; Knowing this, that the trying of your faith worketh patience. But let patience have her perfect work, that ye may be perfect and entire, wanting nothing. If any of you lack wisdom, let him ask of God, that giveth to all men liberally, and upbraideth not; and it shall be given him. (James 1:2-5)

Oh, Joy!

Dreams

Then thou scarest me with dreams and terrifies me through visions: So that my soul chooseth strangling, and death rather than my life.

(Job 7:14-15)

After my brother in laws death, my wife's family's attitude toward me began to turn against me in many forms. I had made all the arrangements for his funeral, and I spoke for the family at the funeral.

My brother in law loved the Lord, and he had served in the Army, then as a police officer for ten years. Had married and had two children. He once told me when he was fourteen that he planned to join the Army to be an M.P. (Military Policeman) then after leaving the Army becomes a Police Officer, and having a family, hopefully having a boy and a girl. He also wanted to serve God and loved to play the guitar, he played music for the children's ministry. He did all that he had aspired to do and then after ten years on the police force, got cancer from agent orange which he was exposed to while in the Army. He spent a long time in the hospital it was his faith in God that held him together. Together we read this scripture, later when he could not talk due to the respirator I would read this scripture to him and pray:

"And the peace of God, which passeth all understanding, shall keep your hearts and minds through Messiah Jesus (Messiah Yeshua). Finally, brethren, whatsoever things are true, whatsoever things are honest, whatsoever things are just, whatsoever things are pure, whatsoever things are lovely, whatsoever things are of good report; if there be any virtue, and if there be any praise, think on these things. Those

things, which ye have both learned, and received, and heard, and seen in me, do: and the God of peace shall be with you."

(Philippians 4:7-9)

My mother in laws heart was crushed; she was furious at God for taking her only son at the age of thirty-three. She did not treat his wife or children with the love one might expect. Before her son died, he had started some repairs around the house for his mom. Some of the work was not completed because he had become sick from cancer. So, I finish what he had started and listened to his mom. She was grieved for the loss of her son; she mourned for him till she passed from this life. I hoped that she did not remain mad at God for the death of her son, but draw close to God and have real peace in her heart.

Death of friends and family became too familiar; I lost eighteen of my co-workers in one year. A very close friend had committed suicide, while another friend drank himself to death. All this leading up to the end of my brother in laws life, and not long after this my great uncle, grandmother, and grandfather passed from this life.

About this time of my life another vision which filled my heart with despair, which caused me to seek God even more in my life. This vision was the most disturbing, even now as I begin to place it on paper.

All the family was in bed; each of my daughters tucked in and my wife now sound asleep next to me as I dozed off and now in a deep sleep. When I heard a strange sound, and I started to get up but, the wall had turned into what appeared as a very dark liquid, and a demon like a figure jumped on me and held me down. This evil looking creature placed his hand on my mouth so I could not talk, then I was unable to move but, I could see everything that was going on in the room.

This demon for lack of anything else to call it; It was about four feet tall skinny and had a much-distorted face. Its eyes were like flames of fire, but it was filled with the darkness of its heart and at times seemed to be afraid of me. The hands and feet were like that of a frog. Then from the wall of the dark liquid one came next to my wife and placed his frog-like hand on her head, then three more came from the dark liquid and rushed into the bedrooms of my daughters. I was unable to go and protect them. I tried to scream a warning but, I could not talk, the words could not come out of my mouth. And with all my might, I could not move, and then I called on the Holy name of God to stop this, and now my mouth worked. I shouted, "In the name of the true and living God Stop!"

At that very instant the demon on me jumped back with great fear, and its eyes had lost the fiery flame. I began to sit up, and the demon next to my wife vanished, and the one still on my legs was shivering with fear and jumped up. Then leaping back into the dark liquid that was on the wall and it closed up behind it. I rushed to my daughters, and they were still asleep as if nothing had happened.

Went to my office at the end of the house and got out my Bible and began to pray. I opened up the Bible where I had left off and started reading:

"Now a thing was secretly brought to me, and my ear received a little thereof. In thoughts from the visions of the night, when deep sleep falleth on men, Fear came upon me and trembling, which made all my bones to shake. Then a spirit passed before my face; the hair of my flesh stood up: It stood still, but I could not discern the form thereof: an image was before mine eyes, there was silence, and I heard a voice, saying, Shall mortal man be more just than God? Shall a man be purer than his maker? Behold, he put no trust in his servants; and his angels he charged with folly: How much less in them that dwell in houses of clay, whose foundation is in the

dust, which is crushed before the moth? They are destroyed from morning to evening: they perish forever without any regarding it. Doth not their excellency which is in them go away? they die, even without wisdom." (Job 4:12-21)

Even then after reading this scripture my heart was still racing and my mind in great wonderment on what can I do? Another vision, why?

Now some time had passed, and the vision of the demons still troubled my heart. But, I had in my heart to serve God even more than before.

At a Sunday service Franklin Graham was a guest speaker and gave a message, and it was then I knew I wanted to go on a mission. In this way maybe I would learn more about God and his people. I had no Idea on how to go about all this, but I know God does.

So I began to pray about it. I wanted to talk to Franklin but, what are the chances. The Church where I was attending had grown to about four thousand people on a Sunday. And after the service, I needed to go retrieve my children from the children's ministry. But, I prayed none the less that I would be able to talk with Franklin.

As always I slipped out the side door to beat the traffic of the other parents to retrieve my children while my wife would visit with her mom and friends and later we would meet up to go to the retirement home where I would be giving a message that afternoon.

As I headed up the stairway ahead of me was our senior pastor and Franklin Graham. The senior pastor's briefcase suddenly opened and papers flew down the stairwell toward me. I retrieved the documents and gave them to my senior pastor, and he then introduced me to Franklin. It was then I told Franklin what was on my heart and they both laid hands on me and prayed.

After arriving home, I received a call from my mother. Dad was not doing well he had fallen and had injured himself and could not get around. We talked for some time; I realized my children had not yet met their grandparents. That night I had many things to pray about as I did throughout my day.

As I went to sleep that night, I had this feeling that my Dad or Mom would pass away without seeing my children. This weighed heavy on my heart. The next day I made arrangements with my wife and my work to take a vacation to go see my Mom and Dad. We spend most all we had in savings, and it was a tight budget. We ate at hamburger places on the way there and back to save money, and I drove straight through. Mom made a place for the children to stay while we visited. The children were able to visit with cousins they had never met.

After returning home, I received a call from one of the pastors at the church. He informed me that they wanted me to go to Burma on a missionary trip. I explained to the pastor we had spent all our money and I used up all my vacation time. He said he would be praying for me he knew God wanted me to go. I said I would pray too, and I would call him back.

I went to work the following day, I was approached by my manager. He informed me I could start a new position as District Technical Manager. And if I wanted I could take off for the next month with pay till I begin the new job. After arriving home, I told my wife who was not quite as excited as I was about the fact I had the time to go to Burma. Her concern was how am I going to pay for the trip and travel arrangements? I was convinced in my heart that God would provide and said, "God will provide."

She said if God provides then, then go! I thanked her and gave her a kiss. Then called the pastor to give him an update, I asked him to keep praying. The word got out and before I knew it the money for airfare and travel had been gathered and given to me. Now, this was my first time to do such a bold thing as going on a mission trip. My pastor knew this was all new to me and gave me a list of things that I needed to take to the church in Burma. I looked at the list; it was filled with a list of books I needed to bring to the Bible College in Burma. This is where I would be teaching the Word of God. I took the list home and showed it to my wife along with the airfare and travel arrangements that God had provided.

My wife looked over the list of books, and she said it is impossible for you to get all these books in the short time I had left to go to Burma. I had my passport, airfare, travel arrangements but, I need to take these books which would weigh over a hundred pounds and my suitcase of clothing which wasn't much and my Bible. I said, "God will provide." But, it was met with silence from my wife. I remembered the scripture about Abraham and Isaac:

"And Abraham said, My son, God will provide himself a lamb for a burnt offering: so they went both of them together." (Genesis 22:8)

This provision was the very reason I wanted to go on this mission trip. I knew in my heart God who provided for Abraham and Isaac, would provide for me. It was the Lamb that was sacrificed for me that now lives in my heart that has to lead me by faith to go forward on this mission trip to Burma.

Prayed about all the books on this list and then I went to the nearest Christian bookstore to count the cost. When I arrive the very first Item on the list was in the discount book bin as I walked in. It was a Greek, Hebrew Lexicon it weighs at least ten pounds. I asked a young lady how much it cost; it was the only Item in the bin that did not have a price on it. She asked me "Why do you want this book?" Then explained about the list and she said: "Don't leave I need to get someone and I will be right back." In only a few minutes the manager of the store and several other people from the store came over and was introduced to me.

Once again I was asked why I wanted that book. After telling the story about the list and what God had placed on my heart. I could see each person there was in great anticipation which now filled the air. It was then the manager told me that they had been praying for the past month that this book would come to some good use in a bible college. Then asked for my list and said come back tomorrow, and we will have everything ready for you. Don't worry; it will not cost you a dime. But, make sure these books make it to Burma to the Bible College.

Went home and told my wife, and she could not believe it. I was to leave in three days. Sunday the day before I was to leave, the church prayed over the group of men going to Burma. I was asked if I had pocket money for the trip, I needed two hundred dollars to exchange when I got to Burma. I didn't have the two hundred dollars. But once again I said God will provide. When we got home, I saw something hanging on the front door. It was a One hundred dollar bill; my wife said "Well, I would have never believed it, if I had not seen it myself. But, that is only half what you need. Before I could say a word, she looked at me and said: "I guess God will provide." I smiled and then we went inside the house. My youngest daughter said to me" Daddy, I forgot I checked the mail yesterday, and you got a letter from someone called Buckshot!

She handed me the letter, and it was from a friend who had been involved with the Bible study we had at lunch time at Disneyland. He was from India, his name is Burchshat. The letter read as follows:

To my dearest brother in the Lord Jesus the Messiah,

I send you this letter to tell you, you were right in saying that Jesus is the Son of God. Remember our wager I would read the Bible and you would read the Koran. Then one of us would have to convert. Well, I believe, and my wife and children do too.

My wife and I are going to India to preach the Word to our Parents; even if it cost us our lives. We love God and what he has done for us. If you do not hear from me again, I will see you in heaven. God will provide.

Oh, we heard you are going to Burma, so we placed this money in the letter. Please pray for us, we understand that even our parents could have a sentence to death for preaching the Word. But, who should we fear? Only our father in heaven. Prays for us as we are praying for you.

Love you brother

Burchshat (Buckshot)

At that moment tears filled my eyes knowing the danger my friend and his wife is now facing. In the letter was one hundred dollar bill. My wife could see I was crying and my daughters too. I handed the letter to her so she could read it as I went outside to have some time by myself. The urgency for prayer and time to be with God was paramount to me at this minute in my life.

"Draw nigh to God, and he will draw nigh to you. Cleanse your hands, ye sinners; and purify your hearts, ye double minded. Be afflicted, and mourn, and weep: let your laughter be turned to mourning and your joy to heaviness. Humble yourselves in the sight of the Lord, and he shall lift you up." (James 4:8-10)

Spirit of Wisdom

My son, if thou wilt receive my words, and hide my commandments with thee; So that thou incline thine ear unto wisdom, and apply thine heart to understanding; Yea, if thou criest after knowledge, and liftest up thy voice for understanding; If thou seekest her as silver, and searches for her as for hid treasures; Then shalt thou understand the fear of the LORD, and find the knowledge of God. For the LORD giveth wisdom: out of his mouth cometh knowledge and understanding.

(Proverbs 2:1-6)

Not much was said about the letter from my friend from that point on. It still weighed heavy on my mind, and I continued to pray for my friend and his wife who were now in India. The world seemed to get smaller to me.

Now, I was headed to Burma not far from where my friend was being a witness to his parents and family. Thought of him willing to give his life to present the gospel gave me courage and hope. Yet, I was in sincere prayer for him and his wife's safety.

After boarding my plane for Burma and saying goodbye to my family. I thought once on the flight it gave me plenty of time for prayer and to read my Bible. But, during this time God had placed a traveling companion in my life.

The conversation started when he asked me if I was a Christian. He was a young man going to Korea to serve there in the Army. I could picture myself some twenty years earlier on a similar journey. My reply to him was yes, I am a Christian. His response was I thought so; you have a bible with you. My response was I could see you are in the Army from your uniform are you going to Korea?

He said yes, told me where he was going to Korea and that he was a Christian too. He was wondering if there were any churches in Korea he could attend that spoke English.

I told him of the Bible study that I had participated in some time ago in Seoul Korea. We enjoyed our time of fellowship as fellow travelers before we parted company we prayed for one another. It was refreshing to see a young soldier who loves the Lord.

"Be not forgetful to entertain strangers: for thereby some have entertained angels unawares." (Hebrews 13:2)

Saying goodbye to the soldier at Inchon International airport then caught my connecting flight to Thailand. I would be staying with a missionary family in Thailand. I would take a couple of days to get my paperwork ready in Thailand and my money exchange to satisfy the Burmese government before entering the country. This leg of the trip I was focused on prayer and reading my bible, I thought.

"To know wisdom and instruction; to perceive the words of understanding; To receive the instruction of wisdom, justice, and judgment, and equity; To give subtilty to the simple, to the young man knowledge and discretion." (Proverbs 1:2-4)

After takeoff from Inchon Korea, I started to read my bible. It was then I could smell smoke. It was coming from the TV monitor cabinet in the front of the cabin. Then rushing to the monitor cabinet air attendant put out the fire with a fire extinguisher. The pilot with broken English he gave a short announcement "We had a little excitement after taking off from Inchon, but do not be alarmed. The problem is under control, and the air system is cleaning the air. When we arrive in Thailand, for those of you continue on. We will be changing planes there. Sorry for the inconvenience. Have a nice trip."

This did not give me a comfortable feeling at all. I then closed my bible and began to pray for all of us on the plane. I continued praying through most of the flight. The fire which had started just after take-off started up again just before the plane landed. This time the smoke was very heavy. Now my prayers did not stop till we arrived in Bangkok Thailand.

Once we landed, we had to leave the plane via stairs on the back of a truck. And alongside the aircraft was a fire truck standing by. As I walked out of the plane the humidity hit me with the hot temperature both of which were 100% humidity and 100 degrees F; it was like walking into a wall of hot water.

As I looked back, smoke was coming out of the plane in both the front and back doors of the aircraft. We were all rushed to the terminal, and the Fireman hurried up the same stairs I had just left behind. After going through the customs, I saw a sign with my name on it. It was the Baptist Missionaries waiting for me. They hurried me to the curb outside the terminal then we rushed off into traffic that reminded me of Korea some twenty years ago. Bicycles loaded with stuff to be sold at market stacked five tears high. Taxis blowing their horns, buses; and the busses, I was surprised – Dae Woo Buses from Korea and they still had the Korean writing on them.

I asked about the busses, and the Missionary told me with a Texas draw it wasn't too long ago a company in Korea sold a whole fleet of these busses to Thailand and Burma. I laughed and said I probably road in one of these busses when I was in Korea.

It was getting late, and when we arrived at their home, the maid greeted us and supper was ready. During the time at the supper table, we got to know one another. The missionary and his wife had been in Thailand for almost eighteen years. They invited me to a service they were holding the next day and then they were going to the prison to pray with the prisoners there. Each time they went to the prison they brought food, clothing, and Bibles. It had to be checked in, and I needed to be cleared to visit. So after the service, we would arrive there at the prison a little early so we would be able to attend and pray with the prisoners once everything was cleared.

I had just entered into God's school of Wisdom:

"A new commandment I give unto you, that ye love one another; as I have loved you, that ye also love one another. By this shall all men know that ye are my disciples if ye have love one to another." (John 13:34-35)

Amazed at the faith and love this missionary husband and wife team. My hope was to glean as much as I could from them, seeing the dedication put into everything they did. Most of all it was the Love they had for others. They seemed to always put others before themselves. This was the love I was seeking in my journey to know God more each day. Their examples of love were a great instructor to me. I could see the joy they both had for others and one another. After spending a couple of days with them before going to Burma, I hated to go. But they told me I could stay with them on my way back from Burma if I wanted. They gave me their contact information, and I said to them I would call them once I returned to Thailand.

After getting on a tiny plane, then buckled up for the flight; only took less than an hour from loading to landing. Waiting for me was David Yone Moe, the founder of the Bible College in Yangon, Burma.

Once I clear customs he hurried me to a church van, and we rushed off to the college. David was very straightforward and asked me if I had my money exchanged. I said yes, he then said give it to me for safe keeping, and I will take care of everything. Then he asked are you ready to teach tonight. I have an interpreter available to be with you at your side when you teach. He then introduced me to Bow the interpreter. David continued and said "after arriving at the college, just leave your baggage in the van, we need to get upstairs to the service will be starting once we arrive. I will introduce you, and then you can share with the students and the church what brought you here from America. We want to get to know you and your testimony. Thank you for coming such a long way to see us.

Told David the large Bag I brought with me was for the college it had everything that was requested; on the list. David then instructed to have that bag taken to the office, but the other bag is left in the van. Next thing I knew I was upstairs, and there were about a hundred people there. And downstairs were as nearly as many there listening to the service over a PA system. David introduced me and says he will now give us our evening teaching and his testimony.

I am sure God could hear my prayers as I stood up in front of the congregation and shared my testimony. Then something unusual happened, it was as if Bow the interpreter and I were one person in heart and language. I knew the Holy Spirit of God was with all of us there that night. After giving my testimony and sharing my vision and love I was searching for, I asked if anyone there wanted that, and I would like to pray for them. Several people came up to the where I was standing, and I prayed with them and Bow interpreted.

"If any man speaks in an unknown tongue, let it be by two, or at the most by three, and that by course; and let one inter-

pret. But if there be no interpreter, let him keep silence in the church; and let him speak to himself, and to God."

(1 Corinthians 14:27-28)

David had a very rigorous schedule set for me. Also, the rest of the team would arrive in Burma late the next afternoon. For the month my plan was as follows:

5AM prayer and breakfast with staff
6AM Third Year students Book of Matthew
7AM Second year students Book of James
8AM First Year Students Book of John
9-10 AM Visit House Churches in Area – Give Devotional
11- Noon Lunch with House Church - Give Devotional
12-1 Meeting with Pastors and Staff – Prayer
1PM Third Year students Book of Matthew
2 PM Second year students Book of James
3 PM First Year Students Book of John
4-5PM Visit House Churches in Area – Give Devotional
5- 6PM Staff Dinner – Prayer
7-9PM Worship Service
10PM Hotel for the night
Every day was the same, but on Sunday:
7-11 AM Morning Service
12- 1 PM Staff Dinner
1-5 PM Free Time
6-9 PM Evening Worship Service

The rest of the team from America showed up at 8:30 PM on a Sunday, after the services they were taken to the hotel along with me. When they arrived, I was giving my testimony and sharing Gods Word with the congregation. The place was packed, standing room only upstairs and downstairs and many people sitting outside in the courtyard listing to the PA system as Bow and I gave the message.

Later, once at the Hotel, we had a meeting with Pastor George. He was going to do some recording at the schools recording studio with the Praise Band, and he was going to give a course on Bible verse memorization. He asked me to fill the gaps if he was busy with the music and studio recording and teaching. His traveling companion was an elder in his church, and he was not going to teach but assist him at the studio. Then there was my roommate he attended the same church I did. He was shy, and Pastor George asked what my roommate was going to teach. He had several large ring binders full of sermons. And showed them to the pastor and said:" My wife wrote all these for me to teach." The pastor said are you sure you want to teach all these? He shrugged his shoulders and said I'll try.

That night after turning in I fell asleep right away. Later that night around midnight we were jolted out of bed. It felt like a truck had rammed the side of the building. Now sitting up in my bed, it happened again, and it hit so hard that it threw me out of my bed and on to the floor. And now sitting next to me with wide eyes was my roommate.

Seconds later the other two men of the group the pastor and the elder rushed into our room, saying it is an earthquake. A lot of excitement outside and we all prayed together then went back to bed. Before going to sleep, my roommate said "I don't think I am going to teach from my wife's sermons. God just answered my prayer, I need to present what God has for me to share from my heart." And, I said Amen.

The days went by quickly, and the team had to leave after 30 days in the country. But, I would stay for three more days. After seeing the team off at the airport, David took me to lunch before returning to the Bible College. He asked me if I would go to the leper colony with him to teach and visit them and pray over them. I told him I would pray about it and give him an answer in the morning. He smiled and said okay; let me know at the Prayer Breakfast with the staff in the morning.

Spirit of Understanding

The fear of the LORD is the beginning of wisdom: a good understanding have all they that do his commandments: his praise endureth forever.

(Psalms 111:10)

The following morning at the Prayer Breakfast with the staff David asked if I was going with him today to the leper colony. After much prayer last night I believe I must go, I would like to go and when do we start.

David said we need to pick up some supplies first then we can go. David said you haven't spent any of your money, would you like to donate some towards the supplies to the leper colony? Sure, use whatever is needed for the supplies; I don't need any of the money for myself. David asked what about your return trip? I have some money setback for my flight home.

After the breakfast, we bought gas for the church van, chickens, ducks, and rice and spices and first aid items and candy for the children. It was a long trip from Yangon to Pegu located in the Bago province where the leper colony was located. Along the way we got stuck in the road, the rain turned the road into the sticky red clay of goo. Along the road was a chain gang of prisoners watched over by the military armed with AK47. I notice one guard had an M16A1 like I had when I was in the Army. David told me to stay in the van and steer the Van while the Chain Gang of Prisoners pushed us out of the mud. David paid the guards, and we were on our way.

Once we arrived in front of the small church, the van was surrounded by people. Children were calling out for Papa

(David) whom you could tell they loved him with a passion. We unloaded the van of the chickens and ducks. Then serval men whom it was quite obvious they were lepers' and with joy unloaded the two large sacks of rice. The ladies gathered the spices and went straight to work on fixing dinner for us. David introduced the Pastor who he assigned to the Lepers. This young man had graduated from the Bible College I was now teaching in. David tells me the story of him and his two brothers.

David said it was about five years ago the three brothers decided to come to the Bible College they heard how people were changed once they entered the gates and left after three years of training. The three brothers were opium attics and were from the Shaun state near the golden triangle. This is where most of the Opium is grown. Tired of life, hearing about the Bible College they set out on foot which was about 150 miles to walk. Once the brothers arrived they were in bad shape, they when into withdrawals from the opium which they had run out of during there long journey.

David said they were in very dire straits, they were brought to his office, and he explained the program to them. They were not allowed to leave the compound for three years if they chose to stay. But, first, they must take a test. He gave each one of them the gospel of John to read; they can remain in the newcomer's room. If they want anything else, they need to ask the room pastor. Then if necessary he will get what they need.

But, they need to read the book of John and let him know what they thought about the book. David said it wasn't long they were very sick with withdrawals from the opium, they were crying out wanting to die. David and the other Pastors as they had done in the past for so many others laid hands on them and prayed for God to take away the addiction and heal them. It wasn't long they were like new people; they read the book of John and had prayed to be born again. David says that is how our program works here. It's a one-step program, give everything to God and be born again.

The brothers studied hard and graduated from the Bible College. Once they had graduated, they are to go out and start a ministry. The oldest brother went back to the golden triangle to start a church, the middle brother was arrested and sent to prison, he did this to preach the gospel to the prisoners, and it was the only way he could get into the prison to share the Holy Word of God. The youngest brother went to the leper colony where David introduced him to me. To build good faith and start a church he married a young leper girl and started a family and then a church. The church we were in was the fruit of his labors.

I had brought my harmonica to play music for the service. Everyone sang the songs I played their favorite of the songs were "At the Cross." After worship, David gave a message, and everyone's eyes were glued to David as he taught from Gods Word. You could hear the silence, between the breaths that David took. Everyone's heart and souls were soaking up every word he spoke. After the service, I was asked to play my harmonic again. Everyone enjoyed the music. Then David called the children to share their memory verses. After each child recited their scriptures to David, he gave them a small piece of hard candy. He started with the oldest to the youngest.

Last but not the least of these beautiful children was a little five-year-old girl who stood in   front of David with her arms folded and reciting the scripture she had chosen. She swayed back and forth to the rhythm of her voice reciting the memory versus she had decided. She took almost five minutes. Then she was finished and received the small piece of hard candy that David had been giving to each child. The reward was the same for each.

I asked David what verse of scripture she did from memory. He said she chose to remember all of Psalms 119. I had tears in my eyes, and David asked me why I was crying. I told David, I am so convicted of this five year old girl, and I should be memorizing the scripture like this.

"Thy word have I hid in mine heart, that I might not sin against thee." (Psalms 119:11)

Each day I have spent in Burma, God has placed me in his boot camp of understanding, faith, hope and love. My eyes are open, and my ears hear the beautiful things God is doing here in Burma. The Faith in action in the lives of each person is shouting the Word of God in my heart.

Now a five-year-old girl's has stirred up a fire in my heart to learn and memorize Gods Holy Word. I asked David why she chose Psalms 119. David smiled and his reply she did not pick it; she said she prayed about which scripture to remember, And God told her Psalms 119.

She remembers the verse for God not the piece of candy like the other children. He said the little girl is an exceptional child. She is one of the only children here who does not have any form of leprosy. Her father has passed, and her mother wants her to leave and not get leprosy. But, she tells us God wants her to stay with her mother. I cannot argue with that, she is a joy to everyone here.

David asked if I wanted to eat, I said sure sounds good to me, I am hungry. He told me lepers had made food for everyone. You don't mind? I said no, I am hungry.

David smiled we prepared to eat in the church. The food served was curry chicken and rice. David asked if I would pray over the meal for everyone, and he interpreted the prayer. I finished the chicken curry in no time. I looked up, and everyone was looking in my direction. David smiled and said they never had anyone who visited eat with them before. I said that this is best curry chicken I have ever had. Before I knew it, another serving was given to me, and everyone was amazed and continued to look at me as I finished my meal.

After the meal, I was asked if I would be willing to go out in the jungle and pray with those who are too sick to come to church. We prayed, and David took a picture of me as I placed my arms around the pastor and one of the elders who had leprosy. As I took my arms of each of the men, I notice some blood and tissue from them were on the sleeves of my shirt. Then this verse came to mind that still, small voice said:

"Herein is our love made perfect, that we may have boldness in the Day of Judgment: because as he is, so are we in this world. There is no fear in love; but perfect love casteth out fear: because of fear hath torment. He that feareth is not made perfect in love. " (1 John 4:17-18)

At that moment I knew beyond any doubt that God had me there, that very moment for a reason. I agreed to go and was warned about the dry land leaches and the concerns that they are known carriers of HIV and other diseases in the jungle.

We spent the last part of the day till it was getting dark visiting each little hut along a narrow pathway in the jungle. I was asked to lay my hands on each of the people and pray for them, I could see the joy of each person despite the harsh and terrible leprosy they each had. I found out it wasn't leprosy that causes their deaths it was other diseases in the jungle such as HIV which was at an epidemic level in the broader community of the lepers. Out of the five thousand lepers in the colony in Pegu, there was a small community of Christians. There were only about two hundred believers in this part of the colony; I found it interesting that the Christian community was geographically right in the middle of all the unbelieving lepers.

The unsaved lepers would mock the Christians, but they would buy food from them, and some came to know the Lord in this process. The living conditions were sad, to say the least, but the Christian community strived to help others and grow food by starting a plantation. I was amazed at how hard they worked even without toes, fingers or lost limbs. David referred to the Christian Lepers as Happy lepers.

David told me the story about how the young pastor started the church. He married a young lady who became a Christian, and the lepers hated him. They tied both of them to a tree in hopes they would die there. The Lepers mocked them, and the pastor and his wife prayed for them and sang songs of worship. Then it began to rain, and it came down so hard that the other lepers raced for shelter. A flash of lightning hit the tree and the ropes of the pastor and his wife were gone. They remained unharmed and continued to praise God and to sing songs of praise. This put fear in the hearts of the lepers and most of them ran back to their village area.

The next day they came back, and the pastor and his wife were eating some rice under a small hut they had made. The other lepers saw them and were afraid of them; they thought they should have died when the tree was hit by lightning. But, instead, they saw the Love of God shining from both the pastor and his wife.

A few of the lepers stayed and asked why they could sing with joy and praise a god that they could not see; did your god cut your ropes and save you? The Pastor was now given an opportunity to share the love of God. And that day and each day, one by one the church grew. The church we met in today, well it is not much but, it is the people here that make the church not the building.

"Praising God, and having favor with all the people. And the Lord added to the church daily such as should be saved." (Acts 2:47)

David said it is getting late and we have to be careful driving out of here. We have to watch for Army patrols there have been some firefights not far from here. The Koryn and the Burmese are still at war. The Koryn are Christians and have been fighting the Burmese Army ever since the end of World War Two. They were promised if they fought against the Japanese they could have their land back. But, that has never happened, and the Burmese have condemned them as enemies of the country. This area is considered a war zone if we leave now we should be okay.

As we traveled the road back to the College, I noticed a small village as we crossed a river. I asked David could we stop and get something to drink. David said we have a little time, sure. We stayed in a little coffee shop which was made out of used lumber and scraps of sheet metal, and old military portable flight line (PFL) which was used for the sides of the building and the scraps of wood were used to form the frames of the wall, and the sheet metal was used for the roof. Inside it was decorated with pictures from calendars and magazines. It was done in good taste. There were six tables, and David and I sat at one, and he orders coffee and some deep fried chicken to snack on.

As we sat there an Army patrol of five men sat at the table next to us. Then another patrol arrived. David was listening to their conversation and told me not to talk. Looking at the uniform, it appeared it was an officer most likely a lieutenant who was in charge of the two patrols. He approached David and asked who the white boy was.

David translated so I would know what the Officer was asking. My name is Jesse, and I offered to shake his hand. He smiled and touched my hand and said:" Why have you come to Burma." I came to share the secret to life everlasting." He was amazed at my answer and then sat at our table.

He talked with David for some time and then asked me another question, what do I think of his country?

My response surprised him, I said the country is nice but, the people are beautiful, and it is for this reason I want to share the good news of everlasting life."

He then shakes my hand and then called all the soldiers to leave on patrol. David smiled and said" this is one of the two patrols I was talking about. This place is just on the outskirts of the war zone. He warned us not to go into the war zone at night and to take you back to Yangon to safety. He said if you truly have the knowledge of everlasting life then share with his people in Yangon.

"Ye that fears the LORD, trust in the LORD: he is their help and their shield." (Psalms 115:11)

Spirit of Counsel

The counsel of the LORD standeth forever, the thoughts of his heart to all generations.

(Psalms 33:11)

David picked me up from the Hotel and asked if I would have my bag ready to go to the airport in the morning as we drove downtown. We stopped at a one of the home churches, and he asked if I would share with them what I had learned in Burma. He said the people you will be meeting all know English and are looking forward to meeting you.

We stopped in front of a five-story building, and as we got out of the church van, I saw a young lady waving to David and said we are ready. The contrast to the jungle and now downtown Yangon seemed like two different worlds. Though the streets were filled with cars, taxis, and buses, yes Dae Woo Korean buses which the Burmese did not bother to change the Korean writing on the bus. I saw one buss with a Seoul train station written on it. Still, this part of the city seemed very new. Noticing that the cars parked outside were all new cars. The area where we had stopped was well kept with some trees and a nice sidewalk.

We went up the stairs to the home church which I was to speak, and I found it was the home of one of the pastors from the college. The building we were in was for government employees and their families. The pastor's father was retired from the government and had served there for some 35 years. The pastor's father, mother and their son and the family lived in this charming apartment. David introduced me to the family and not much later two other families arrived.

David led everyone in prayer, and the young lady who had waved at David through the window sang an old hymn. The each of the children said their memory verse. Then David said this is the American which you have been praying for each day to come to Burma. He will be leaving in the morning. If you have any questions, this is the time to ask, and he will be glad to answer.

The pastor's father asked me;" How did you find the means to come to Burma?" I smiled and said" I had no means to come to Burma. But, God provided for my every need and more." I then told the story of how God had placed it on my heart for a mission trip and how God provided for my every need.

I asked them to pray for Buckshot and his wife in India and their safety. The next question was from the pastor; "How has this affected your life." With tears in my eyes, I said "I have learned more about God and his hope, faith and love here in Burma than I have all my Christian life. Please pray for the Christians in America to wake up. The passion you have as believers in Burma is wonderful; I feel the church in American needs to be humbled by God to know the truth of His Holy Word.

After the meeting and the excellent food that was served David and I returned to the College for me to say my goodbyes to the students. Each class I gave a devotional and prayed over the Students in the class.

Then David said there is someone I want you to meet. He took me to a room next to his apartment on the campus. There on a small bed laid a very old woman in the fetal position, crippled from old age. She had a big smile on her face and spoke perfect English. She said, I have been waiting for you and praying for you. David said she is our prayer warrior she prays for us all the time. We care for her, and she is almost one hundred years old. The lady smiled, and David left.

She said she had something to tell me. I sat a listen to every word she spoke. I held her hand, and she began to reveal how she had been praying for me before I even left America. She told me that David and the college needed some books and materials for the college. Also, they wanted someone from your church to come. I prayed for several months, and God assured me he would send you. You were to arrive early and to leave later than all the others. You would find joy in the hearts of our people, and we would find comfort in you from the Holy Spirit of God. You would go to the leper colony, and God would teach you of his perfect love you have been seeking most of your life. In return, you would someday return to us with what David will ask of you once you leave. My eyes cannot see the present, but I had seen you before you left America and that you will return, but I will be going home while you are gone, complete the mission that God has in store for you. Listen to David and do as he says, I will see you face to face someday. After this, she said she was tired, and I could go.

"I know that whatsoever God doeth, it shall be forever: nothing can be put to it, nor anything was taken from it: and God doeth it, that men should fear before him. That which hath been is now; and that which is to be hath already been; and God requireth that which is past."

(Ecclesiastes 3:14-15)

After taking a walk to clear the tears from my eyes and pray. Then I returned to the College office to meet up with David. I saw David sitting in his office, and he had some people there he was talking to. He waved for me to enter and introduced me to some new students that just made a commitment for three years of study.

David said this young man and his wife and small child are our latest students. He is blind, and his wife and young daughter are here to help him go through the program. Would you pray over them and I will translate. Praying the words that came from my mouth were only from my heart and soul as if God had picked each word by His Holy Spirit. I was now overwhelmed with the prayer, and their prayer warrior whom I had just met and God have given me a humble spirit that now the counsel of God can work through me.

"Praying always with all prayer and supplication in the Spirit, and watching thereunto with all perseverance and supplication for all saints; And for me, that utterance may be given unto me, that I may open my mouth boldly, to make known the mystery of the gospel,"

(Ephesians 6:18-19)

David then took me to my Hotel and said he would pick me up in an hour to go to dinner. After he left me off, I remembered the old lady said David had something for me to do. I wondered what it might be. I retrieved my Bible from my room and sat outside in the courtyard in swing chair praying. As I sat there, I was drained physically, mentally and spiritually tired, but a great peace that rested in my soul was my strength.

As I sat there, swinging back and forth and for the days of my visit to Burma rushed through my mind. The love I had in my vision as a young teenager was here and alive in my heart in Burma. I wanted more, and I wanted to stay and not leave. But, I must go; I have a family and a job to go back to. That moment was both the most wonderful moment of my life and the saddest too. My emotions were filled with the Love and joy that comes only from the Spirit of God. Then I read this passage which humbled me even further:

> "But the fruit of the Spirit is love, joy, peace, longsuffering, gentleness, goodness, faith, Meekness, temperance: against such there is no law. And they that are Messiah's have crucified the flesh with the affections and lusts. If we live in the Spirit, let us also walk in the Spirit. Let us not be desirous of vain glory, provoking one another, envying one another." (Galatians 5:22-26)

Now I realized this mission trip was more for my benefit that it was for all the people I had met in Burma. Then, I looked up it was David, Time had passed so quickly. He asked are you ready and I smiled yes, and we left for Dinner.

We arrived at a food place, and David escorted me to a large room, there sat the whole staff of the college. They all greeted me each one, they prayed over me and then David Prayed for the meal. It was indeed a magnificent banquet with all the trimmings. David said we have observed that you like all the foods we have placed before you. So we all agreed you would want the menu tonight. My response was slow, but I did respond to this table is fit for a king. David said all of us here are the sons of the King Jesus the Messiah, enjoy.

After leaving David said we need to go to my office. There he handed me a Burmese Bible. He said" This the last one we have here, there were one thousand of these smuggled into the country through Bangladesh. They were sent here from Franklin Graham. Only eight hundred made it here. I want you to take this Bible and bring back as many as you can. God will provide, and when you have them ready I will meet you at the airport, and you can revisit us. Remember this God will give you all you need to bring Bibles back to Burma.

The next day I arrived at the airport, I had the one bag that had my clothing in it along with my Bible. David said "I have your other suitcase here and we placed a few things in here for you to have as gifts from each of the staff. We checked in the bags, and then I left for Thailand. After arriving in Thailand, I found a phone and called the missionaries. The maid picked up the phone and told me it will be a while but, they will be there soon. I sat waiting after my trip to Burma how I longed to be with them there, and I missed my family – it was a dilemma, and I was torn, but I was at the same time filled with Joy knowing God has plans for me to bring bibles to Burma.

"Hear counsel, and receive instruction, that thou mayest be wise in thy latter end. There are many devices in a man's heart; nevertheless the counsel of the LORD, that shall stand." (Proverbs 19:20-21)

Spirit of Strength

The LORD is my rock, and my fortress, and my deliverer; my God, my strength, in whom I will trust; my buckler, and the horn of my salvation, and my high tower.

(Psalms 18:2)

I am now waiting for the missionaries to arrive sitting outside with the luggage. Sitting on a cement bench which was not very comfortable, but it served its purpose. Thoughts are racing through my head about the family at home; wife, and children what they might be doing. Now praying for family, Buckshot and his wife in India, the Bible College and the Missionaries in Bangkok Thailand as thoughts raced in my mind.

The thought kept returning to the old lady, the prayer warrior for the Bible College and how she gave instructions to do as David asks. These thoughts of her praying for me, the knowledge and understanding about me even before coming to Burma was amazing. Also, the fact that she knew just what I was to accomplish while in Burma. Tired all over, even so, could feel deep inside my soul an inner strength which had been placed there during the stay in Burma. Spiritually I knew that this was growing pains in my faith, what a beautiful thing.

Time passed quickly; the Baptist missionary and his wife had appeared with their van and parked right in front of me. Before I could pick up my bags, the big Texas missionary had them loaded in his van. Off, we went. He said before we go home we have a service to attend and you are welcome to join us. Returning to his response with a smile and said would be honored to participate.

It was not long, and we arrived, and the building was beautiful, had plenty of parking spaces. It was a pleasant afternoon as we entered a schoolhouse and one of the large classrooms which the missionaries have been using for a church.

Asked him how you can have a church service in a school? Isn't that a hard thing to pull off? With his thick Texas accent, he said, yeah in the states that can be hard thing to do these days. However, here in Thailand, well we are teachers of the Bible and many people including the school system think it is a good thing. We teach English, the Bible, and Music in this classroom. The music is gospel and Hymns, the English we use the Bible as a textbook and well as you might expect we use the Bible to teach Gods Word. It seems to be working quite well. Would you like to start us off with prayer and do you sing? My answer amused him "If I sing people pray I would stop, but I do play the Harmonica."

The service began after about thirty people arrived for the class all sitting in the chairs we had arranged in advance. I was asked to say the opening prayer, and I would play a song on the harmonica, I played "At the Cross" Everyone sang along knowing every word. Then the Texan stood up and played the Trumpet; the song was "When we all get to Heaven." While his wife played the piano, the missionary lost his Texas accent and began to teach in the Thai language, and I was in awe. He taught the Word of God with the Baptist heart and Texas boldness but in Thai. The people all love his sermon. After giving the message his wife played "In the Garden," and everyone stood and sang it in English, and I sang along too.

After the service, the Missionary told me he heard me singing. He refrained from praying for me to stop. Then he laugh, meant to tell you the truth that's why I play the trumpet. I cannot sing a note. Then the English class started in the same room.

When we left school to go to their home in Bangkok to eat and get ready for the next day. I was asked when my flight leaves for the states? I leave in two days on Korean Air Lines; the flight leaves at 9 AM. The missionaries said I could join them as they visit the prison the next day. Then in the afternoon, I could rest for my trip back to the states.

Early the next mooring after a good night's sleep I joined the missionaries at the breakfast table. The missionaries went over the plans for the day, and then we prayed. The plan was simple we would gather the bibles, food, and clothing for the prisoner's and then we would spend most of the day visiting with the prisoners.

Once we were in the prison visiting area, it could be overwhelming. The visiting area consists of three regions, the center court area which the visitors are allowed to enter and are escorted by guards for their protection according to prison policy and protocol. This area is horseshoe shaped and parallel to the railing which gives a space of four feet between the visitor and the inmates. It can be overwhelming to the visitor at first because there are about two hundred prisoners to visit each hour. They are all behind iron bars directly in front of the visitor where you must speak in a loud voice to communicate with one another.

At times this can be very difficult. However, the guards' demands silence unless they are being visited. Halfway through my visit, the missionaries said I could stay and visit; they have been granted to visit the prisoners on death row.

This is something they must attend when allowed. After their visit, the prisoner is led to the gallows and is hung.

The missionaries said this could be the hardest but, sometimes the most rewarding visits. They remain after the executions to comfort loved ones. Most often the prisoner is from a foreign country, and the crime is drug trafficking in Thailand which carries the death sentence. The missionaries are allowed to speak with the prisoner and pray with them before the execution. Families and friend rarely show up because of the travel expenses. But, when they do visit, the missionaries are there to comfort them.

I remained and took notes and address of eight prisoners who wanted me to send them a letter. One man stood out to me he wanted to have a computer to learn on. I told him that I would look into it and got his address. I poured out my heart in prayer and sharing the Word of God with all I could. When we returned in the late afternoon, we had an early dinner, and I returned to my room, and I was entirely spent.

The morning arrived quickly as I woke up, heard a voice saying it is time to get ready to go to the Airport, and I could smell breakfast. Got dressed and organized my things and placed them in the luggage. We all gathered at the breakfast table and prayed.

Next to my plate was a flier as I picked it up. The Texas missionary had a smile on his face, and said "Have a thousand of these printed up at a professional print shop, and then send them to me. I want to hand them out when we go to northern Thailand. I would be most grateful. I put it in my pocket, and I agreed to get it done as soon as possible.

Then I asked what else do you need? He responded with a great deal of excitement, Bibles, all the Bibles you can send. I responded "I will do what I can. I handed him my list of the eight prisoners who wanted me to write, along with their requests, along with their address. The Texas missionary told me to send the letters to him. This way I can make sure they get the letters; otherwise, they could get lost or discarded in the government red tape. The Missionary response was "If I hand carry these letters, I know they will reach each one of the prisoners."

It did not seem long at all, and I was on a plane to Korea where I would make a connecting flight to California. When I arrived in Korea, I landed in Inchon, and I could spend a little time in Korea. I was amazed in the changes Korea had made as a country in the last few years from 1989 to 1992 and even more the changes I have seen since I was in the military 1971-1975 it was a whole new world.

When I arrived at LAX airport after leaving customs I could see my wife waiting, she had lost much weight, and I was a bit concern. I asked how the children were, and she said they are with Mom right now and we can spend some time together. We stopped and had lunch together, and I got caught up on what was going on at home with the kids. I did not have to be back to work for a couple of days, and I could spend it with my family.

Something strange happened after returning to California, I became very depressed, and I was crying whenever I was alone. I looked up Pastor George, and he told me the same thing happened to him and the rest of the team. He said "we had a lot of prayer cover and each of us knew we were there for a purpose. Well, now we go home the prayers stopped, and life is back to the way it was. He paused and was choked up, then said we no longer have that prayer cover we had, and the joy we had doing God's work is over for the time being."

"Sorrow is better than laughter: for by the sadness of the countenance the heart is made better."

(Ecclesiastes 7:3)

Before returning to work I looked over the Burmese Bible that David had given me. Then the flyer that I had placed in my pocket needed to be printed and sent to Thailand along with as many bibles I could gather up. Then my heart went out to the prisoners who wanted me to send them a letter. Also, the prisoner who wished for a computer with lessons materials to learn about computers. I could get overwhelmed but, I decided I need to pray and share with my friends at church.

That Sunday I took my time and visited with as many of my friends as I could and answer their questions about my trip to Burma. Then as a family, we went to the retirement home and gave a service to my friends there. I gave an update about my trip and what God had placed before me to do. The prayers from my friends in the faith encouraged me and gave me the strength to accomplish what God has placed before me.

"The LORD is my strength and song, and he becomes my salvation: he is my God, and I will prepare him a habitation; my father's God, and I will exalt him." (Exodus 15:2)

Spirit of Knowledge

The fear of the LORD is the beginning of knowledge: but fools despise wisdom and instruction.

(Proverbs 1:7)

The new position I took as a District Technician seemed to be going well. My new position took on a roll of Tech support for the other six Technical managers in my district, along with moral support as well.

After some time I received a call from one of the Technical managers, and I could tell he was distraught. After talking to him for some time, he asked me how I can be so calm and understanding. I said," To tell you the truth it is not me, it is Messiah who lives in me." He wanted to know more about God and my relationship. He asked if I would pray for him and he told me that he was going to end his life if he could not get things straight after this call. We talked for some time and before finishing the phone conversation he told me he was not going to kill himself. I visited him at his office the next day, and we had lunch. I said to him he is not alone to call me if he needs prayer or just someone to talk with. He agreed, and over the years he devoted his time and energy to serving in his church, and later on, he married a nice Christian girl. But, now he had a church family and a new set of problems, and it wasn't anything God could not handle.

During this time I had been writing to the prisoners in Burma, and one of them was released to go home. He had spent five years in prison, and the country of South Africa requested his release, and it was granted. I still wrote to the other seven every other week. When I had received a letter from the prisoners, I would pray over them and reply. I was sending a bag of Bibles about every month to the missionary in Thailand and had sent him the flyers he requested.

In my office, I had set up a scanner and started to scan in the entire Burmese bible and made each page into a tiff file so it could be printed out via a computer of any printing device available. The plan was to get all the files on a diskette then transfer the information to a computer media that could hold all the information. This project took me two years to accomplish with Gods strength and Knowledge. As the time had passed, updated my computer and add a streamer tape then transferred all the files to the tape. I began to pray about the next step of the project of preparing to print Bibles in Burma.

With work and the family, I still managed to find the time to gather Bibles from thrift stores and send a Mailbag to the missionaries in Thailand every month. I had many friends praying for the project to print Bibles in Burma. An Engineer in Colorado said he could put all the files of the Bible to be access to print by placing them on a CD. So I sent him the streamer tape, and he made several CD's each having the entire Burma Bible on them to be printed. At the same time, a Program developer gave me a handheld computer and all the manuals and lesson step by step to be given to the prisoner in Burma. I sent this to the missionary in Thailand, and he made sure it got to the prisoner so he could learn how to program the computer. He was released late that year. He gave the handheld computer to his roommate in prison so he too could learn on the computer. I kept in contact with the prisoners for many years until they were released, or passed from this world to the next.

Now I had all the information I needed to print Bibles in Burma. I started to make plans to go, could not find one brother in the church that was willing to go with me. But, I did not give up hope in a church this big with more than four thousand attending you would think someone would step up. Everyone was willing to give money for my trip, but none would go. I checked with some of my friends from Disneyland bible study, and that is when I found out that Buckshot and his wife were killed in India. Their family turned them in, and they were killed for teaching the Bible.

Could not let this stop me from going to Burma, my wife and the children were praying with me, and middle daughter wanted to go with me. My wife said no way. My wife was now pregnant, and I wasn't going to argue.

While the engineer in Colorado was making the CD's I need to take to Burma, I prepared to take a printer and computer with me as a donation. Then I was notified that my position at work was being consolidated with another district.

So, I looked for another means of employment. My friend that I led to the Lord during the storm who was in the Bible study at Disneyland wanted to go on vacation but, there was no one to take his place. He asked me if I would be willing to work at the hospital for the next three weeks as a Biomedical Technician for a company near my home. I made arrangements when I was hired, to advance the vacation time so I could go to Burma. It was agreed that I would be paid during my trip to Burma after my friend returned from vacation. Then they would place me at this hospital as Director of Clinical Engineering. Then the company would assign my friend as a Director of Clinical Engineering in a hospital in Los Angeles, California. It seemed to work quite well for the both of us.

"Commit thy works unto the LORD, and thy thoughts shall be established." (Proverbs 16:3)

Started working at the hospital and my friend showed me what my duties were he trained me for a month, and then left for vacation, once he returned I would leave for Burma.

I met a very kind Doctor who liked the way I did things, Dr. Reynold's heard I was going to Burma, and he shared that his mother and father were missionaries there before and after World War Two. After finishing medical school, he took his residency training in Yangon, Burma. I shared with him about the Bible College and David who is diabetic and needed insulin it was hard to come by in Burma. He made up medical supplies as a donation for my trip. All medical supplies I would need in Burma for David and the leper colony. I was to pick it up the day I left for Burma.

The many Delays to Burma were Devine intervention I believe. The first attempt to leave I had to find new employment. My family and I were watching the news together, and the time I would be arriving in Thailand serval commercial aircraft with passengers aboard was washed down the river from flooding.

The second attempt was while I was working at the hospital. I was asked to wait another month before leaving for my trip to Burma. I had a ticket and arrangement's to part with my connected flight from Thailand the next day to Burma. I canceled the flight and set it up for a month later. Once again on the news, we heard that the small plane carrying people from Thailand to Burma was shot down with a rocket. I was grateful that I was not on that plane. Friends and family kept praying if I should go, I had no one to go with me, but I knew I must go, everything was ready to take to the Bible College in Burma to print out Bibles.

"A man's heart deviseth his way: but the LORD directeth his steps." (Proverbs 16:9)

The day finally came; I left on Korean Air Lines to Inchon Korea. After a layover, I would take China Air Lines to Taipei then on to Thailand. There I would meet my old friends, the missionary and his wife at the airport. We spent the evening together, and I would go back to the airport the next morning to go to Burma. Everything was going well, but it wasn't going to last.

The next day I boarded a small aircraft for Yangon Burma. Once I arrived, I went through the first checkpoint where the government checks my passport and my visa. Due to the delays going to Burma my visa had expired, and now I was escorted to a holding area by the corporal.

Then in came a stern and with a bad attitude a Sargent who spoke perfect English. He asked me why I was in Burma and I told him I was going to the Bible College in Yangon. What he said is there someone waiting for you at the airport. I said yes, David from the college. He said for me to stand and he searched me and told me to sit till he returns.

Then I was taken to a Captain of the guard who could speak perfect English. He asked the same questions and told me they were searching my bags and staying in my chair till he returns. He returned sometime later and took me to the General of ministry and travel.

He had a big office with many awards and pictures on the wall. His desk was made of wood which looked like dark alabaster. He had on a military uniform with more medals than I have seen on most military uniforms. He had me sit in front of his desk; there were two soldiers one on my left and one on my right.

"He shall cover thee with his feathers, and under his wings shalt thou trust: his truth shall be thy shield and buckler." (Psalms 91:4)

The general of ministry looked up from his desk and told the two guards to leave the room. He had my passport in front of him and was looking it over with a fine tooth comb. Then he looked up and stared for a moment "and asked the question" are you, Jesse Joseph Engel?" Yes, and a long pause, as the general of ministry continued to look at my passport. He then asked, "Why have you come to Burma?" I said, "I came to visit David at the Bible College here in Yangon, and he should be waiting for me outside."

The general of the ministry continued with his investigation "So what's the purpose of your trip?"

I responded, "To teach at the college."

Then he said "you know according to your visa it has expired. This makes you an ill legal alien, and I must contact David at this time and see if he is willing to take you as his responsibility. Then the following day you are to report to the adjutant general of immigration in downtown Yangon. This all hinges on the fact that David is willing to take you has a responsible citizen.

One last question, are you a Christian?" I answered the general of ministry "yes I am." The general then said, "This could complicate things." Then he picked up the phone and called someone using the native language which I believe was Burmese. We waited for some time than a knock on the door. The general said something in Burmese in the door open. There were two guards with David and escorted him to the chair next to me. The general and David talked for some time. And David said to me "this is not America you need to be careful in this country." The general then said in perfect English "David here is my pastor and we have been friend since we were children. Do as he says and everything will be okay all your luggage has been impounded till the general of in immigration gives you the authority to pick it up from the impound. You will be released to David's custody and please do everything he tells you to do, or you could be in big trouble. You are not to say anything about David being my pastor or friend. This could be harmful to David and me. If everything goes well will be able to continue working with David. If not, the general of immigration can have you in prison. So be very careful of what you say and do. You can go with David now."

Not a word was spoken as David, and I walked from the general's office and through the airport and out the front to the college van. Once we got underway, David looked at me and said "you really need to be careful. Here in Burma, the military runs everything you are fortunate on how things went today. Hopefully, things will go better tomorrow with we go see immigration. David asked you have money that has been exchanged?" I said, "Yes David here it is." Then I will take you to your hotel at this time. Do not go outside the hotel grounds. But remain at the hotel and tomorrow if everything goes well will get your passport back and you will be able to teach at the college."

"All the paths of the LORD are mercy and truth unto such as keep his covenant and his testimonies." (Psalms 25:10)

Needless to say, I did a lot of praying that night. The next morning David took me to the general of immigration. We went to downtown Yangon and then into a military compound area. All the buildings were made of concrete, and there wasn't any paint on any of the buildings.

I noticed coming into the building it appeared to have indentations made from rifle rounds, but they were quite old. The building itself looks to be over 70 years old, but that was my guess. Vines were growing on the outside of the building, and when we entered the building, we went through a security cage. Then we were escorted by armed guards, and then we went down a hall to a holding area after going through another security cage. Seemed to be heavily armed guards everywhere, I was wondering if this was a prison or an office building from where I was sitting it didn't much matter. Later I asked David about the premises, and he said these buildings were part of a Japanese military base during the Japanese occupation of Burma.

Before going inside, I was placed in a holding area with two guards locked and loaded with their AK-47 standing in front of the holding area. Then another guard came and talked with David, and they left and went down the long hallway and into a door on the left. They were gone for only about 15 minutes, but it seemed an eternity to me with these two guards armed and standing at attention in front of my holding area.

Then a guard and David came to the holding area, and all of us went down the hallway with one guard in the front and two in the back, and David and I in the center. Once we reached the door on the left, the two guards stood outside the door one on each side. The other guards knocked on the door. I heard a voice then we entered with the guard leading David and me to the front of the desk where two chairs. Then we were told to sit down by the general of immigration.

The silence in the room was almost overwhelming unlike the office that I saw at the airport, this office had bare walls and a small desk for the general of immigration. There was one hanging lamp above his desk to light the room which had no windows. Seemed to me like something you'd see in the movies where you were taken the prisoner for interrogation.

David and the general spoke in Burmese for a brief time. Then the general asked me why I have come to Burma. My response was simple "I came to teach at the Bible college that David operates." Then he asked, "Do you like our country?" I smiled and said, "that's why am here is to teach students in the Bible college because I like this country." The general then asked, "which is that that you love more, the country or people?" I was a bit puzzled by the question, but I gave this response "the people are the country, and that's what I love about Burma is the people."

There was silence for a moment then the general looked right at me and said "how would you like to be able to come and go in this country as you please. What I mean is have the freedom here as all the citizens?"

I smiled and said, "I would like that very much." The general then took out my passport and ink pad and a huge stamp and stamped my passport. He handed the passport to David and said you could give this back to him once you leave the compound." The general turned his head towards me and smiled "I want you to listen and do exactly what I have to say and never repeat this to anyone. I have known David for many years, and it is because of him and the college that we could build relationships with countries like America. I am a Christian and David is my pastor and several people in high positions are Christians just waiting for the right time to change this country. I guess you could say we are secret agents for the Lord Jesus Christ. Please understand how delicate the situation is and be very careful while being in our country. I just stamp your passport to show that you have the right to work and live in this country indefinitely. You will be treated as a Burmese citizen by the authorities but, be very careful. You and David could go pick up your luggage in the impound area which is near the shipyard. There are some items in your luggage which we could not identify. Be careful when asked what these items might be. You can go now David, I stood, and the general called for the guards, and they escorted us out of the facility.

David and I went to the impound yard by the shipyard downtown and picked up the luggage where the uniformed guard had me sign that everything that was in the luggage was still there.

Then we drove to the college, and I took in the computer and printer the CDs and set up the computer for training. I spent the month teaching how to use the computer and how to set it up to print the Burmese Bible utilizing any type of printing device that they would hook up with RS-232. The programming was very simple, and the methodology of printing out masses amount of Bible pages to make Bibles are now made available for the Bible College.

I explained how to use the CDs which no one had ever seen before in Burma. I had several extra copies of which they would want to keep in a safe place. Once I showed all this to the students in David realized that no longer they had to worry about smuggling in Bibles. The old lady who was a prayer warrior prophesied I would bring Bibles to Burma. But now they could print their own Bibles, what could be better?

"That I may publish with the voice of thanksgiving, and tell of all thy wondrous works."

(Psalms 26:7)

Fear of God

If thou seekest her as silver and searchest for her as for hid treasures; then shalt thou understand the fear of the LORD, and find the knowledge of God. For the LORD giveth wisdom: out of his mouth cometh knowledge and understanding.

(Proverbs 2:4-6)

The day after I had received the stamp in my passport, I was walking in the garden of the hotel and across the street, just five hundred feet or so caddy corner from where I stood I saw a black car pull up to the gated home of what appeared to be of someone quite extraordinary.

Not long a crowd was gathering about thirty or more. And it seemed more were coming up the street to join them. Then several military vehicles appear, they appeared to give an escort to the black car. Coming out of the house and gate were several people escorting a lady to the black car parked in the front of the entrance, and then there began sounds of loud shouting . There was a lot of confusion and people running in several directions. And the same people carried the Lady back into the gated area. Later I found out that it was Aung San Suu Kyi on house arrest. The visitors from government in the military vehicles were most likely the leaders of Burma, General Shwe and or General Nyunt.

That night there was a lot of noise in the hotel. The military rounded up all the American citizens and put them on a plane to Thailand to be sent back to America. In reply to President Clinton signed mandated sanctions if the Burmese military commits "large-scale repression" against the democratic opposition or if it again detains the opposition leader, Aung San Suu Kyi.

I was left because I had the rights of a Burmese citizen stamped in my passport. I was then able to continue to teach at the Bible College. David picked me up at the hotel and said until things cool down I should restrict my visits to the College until further notice. I agreed, and this will work out just fine to teach how to publish Bibles and teach the third year students the Book of Matthew.

When I arrived at the hotel, the UN Delegation teams were assigned rooms. The following morning, I went down to have breakfast, and the delegates of UN were already at the dining table. They ask me, "Who are you?" I introduced myself, and they asked me are you an American? I said yes, how did you manage to escape the deportation of all the other Americans. I asked the desk for my passport and showed them the stamp that was in my passport. They then told me, we don't see how this is possible, you are allowed to remain in Burma, and the U.S. Ambassador cannot enter the country at this time, so we hope to issue him a UN Passport. Maybe he can then join us to work out this mess. Who gave you the authority to be here we had a hard time getting in the country. My response, if you really want to know, I will tell you, but you will not believe me. Silence, then one of the ladies in the group said: "Try me!" I smiled and said, "God he made all the arrangements." You could hear a cat walking on a carpet a mile away with the silence in the room. Perfect timing the manager from the desk approached the dining table and said: "Mr. Engel your ride is here."

I said goodbye and left for the Bible College. David was waiting for me in the van and said "We must be careful there are civil and military problems in the city. We will take another route to get to the College today. I must go see a friend.

First, he knows you're here and why, but we must be cautious, too much is going on right now. As we passed by the house where the trouble was yesterday, I asked who lives there and told David what I saw.

He said now I am sure there is going to be trouble. The Lady that lives there is an old friend we when to High School together her name is Aung San Suu Kyi. He explained how her father Aung San was assassinated in 1947. He filled me in on all the details and what he could remember about what had happened during those days.

We arrived at a villa with a high wall all around it and a gate with an intercom. David pressed the button, and he said something but, I could not make it out and the gate opened. We drove the van in the gated area and parked then walked to the front door of this beautiful home. There was a grand garden of flowers and fruit trees surrounding the house.

Once inside we took off our shoes, and I was introduced to a man who seemed to be very wealthy. He invited us to his front room that was designed for visitors. There we sat and had tea and some finger sandwiches as David and he talked over some business in Burmese. Then the man of the house crossed his legs and leaned back in his chair and said" I apologize for conducting business in Burmese while you sat there.

You are an American?"

I said, "Yes, I am."

David tells me that you are teaching at the bible college.

I must not be rude. I am a banker that is my trade in life. I am from Indonesia, and if there are any problems, you can come here, and I will help you get to safety." If I were in your shoes, I would not want to go to the American Embassy."

I said "Thank you, I am sure I can find this place again if I have too, and you can be sure I will not go to the American Embassy. I have my own reasons for that, and I will place my trust in God and Him alone."

"And he said, The LORD is my rock, and my fortress, and my deliverer; The God of my rock; in him will I trust: he is my shield, and the horn of my salvation, my high tower, and my refuge, my saviour; thou savest me from violence. I will call on the LORD, who is worthy to be praised: so shall I be saved from mine enemies." (2 Samuel 22:2-4)

The Banker looked at David, and he said" I see what you mean David. He is the one that was chosen to bring bibles to Burma!"

David then turned to me and said" Our prayer warrior before she went home to be with the Lord told us you would bring an unlimited supply of Bibles. We could not understand how that could be?"

I explained the means with the CD and the computer and how they could print all the Bibles they would need. But it would take time to train the students and find the printing machine or printer that would work. Then it would be up to the Bible College to use that information and equipment to glorify God."

A long moment of silence as we all leaned back in our chairs, took a drink of our tea. The Banker said," I can acquire the equipment and money, David and I will work out the details you need to teach the students how to operated and set up the equipment.

"My reply "That is why I am here." David said if the government hears of this, we are all faced with Jail or worse. A man from Australia brought a FAX machine into the country and was using it without government approval, and he is going to be executed. This is not a game, if you want out now is the time."

I stood up and said, "God has sent me to do this job, then why all the fuss let's get to work."

Ye are of God, little children, and have overcome them: because greater is he that is in you, than he that is in the world. (1 John 4:4)

After leaving the Bankers home, we took the long way to the Bible College, and I started the process of teaching the computer to 40 students on how to hook up the computer to the printing device and how to test it. The class was focused on how to print out the pages of the Bible, and then how to use the pages to make the bibles.

Later that evening as David took me in the van to the hotel he asked me if I could find the bankers home again. I said yes before I left the States I had a thought about what I would do if trouble happened in Burma. Everyone was so concerned about my safety and what I was doing was very risky. So, I studied maps and the possible way to get myself out of trouble. With my past military training, I would never go to the American Embassy, which would be foolhardy.

It's nice to know that going to the Bankers is an option. But if things get that bad, well I think I will do what General Stilwell did in 1942 he personally led his staff of 117 men and women out of Burma into Assam, India on foot. He was a pretty smart man, and he played the Harmonica maybe as good as I can. But, let's hope it doesn't come to that. I trust the Lord, and he has me here for the purpose of printing Bibles for your people.

"There is no fear in love; but perfect love casteth out fear: because of fear hath torment. He that feareth is not made perfect in love." (1 John 4:18)

"Giving thanks always for all things unto God and the Father in the name of our Lord Jesus the Christ (Master Yeshua the Messiah); submitting yourselves one to another in the fear of God." (Ephesians 5:20-21)

Time moved swiftly and I had taught all 40 students how to set up and print Bibles. The third year students were ready to graduate and my class on book of Matthew was complete. David said I want to take you on a trip south of Yangon to the Delta area. It is here where the tribe of Palaung resides. You might have heard of them they have rings that they place around their necks and stretch it so they appear to have a long neck. I refer to them as stiff necked Christians.

A new generation of the Palaung tribe, no longer practice this form of disfigurement, but those who have cannot remove the rings in fear of death or other health problems for doing this for such a long time. They have a church there and I will interpret for you, are you willing to go? I agreed, David said we will leave early in the morning.

My time in Burma was drawing to an end; I will be leaving in three days. Going to teach in the Delta area seemed like a good Idea. That night I slept sound as a baby. That next morning David arrived, I had just finished breakfast with the UN Delegation.

The news that the US Ambassador would be arriving that afternoon, and this was the main topic at the table. I excused myself and they asked me "What do you do here in Yangon?" I smiled and said "I teach at the Bible College." Smiled and left noticing several of their jaws hitting the table and left speechless as I excused myself from the table.

David was waiting in the van and I was asked to ride shotgun. He said we need to stop of at the college before leaving for the delta area. When we arrived he asked me to change my clothes put on the clothing of a native Burmese. I put on the clothing which included handmade sandals and a bamboo hat. David said we are going to a war zone in the delta and if you see soldiers do not speak I will talk for you, and by all means stand in the mud so they do not see your white feet.

We can only drive so far then we must walk several miles on foot along the river. When we get there you will give a message that God has placed in your heart. Tomorrow morning we are holding the graduation party at a new location we have bought and built an orphanage for the children of the leper colony. They are eager to hear you play your harmonica again. It will be a day of celebration. Then we will select some of the student you taught to print the Bibles to go to Mandalay and set up printing in our Northern Bible College.

"A man's heart deviseth his way: but the LORD directeth his steps." (Proverbs 16:9)

After couple of hours on dirt roads we arrived near the river and David said we will walk now. Two other pastors from the college went with us and a third stayed with the van. David led the way, on a jungle path along the river. David had taken point and one of the younger pastors took up our six. The four of us, David then John, myself and Timothy walking in this order along the trail to the church couple of miles along the river then into the heavy jungle area for a half a mile. When we arrived everyone spoke in whispers and I remained silent.

We were taken into a hut which was about 250 square feet and was standing room only. I stood at the front and could see clearly outside the doorway which was about 15 feet wide and open to the roof. It was beginning to rain and David spoke and said a prayer then asked me to give a message and I read this Scripture and shared what was on my heart:

Ye have heard that it hath been said, Thou shalt love thy neighbour, and hate thine enemy. But I say unto you, Love your enemies, bless them that curse you, do good to them that hate you, and pray for them which despitefully use you, and persecute you; That ye may be the children of your Father which is in heaven: for he maketh his sun to rise on the evil and on the good, and sendeth rain on the just and on the unjust. For if ye love them which love you, what reward have ye? do not even the publicans the same? And if ye salute your brethren only, what do ye more than others? do not even the publicans so? Be ye therefore perfect, even as your Father which is in heaven is perfect. (Matthew 5:43-48)

As David finished reading the scripture in Burmese, we heard gun shots not far away along the river. I continued to share what this scripture meant to me. And how many times in my life I could have got revenge but, the Holy Spirit of God tugged at my heart and I listened. Even Yeshua famous last words were "Father forgive them for they no not what they do."

We need to be like the Son of God who became the son of man and forgave us. As I was sharing and David was speaking all I said in Burmese. I looked up and five men stood at the door with AK47 rifles and were listening. I continued to share Gods Word. Then I shared my testimony on how God revealed His love to me in a vision and that perfect love is why I was in Burma to share it with them because he loves them.

I caught out of the corner of my eye that four of the soldiers had left and one remained. I was praying in my heart that this was a good thing. Once I had concluded my message and testimony, said if you have any question after the service please come up and I will try to answer them.

Everyone was silent as the soldier from outside walk up to where I was and laid down his weapon and asked David something in Burmese. They talked for some time, and then the congregation began to say Halleluiah over and over again.

David looked at me and said "He just came from a raiding party on the other side of the river where they burnt down a missionary's school for refugee which are most are of women and children. They killed the men and the cattle and returned back across the river and stopped by here. He is the squad leader and he sent his men away. God has touched his heart and he wants you to forgive him. And tell him how he can find that Love you have.

A moment like this, I never thought I would be in. I placed my hand on his head and prayed for him and David and I worked together as I spoke English and David spoke Burmese. The stiff necked Christians had tears in their eyes and where praying with all their hearts. I shared about the man Jesus (Yeshua) healed:

"Afterward Jesus (Yeshua) findeth him in the temple, and said unto him, Behold, thou art made whole: sin no more, lest a worse thing come unto thee. The man departed, and told the Jews that it was Jesus (Yeshua), which had made him whole." (John 5:14-15)

Then I explained that I can forgive him, but the forgiveness from Yeshua the Messiah is most important of all. You need to seek His love and forgiveness and you will find it. So I turned my Bible to this scripture and read it and David did the same.

"Ask, and it shall be given you; seek, and ye shall find; knock, and it shall be opened unto you: For every one that asketh receiveth; and he that seeketh findeth; and to him that knocketh it shall be opened. Or what man is there of you,

whom if his son ask bread, will he give him a stone? Or if he ask a fish, will he give him a serpent? If ye then, being evil, know how to give good gifts unto your children, how much more shall your Father which is in heaven give good things to them that ask him?" (Matthew 7:7-11)

The soldier left his rifle on the floor and walk back outside, and out of sight. David said "He will come and see me soon in Yangon. I have some pull with the authorities and I will try to have him place in my custody as I have had done with other soldiers in the past. We closed in prayer and then we ate and took the jungle trail back to the car and to the college. I was worn out and was glad to get back to my room and take a long hot shower, then getting a some sleep and be well rested for the graduation event and opening of the orphanage for the children from the leper colonies throughout Burma.

"I will bless the LORD, who hath given me counsel: my reins also instruct me in the night seasons. I have set the LORD always before me: because he is at my right hand, I shall not be moved. Therefore my heart is glad, and my glory rejoiceth: my flesh also shall rest in hope."

(Psalms 16:7-9)

Living in the Spirit

That the righteousness of the law (Instructions) might be fulfilled in us, who walk not after the flesh, but after the Spirit. For they that are after the flesh do mind the things of the flesh, but they that are after the Spirit the things of the Spirit.

(Romans 8:4-5)

Got up early and packed my bags to leave early the next day for home. I went down for breakfast, and no one was there. I went to the front desk and asked if they were serving breakfast today. The manager said yes what would you like, you're the only one left in the hotel, the others have left very early this morning to the American Embassy. He handed me a menu, and I ordered breakfast and went back to the dining area in no time my meal was brought to me. Steak and eggs, a glass of OJ and I was set to go.

I went outside and sat in the front garden where a koi pond was located, and from there I could see when the college van would arrive. The van came but, David was not there, the driver said we will meet David at the orphanage compound. He is preparing for the graduation and the opening ceremony to the orphanage.

My mind was filled with the thought of my visit and what was I going to do when I got home. As I pondered these things, we drove along the river to a Bridge which took us over the river and to the compound. My reflection on the events which have happened during my stay gave me strength for the future, and I knew this.

But, the question that was haunting me what was I going to do when I got home. I had spent most of my time for the past two years preparing for this trip. So, now what is the priority, what is it God has for me to do that I can show my love?

I know I will have more time for my family and work. But, I know there is much more to life than that. Yes, I love my wife, children and I enjoy my job and I am good at what I do and do this because I love God. I know there is much more that God will place in my life to honor and glorify Him.

These thoughts left me with this question in my soul, with longing for direction in my journey to serve God with all my heart, mind and strength. I know now, more than ever, the Love of God, it is this Love I want in my life and for the lives of all I know. This Love is filled with meaning that fills the emptiness in life, and the pursuit of this Love is the journey we are all faced with.

I thought of the prayer I had learned while serving with the messianic congregation in California, this prayer I learned was to be said each morning and evening to remind the believer to listen to God and what they should do, daily. It is this prayer that now I hang onto:

"Hear, O Israel: The LORD our God is one LORD: And thou shalt love the LORD thy God with all thine heart, and with all thy soul, and with all thy might. And these words, which I command thee this day, shall be in thine heart: And thou shalt teach them diligently unto thy children, and shalt talk of them when thou sittest in thine house, and when thou walkest by the way, and when thou liest down, and when thou risest up. And thou shalt bind them for a sign upon thine hand, and they shall be as frontlets between thine eyes. And thou shalt write them upon the posts of thy house, and on thy gates." (Deuteronomy 6:4-9 The Shema)

We arrived at the compound, and many of the students gathered around the van and unloaded the contents to set up for the event. David came to the van and asked me, "How are you doing today? We will miss you and will be praying for your safe return home. Please come with me, and we have much to do to prepare for the meeting. Also, one last thing would you play your harmonica; with the praise band? They want to know what songs you want to play and the pastors want to sing with the praise band.

The whole staff will be here to celebrate the opening of the orphanage and the graduation of students. Hurry we must get everything ready." This excitement placed my thoughts on hold. I spent the rest of the day with my friends even though I might not see them again for some time if any. The Love and joy I have found in the Christian believers in Burma. They remind me of what I have read in the scriptures of the first-century church.

'And they continued steadfastly in the apostles' doctrine and fellowship, and in breaking of bread, and in prayers. And fear came upon every soul: and many wonders and signs were done by the apostles. And all that believed were together, and had all things common; and sold their possessions and goods, and parted them to all men, as every man had need. And they, continuing daily with one accord in the temple, and breaking bread from house to house, did eat their meat with gladness and singleness of heart, Praising God, and having favour with all the people. And the Lord added to the church daily such as should be saved." (Acts 2:42-47)

The sweetness was filled with sadness after this evening. Leaving the next morning I might not see my brothers and sisters again. I now know what must have filled the heart of Paul (Sha'ul) as he left knowing he would not return to the brethren but, he must continue his journey and walk the road with his Messiah even unto death. This sharp reminder went before me as I said my goodbye to the staff and friends. I would be going to Thailand and my flight home on China Airline would leave within the hour and I would not be able to visit the missionaries in Thailand again.

"And when he was come unto us, he took Paul's girdle, and bound his own hands and feet, and said, thus saith the Holy Ghost, So shall the Jews at Jerusalem bind the man that owneth this girdle, and shall deliver him into the hands of the Gentiles. And when we heard these things, both we, and they of that place, besought him not to go up to Jerusalem. Then Paul answered, what mean ye to weep and to break mine heart? For I am ready not to be bound only, but also to die at Jerusalem for the name of the Lord Jesus (Master Yeshua). And when he would not be persuaded, we ceased, saying, the will of the Lord be done." (Acts 21:11-14)

Once I arrived in Taipei, I was told I could not go to the main terminal and was escorted to a large area where other passengers were also waiting for Korean Airlines. We were isolated for our own safety due to some unknown emergency unrest we must remain in this area. We continued there for 10 hours, no water or food then we were escorted to a loading area, and we received bottles of water. Then we were to board Korean Airlines to Inchon.

Once we were airborne the Captains voice came over the intercom and said "We are now leaving Taipei, most of you who have arrived by air in Taipei may not be aware of the earthquake could be felt in Hong Kong and Macau, and the intensity recorded in Hong Kong was believed to be 7 or 8. Also, the threat of a tsunami was triggered by the earthquake. The heights of the tsunami were recorded as 38 cm in Penghu, Taiwan, and 18 cm in Dongshan, Fujian, China. We are happy to have you on board Korean Airlines; we will be serving snacks it will be followed by a nice lunch. Please enjoy your flight."

The layover I was hoping for in Inchon to visit friends in Korea was shortened from my ten-hour layover in Taipei. I had only three hours for my flight, so I had a Korean dinner with all the trimmings and then made my way to my connecting flight on Korean Airlines to LAX International airport in California.

Got sick, and was very ill most of the flight. I spent the majority of my trip in the restroom. Arriving in California now I was so weak, I could hardly make it through customs area. I went through customs, and I didn't see my wife or the kids. I went through the main terminal and sat out front hoping someone would arrive soon. My wife drove up to the terminal, and I was very sick, then we put my bags in the car. She asked me if I wanted to eat, and I said some soup might help. My wife told me she had made a reservation at a hotel and we could spend some time there before going home. She said," We have a lot to talk about; we can get some soup for you then you can rest."

Troubles

The troubles of my heart are enlarged: O bring thou me out of my distresses. Look upon mine affliction and my pain, and forgive all my sins.

(Psalms 25:17-18)

After arriving at the Hotel and getting some hot soup to settle my stomach, the Idea of spending time with my wife had become very appealing. My wife was waiting to break some news to me which I had a deep feeling wasn't good news. After taking a shower, and getting dress we sat at the little table in the room, and she began to tell me while I was gone to Burma she had miscarried. I knew this event was going to be rough on both of us, but the emotional and mental effects it has on a woman I cannot imagine. The loss to me was real, but the damage of this event left scars on her heart. This was the second event she had miscarried since we have been married.

My mind flashed back to the first time and how I thought she might not recover at all. She had placed a wall between us; everything for that time was hard for her and me to communicate and to show our love to one another. Even trying to comfort her was difficult, so I just placed my faith in God and loved her as myself. She bore the pain for both of us, and for me to show my loss was not acceptable to her. She wanted me to be strong for both of us and the children. She told me not to quote scripture; she has heard enough from friends at church. She wanted me to know that she needed time and space to heal.

"Submitting yourselves one to another in fear of God."
(Ephesians 5:21)

She explained that mom is watching the children and they are all doing ok. I just need time to sort this all out. Nothing I could say, but what I could do is to submit to her request in love. It was a hard time around the house.

Almost six months had past and spring was on its way. The loss was not forgotten, but the separation of the time and space she needed to heal led to us taking a weekend without the children.

She wanted to have more children; she had a dream that she would have three sons to raise along with our three daughters. She had placed all her hope on this dream, and I could really understand. My vision has led me to the Love of God, Dads dreams were prophetic, and he was never wrong, which gave me hope for my wife. I began to pray for sons, and if this dream is of God, it will come to pass.

Three months later we could tell she was pregnant again. This time she was sure that it would be a son. A couple of months when by and I brought home an ultrasound machine which I had trained on at the hospital and the whole family took a look at the baby. As I operated the Machine, we could hear the heartbeat and see that this was going to be a son. The joy-filled the house and some with mixed emotions. My youngest daughter was in despair she would no longer be the baby of the family.

Later that week I got a call from my Dad, he never called me before. I could sense the urgency in his voice. He told me son your mom is really sick and she wants you to come to Idaho to see her. We talked for some time he explained to me that Mom had fallen and broke her arm and hip. The doctors are going to let her know what the problem is and she wants you to be here for her. You're the oldest, and we want you here to help us both.

After hanging up the phone, my wife asked me what is going on. I told her I need to go see my parents they are having problems and mom is not doing well. Remember, why we went to visit them not long ago? I had felt in my heart when I was going to lose one of them very soon. And I wanted the children to meet their grandparents.

Before I could finish I received a call from the company I was working for at the hospital, the company had sold out to another company. I was no longer needed there; I was instructed to report to the new company. Further, I was to train my replacement. I would receive severance pay for 90 days.

I explained, that I have a family emergency and that I needed to go to Idaho. Arrangements were made for me to give over the keys to the office. When I returned, I was to train the new guy to take over my position at the hospital. I went to the central office, and I received a check and cashed it and headed home.

My wife had packed my clothes and had everything ready for me to go to Idaho. The plan was I would drive straight through. Once I knew what was going on, then I would call home. I kissed my wife and told my daughters to take care of their mom. I hope to be back soon, please pray for your grandparents and me. I took my bag which had my clothes and harmonicas in it to the car and computer laptop which is nothing like what we have today.

Driving the 14-hour drive from Riverside, California to Nampa, Idaho gave me plenty of time to pray and think things over. This part of life's journey was very personal to me. Apart from God helping me through this, I do not know what my strength and faith could endure; I knew I must continue to ask for God's Devine intervention.

After arriving at my parents' home in Nampa Idaho, I went to the door and noticed my dad sitting at the kitchen table. His eyes met mine about the same time; he waved for me to come on in. As I entered the kitchen, my dad says "you're probably pretty tired from that long trip. Looks like you made good time." My reply to my dad was "yeah I didn't run into too much trouble along the road. I drove straight through I'm a little tired but bring me up to date what's going on." In a tired and concerned voice, my dad says "Mom is resting in the other room, but she's awake. You could go in and talk to her. I am sure she'll like to let you know what's on her mind."

I walked to the opening of my parents' bedroom where I saw my mom propped up in bed she had a big smile on her face.

She said "I'm glad you're here. Now come and sit down beside me here and we'll talk." We had a long conversation; she asked me how the children and the wife were. She had informed me that she had a doctor's appointment the next day and wanted me to be there. My two brothers and my sister would be there when the doctor gives his diagnosis and prognosis.

I spent several hours talking to mom and until she needed to get some rest. Then I went out to see my dad, still sitting at the kitchen table having a fresh cup of coffee. We talked a little, and then he told me that I can go upstairs. A place for me to sleep in a single sized bed was set up for me in my nephew's room. My sister her boyfriend and her sons were living upstairs, they had prepared a place for me this stay.

I noticed from the posters and books in the room that my nephews are very interested in Dungeons & Dragons. It appeared that I was going to be sleeping with my two nephews. By this time I was exhausted, I put my bags alongside the small single bed and got my shoes off and the next thing I knew I was asleep.

The next morning dad had made breakfast, and my sister and her boyfriend and her two sons were at the table ready to eat. Before eating I said grace I could tell everyone, but dad was very uncomfortable with the fact I was praying. But as I looked to my right dad had bowed his head in prayer with me. I prayed for a blessing on the house the food and also for my mother and my father. Then pray for the whole family that God's will would be done; That we would be prepared to do whatever he had placed before us knowing that he is in control of everything.

During breakfast, my dad spoke up and said "Son where going to go to the doctors this afternoon about 1 o'clock. Everyone's going to meet there to hear what the doctor has to say about mom. It seemed to me that there was a lot more being said in that statement. It was as if he was making sure everyone would be there and not doing something else. Dad telegraphed this message toward my sister and her boyfriend. I could see the overwhelming concern that my dad had for mom. The love my parents have for one another has been an inspiration to me throughout my life. Their passion has held the family together all these years through many troubles and trials. Yet dad now a new believer; the real concern dad has that mom still does not believe in God. This was a conflict in their lives now. Because of this I could see the worry and stress that my dad had for my mother.

As I went in to see my mom after breakfast, I noticed she hadn't had much to eat and I asked her if she was hungry. She informed me; no I'm fine your sister has been making sure I get food. At that very moment, I could see my mother's health and the color of her skin; I had seen this before on many people who were about to die.

Over the years I had seen many people before they died. To me, it seemed that I could see death as it was hovering over my mother. I didn't say anything about this to mom. I give her a kiss, and we talk for a while. She wanted to take a nap to be rested before seeing the doctor this afternoon. She asked if I would play my harmonica. I played several songs, as she drifted off to sleep. I left quietly not to disturb her so she could get her nap.

I went outside, and I noticed my dad was setting out by the toolshed. He had been crying because of the songs I played on my harmonica for my mother. The last song that I played before she drifted off to sleep was their favorite song; it was actually the song that they called their song. When I stood in front of my dad, I could see his eyes were full of tears. He said "thank you, son," I sat with my dad for a while nothing was said, nothing needed to be said. Dad and I both knew that mom wasn't going to make it.

The doctor asked mom "is this everyone that you wanted to be here or should we wait?" Mother said, "No everyone is here that I wanted to be here." Then the doctor said I will begin. What I am about to tell you, your mother and I have already talked over. She told me not to hold anything back and give it to you straight.

My diagnosis in simple terms is your mother has lung cancer, and it has metastasized to her bones. Because of this condition that bones have been weakened in your mother's body. So when she fell at home, she broke her arm and her hip. Cancer has spread throughout the lungs and the entire bone structure of her body. Cancer is actually eating up the bones. My prognosis is that your mother has about 30 days left on this earth. At this moment you could hear a pin drop as the news began to sink into our hearts.

My sister broke the silence and asked the doctor is there anything we can do to help extend her life, for another month or maybe six months. The doctor very calmly explained to her that she has only 30 days at most. Most of all he is amazed that she's lasted this long. Your mother asked me to talk to all of you, so you understand that she is going to die. I could see that my sister's heart was broken and she held onto my mom's hand.

I asked the doctor because of this prognosis is there any recommended treatment you would want my mother to consider. The doctor's response was "I have talked it over with your mother. I have arranged for hospice, they will be coming over to the house this afternoon.

They will set up a pump for your mom with pain medication that she can control. This should help her be comfortable and able to rest. Your mother if, she decides to take some radiation treatments may slow down cancer some, but I don't see where that would be very useful at this time because cancer has gone too far.

My sister now desperate said mom, please take radiation treatments. Mom's reply was I will think about it. It's time to go home now.

After returning to my mother and father's home my sister and I help my mother to bed. She asked sis to leave the room and close the door behind her she wanted to talk to me.

Mother said "So I need you to take care of some things for me. First of all, we don't have a lot of money, and I need you to make arrangements for my funeral. We're behind on the bills in the rent, and we also need your help if you can. Also, I want to have my body donated to science for research on cancer. She handed me some information about the cancer research center in Utah. When you have completed my final arrangements, we can continue this conversation later. I need to rest now, I love you son.

Went upstairs and got my laptop, then return to dad's desk downstairs. After asking dad what bills were due? I proceeded to make a spreadsheet to create a budget with the statements that had to be paid and the cost of the funeral arrangements. I then use the phone and called my wife and told her what was going on. Mom and dad were in a bad way financially and that I would be making up the final arrangements for my mother. It appears that mom won't make it through the month so instead of coming home and right back again I think it best that I stay.

I could stay with my brother for a while if I need to. My daughter is in town, and I need to talk to her about what's going on with mom. My wife said that your daughter called and she needs to talk to you right away. So I got her number from my wife, and I said I'll call soon as I can.

Thought to myself what next, then I just started praying about the situation. I know God will provide he always has. Just how I don't know but I know he will still provide. He has never let me down. I know I have let him down, But He is never let me down what an awesome and holy God I serve. Then I completed an estimate of what was going to be needed for paying the bills and helping with the funeral.

I called my daughter. She asked me to meet her at the hospital there in Nampa. So I got in my car then drove to the hospital. Went up to the intensive care unit where I found my daughter sitting at the side of her fiancé. She explained to me her fiancé' was going to be transported to a hospital in Seattle. Where they could remove cancer, they found.

My daughter asked me to be praying for her and her fiancé. She was going to go with him and stay at his side. She asked me how her grandmother was. I told her what happened at the meeting and what mom asked me to do. She said to me that they would be going to Seattle tomorrow and please remember them in prayer. I prayed with both of them and gave them my blessing. My daughter told me I could stay at her house until she gets back, or till I have to leave.

Later after they arrived in Seattle they made arrangements to get married at the hospital in Seattle. Both my daughter and my new son-in-law are born optimists whom trust the Lord God. They both have placed their faith in God at a young age. My son-in-law, his father, was a pastor for many years before he passed away. And now my daughter is picking herself up by her bootstraps with the faith that she received while she lived at home. I told them how much I love them then I had to go to make arrangements for mom.

Went to a Cavalry Chapel in Nampa and talked with the pastor there and we prayed together. I explained to him the situation with my mom. I would like to hold a service here once I know the timeframe. Then I went to the funeral home and made arrangements there to have her body transported to the medical facility that would do the research on cancer in Salt Lake City.

Thinking the reason why my mother wanted to donate her body was twofold one to save money in the other that it would be for a good cause; that she gave her body for research. I did not reveal the details of how much it cost. I proceeded to pay for my mom and dad's rent and utilities, and I spent a month in advance as well. I hoped that this would give dad some breathing room, before having to deal with the finances.

Dad made a request that I would write the eulogy and obituary. He asked that I would place the obituary in the local newspaper once mom had passed; he gave me a copy of a picture he wanted to use in the press with the obituary.

Meanwhile, my mom had made arrangements for her brothers and sister and her mom to come and visit her. I was asked to take pictures and make sure everyone got copies. My mother instructed me that her brother that was just younger than her not to be drinking around dad. I said I'll take care of it.

I had developed a relationship of sorts with my uncle while working with him in California. But the truth be known, both he and his brothers were all alcoholics. And the three of them there would be drinking buddies for sure and my dad would not stand for that. So when my uncle showed up, I had a talk with him and his brothers.

As I walked toward my uncles when they arrived I walk toward them and I noticed a shovel lying on the ground and picked it up. I made my request that they not drink at the house. My uncle asked me what you are going to do, what if we don't do what you say. I said do you really want to find out it's not going to be pretty! He noticed the shovel in my hands and I believe he got the drift what I meant and said okay.

When my aunt and grandmother showed up, they went inside, and I took pictures. Despite my warning to my uncle each of them pulled out a beer and gave one to mom and said let's have a last drink together. I was prepared then to clean some clocks, and mom said its okay son will have one drink with them that's it. I took pictures of mom and her brother's sister and grandma so they could have copies of these later when I had them developed.

After that, I made myself scarce and told my dad I was going to leave to finish work on the arrangements that mom wanted me to make. It was then that my dad gave me three pawn tickets and said he found these in my sister's room. Check on these see if this is my hunting rifle and pistol, and the 22 rifle that you used growing up. I had reported them stolen last month. Told my dad I take care of it, and I try to find out the details and get back with him.

Went to the pawnshop and sure enough, the rifles and the pistol were my dad's. I inquired who brought them there, and he said it was your sister and her boyfriend. They said they were going to use the money to pay some bills. When I returned with the rifles in the pistol and given them to my dad, we lock them up. Then I proceeded to tell him what I found out at the pawn shop. It was sis, and her boyfriend took them to the pawn shop he told the guy there that they wanted to pay some bills.

Did you know about this dad did they pay any bills.

Dad said I knew nothing of it; I reported this to the police that they were stolen. I guess I better let them know that we found the rifles and pistol. Okay, dad, if you need anything else, let me know.

The next day I went in to visit with my mother, and I told her I had taking care of the bills and the funeral arrangements. She should not worry; everything's caught up for the next couple months. I'll make sure dad's okay.

Then I said I do have a question for you mom when you die you know where you're going and why?" Her response was "I've seen how your life is changed son and the things that you've gone through. I couldn't be more proud of anyone than I am of you. To answer your question I want what you have."

God had opened the door of her heart. She wanted to receive the love and forgiveness that I had received from God. I explained to her about the thief on the cross and how he was invited into heaven at the last moment by Yeshua who was next to him on the cross.

"Mother said, "That story is about me, at the last minute I want to steal my way into heaven."

Said mom you don't have to steal it was freely given, Yeshua was the perfect Lamb of God, and he died on that cross for you." She then asked "Could we have communion tomorrow? Just your dad, you and I Also there was a book I wanted to read when I was a young girl if you would get that for me. I asked what book is that she said it is Pilgrim's progress. I told mom I know the book, I will get it for you, and I'll bring it to you tomorrow when we have communion. We prayed together, and she asked with all her heart, soul and strength to be forgiven and have a love of God in her heart.

*"And one of the malefactors which were hanged railed on him, saying, if thou be Messiah save thyself and us. But the other answering rebuked him, saying, Dost, not thou fear God, seeing thou art in the same condemnation? And we indeed justly; for we receive the due reward of our deeds: but this man hath done nothing amiss. And he said unto Jesus (Yeshua), Lord (Master), remember me when thou comest into thy kingdom. And Jesus (Yeshua) said unto him, Verily I say unto thee, today shalt thou be with me in paradise."
(Luke 23:39-43)*

Standing at the door was my youngest nephew after hearing what I had told mom about God, he was with me most of the time tagging the long with me, Then gathered my bag and stuff that I would need to stay at my daughters' place while she was in Seattle. After arriving at a Christian bookstore to get the elements for communion and bought "The pilgrim's progress from this world to that which is to come - by John Bunyan, 1628-1688" the book my mother had requested.

My nephew was looking at the Bible's; he said this is a really lovely Bible. I ask him do you have a Bible. He said no this is a nice one, I said bring it with you, going to the counter. We paid for the Bible and the book that mom wanted at the checkout stand. Also purchased a small communion set. Asked how much it would cost to put my nephews' name on the cover of the Bible.

That second I could see his eyes light up. After paying all this, once my nephews' name was printed on the cover of the Bible we gathered the items that I purchased and headed back to my parents' home.

"A new commandment I give unto you, that ye love one another; as I have loved you, that ye also love one another. By this shall all men know that ye are my disciples if ye have love one to another." (John 13:34-35)

Joy

My brethren, count it all joy when ye fall into divers temptations; Knowing this, that the trying of your faith worketh patience. But let patience have her perfect work, that ye may be perfect and entire, wanting nothing. If any of you lack wisdom, let him ask of God, that giveth to all men liberally, and upbraideth not; and it shall be given him.

(James 1:2-5)

After delivering the book my mom wanted. Mom asked could we have communion now. I said sure mom. As I retrieved the elements for communion, I asked dad to come with me. I explained to mom and dad the meaning of communion and also the warning which comes with observing communion.

"And when he (Yeshua) had given thanks, he brake it, and said, Take, eat: this is my body, which is broken for you: this do in remembrance of me. After the same manner also he took the cup, when he had supped, saying, this cup is the new testament in my blood: this do ye, as oft as ye drink it, in remembrance of me. For as often as ye eat this bread, and drink this cup, ye do shew the Lord's death till he come. Wherefore whosoever shall eat this bread, and drink this cup of the Lord, unworthily, shall be guilty of the body and blood of the Lord. But let a man examine himself, and so let him eat of that bread, and drink of that cup. For he that eateth and drinketh unworthily, eateth and drinketh damnation to himself, not discerning the Lord's body."

(1 Corinthians 11:24-29)

After communion and many prayers over mom and dad, I saw my youngest nephew who was only eight at the time, standing at the door waiting for me. He asked if he could stay with me for the day, and I said Okay let us go. I took him with me to my daughter's house so I could take a shower and get some rest. When we arrived, he had a lot of questions.

What were you doing with grandma and grandpa? So, I explained it to him, and I noticed he had his bible with him and I showed him in his bible were he could read while I took a shower. After my shower, he had another question.

The other day you prayed with grandma, she said she wanted what you have, what is that? I explained it to him and asked him to read the story about Jesus and how to be born again. John Chapter three.

And I took my nap before going back to my parents' home. I left my nephew on the couch he was reading the scriptures I had told him to read.

When I woke up, I went into the living room and found my nephew reading his bible. He saw me, and when our eyes met, he said I want what grandma has. We prayed together, and he asked where he should start reading the bible. He said he wants to learn about God, and what God wants him to do with his life. I instructed him to read the book of John and then we can talk, okay?

His whole face was one big smile. I asked him if he would like to go to church with me on Sunday. He was so excited, and his reply reminded me of myself when I was young. He said I never been to church. My response" Then it is about time to get started, right." I could see the joy in his heart, through that smile as big as life itself.

Sunday came, and my nephew was right by my side, he sat there like a real gentleman, drinking in everything he could from the service. During worship, it starts to sink in that my mother was going home soon. I was indeed very joyful that she would be going to be with God. But, heavens gain was now my loss I began to cry, my nephew asked me why you are crying, uncle.

I said I am happy that grandma is going to heaven, but I am going to miss her. My eyes full of tears and I feel a hand on my shoulder, and I looked up and saw an elderly man standing next to me.

I stood up, and he held me as I cried. He said "What seems to be the problem, I would like to pray for you. My name is Roy Horn and what is your name?" I looked up, and it was my great Uncle Roy Horn my Dads uncle. I told him everything. He said" I had lost track of your mom and dad for years. Then the service began, and we would talk after the service. Only God could make a reunion like this.

After the service, we talked for some time he was in his late 80's then. After mom passed, he spent time with my dad. They would go fishing together. Dad told me that when Uncle Roy was 92 years old, they went fishing together all day. It was the best day ever, and when he got home, he did not have to clean fish. That day they bared their hearts out with one another. It was the last day that Dad saw Uncle Roy before he went home to be with the Lord.

"Many sorrows shall be to the wicked: but he that trusteth in the LORD, mercy shall compass him about. Be glad in the LORD, and rejoice, ye righteous: and shout for joy, all ye that are upright in heart." (Psalms 32:10-11)

During this time it was the Word of God that gave me hope. I know that in this world we will have trouble, but God would be with me through it all. Knowing this gave me joy, comfort, hope. It made me think I should have my affairs in order so when my time comes to go home, those left would not be preoccupied with bills and arrangements and such. But, reflect on the hope they too have in Yeshua.

The time had come, and my mother was very sick. She asked to be taken to the hospital the pain was too high. She was taken to the hospital and my youngest brother Harold, his girlfriend and myself spent the entire night with mom.

Mom had sent my brother Steven to go fishing the idea of seeing mom pass was too great for him. Sis and her boyfriend were at home with dad.

It was early April 2nd, 1995, during the night she said she wanted to wait for dad and say goodbye. Through the night before she could no longer talk she asked me "Tell me what happens to Christian in the last chapter of the book, Pilgrims progress?" I said "Mom you are about to do just what Christian did as he crossed over to the Celestial City where he will meet his Saviour Yeshua. You are living the last chapter yourself. These were the last words I heard from my mother, then she smiled. My brother said I should go and take a shower and come back, we will wait here with mom. So, I dashed to my daughter's home took a shower and went back to the hospital.

The cancer had eaten up most of the Skelton structure on her left side. Half of her skull, left arm left hip and leg were almost all gone. The whole family was there by my mother's side. A moment before I opened the door to the room through the window in the door, I saw my mother sitting up and then lay down. My dad said she saw something at the foot of her bed and smiled. Then she sits up and smiles a big smile and looked at me. She gave me her hand as to say goodbye and laid down closed her eyes and stopped breathing and was gone. She was at such peace! Now the family all but my youngest nephew, Dad and I understood. The rest of the family was crushed and crying uncontrollably. Death was something the world fears, but the believer it's the next step to a beautiful journey forever.

Dad sat by Mom for a while then; he got up and asked me to come with him. We went to the cafeteria to have coffee. We drank our coffee, and it was silent for a few minutes. My dad turned to me and said" Son I was praying God would take her fast. Was I right in praying for this?" My reply" Dad I was praying the same prayer, and the answer it is okay." We just sat there, facing each other drinking our coffee. Dad asked" Did mom say anything to you last night?" my reply "Yes, she wanted to wait for you this morning before going home." Tears filled his eyes and mine as he reaches out to hold my hand. That day our relationship with God and one another had grown and continued to grow.

Stayed with dad the best part of the day then I had made arrangements for mother's body to be moved to the funeral home to be prepared for transport to Utah. I went to the Newspaper and ran the obituary after making plans for a service that next week at the church.

At the service, I saw many of my mothers and fathers friends and family. The service was a tribute to my mother. I gave a message about how she gave her life to the Lord and how she left this earth. My brother Harold sang a song he wrote for mom. His daughter read a poem about grandma. After the service, my grandfather's wife, he had remarried before his death and his wife was very concerned about her husband in heaven.

She very seriously asked me "You know your grandfather was a pipe fitter and he has many good friends. Well, this friend passed away, and they go to the same Mormon Church as we did. She was distraught, and I asked her what was on her mind. Her reply shocked me! You know my friend's husband was an undertaker for many years. The

Church has always taught that when we get to heaven that what we do on earth will be our vocation in heaven. He will be bored having nothing to do in heaven. Grandmother asked me, how this can be. I told her that is not true and there is nothing like that in the bible. God makes everything new, and the former things have passed away.

"And God shall wipe away all tears from their eyes; and there shall be no more death, neither sorrow, nor crying, neither shall there be any more pain: for the former things are passed away. And he that sat upon the throne said, Behold, I make all things new. And he said unto me, Write: for these words are true and faithful. And he said unto me, it is done. I am Alpha and Omega, the beginning and the end. I will give unto him that is athirst of the fountain of the water of life freely. He that overcometh shall inherit all things; and I will be his God, and he shall be my son."

(Revelation 21:4-7)

Conviction

Therefore shall ye keep my commandments, and do them: I am the LORD.

(Leviticus 22:31)

After the service and saying my goodbyes to my dad and family and friends I returned home. The drive home gave me plenty of time to reflect on what had happened and be prepared to face life ahead of me. Knowing I would be seeking new employment and preparing for a new child to enter the home. Comforting my family and sharing with them the wonderful things God had done with mom and my nephew. These things alone could make me overwhelmed.

I had the Bible on cassette back then and listened to it most of the time as I drove from place to place. This was an excellent time to listen to the scriptures. Hoping this would drown out the feelings and thoughts that might get between me and God. It is my desired most of all to look to God for all my needs. Hungry for God's Word it was the only thing that could quench my hunger in my soul.

"Jesus (Yeshua) answered and said unto him, if a man loves me, he will keep my words: and my Father will love him, and we will come unto him, and make our abode with him. He that loveth me not keepeth not my sayings: and the word which ye hear is not mine, but the Father's which sent me." (John 14:23-24)

I had finished listening to the Book of Revelation when I arrived in Idaho. Now it was time to listen again from the beginning, Genesis. The creation story has always fascinated me. The very first words in the Bible "In the beginning

GOD; I realized this is the big problem with most of us in life. If there is a God, I must do what He says. No God, I don't have to do what he says. Thus I can be my own god. As I continued down the road listening with a desire to know God in a more personal way that would change me. Make me more like Yeshua; this is my prayer and desire every day. Then this scripture gripped my heart:

"Thus the heavens and the earth were finished, and all the host of them. And on the seventh day, God ended his work which he had made, and he rested on the seventh day from all his work which he had made. And God blessed the seventh day, and sanctified it: because that in it he had rested from all his work which God created and made. " (Genesis 2:1-3)

Wow, I just got it; Sunday is the first day of the week. The Seventh day is Saturday then why does the Christian church worship and call Sunday the day of Rest? I was deeply troubled by this. I continued to listen and realized that Adam was the first man and he wasn't a Jew or a Gentile. Adam represented all mankind until the second Adam came to straighten everything out.

"For as by one man's disobedience many were made sinners, so by the obedience of one shall many be made righteous." (Romans 5:19)

It was at the forefront of my mind when I got back to Riverside, California. I would ask my friend and pastor who was over the ministries I was serving. I will pose the question of the Sabbath day of rest and then why do we observe it on Sunday as the day of rest? I pulled over the car and prayed and took out my journal and made a note so I would not forget this critical question.

As I traveled I had finished Genesis, Exodus and was now in Leviticus almost home I hear this verse:

"Therefore shall ye keep my commandments, and do them: I am the LORD." (Leviticus 22:31)

I had already listened to the Ten Commandments in Exodus and mentally tried to name them off:

1. I am the Lord your God
2. Have no other Gods before you
3. Keep my name, Holy
4. Keep the Sabbath day Holy
5. Honor Mother and Father
6. Shall not murder
7. Shall not commit Adultery
8. Shall not steal
9. Shall not lie
10. Not to Covent your neighbor's stuff.

I truly believed that the Ten Commandments are just the basics of His divine instructions to me and all mankind. As I was listening to the Books of Moses, It was Friday afternoon, and I arrived home. The instructions that were given to Israel after leaving Egypt began to sink deep into my heart, and I had more questions than answers. But, I was taking notes and was going to find out the answers. My friend and pastor loved to teach the Books of Moses, and he did it with such passion, I was sure he would give me answers to my questions.

My family was waiting for me and supper was on the table. After coming into the house my children were very excited to see me, and when I saw my wife, wow she had become so big. There were no doubts that she was pregnant now. I went to the bathroom and freshened up then returned to the kitchen table where everyone was seated and ready for me to say grace. We held hands and I said the blessing, there was so much to be thankful for. This time I spent with my family was one of the best I can remember.

Later on, I made a lunch date with my friend and pastor. I asked him about the Sabbath day. He smiled and said "Yes you are right; the Shabbat as it is called is on Saturday. Christians celebrate it on Sunday for two reasons:

1. They call it the Lords Day because he rose from the grave that day and that is why they worship him on Sunday.

2. Historically, it was First Sunday Law enacted by Emperor Constantine - March, 321 A.D.

My question was to him then why do you observe Sunday? His answer was" I rest on Saturday as my family has for many generations; I am from a Jewish family. I have not found a synagogue yet that observes the Torah (The Books of Moses) as I believe that Yeshua is the Messiah.

It is my heart's desire to share the gospel with as many people as I can. The Christian community gives me this opportunity. We talked through lunch that day and set a standing lunch date on Wednesdays when I would be counseling, and he would be on staff, we would have lunch together. I remained puzzled why the church and the leaders of the church knew the truth why would they continue this practice.

Over time and observation I found the motivation was not the truth, but to fill the pews and coffers of the church. When this church had started, it had a menorah in the front of the church. Some of the staff was Jewish believers. Over the years the menorah was replaced with a cross as the Jewish believers' left. It became more focused on reaching large crowds of people.

Still presenting the Gospel and building projects and the focus was on building buildings, groups and not the discipleship of individuals. The inner circle became removed from the congregation one on one. But, they focused on the masses of people. The personal touch was being replaced with religion and position, and then it became a form of entertainment for the people, concerts, guest speakers, singers.

Halloween was observed as harvest night, people dressed up as people from the bible, but still, you could see children and adults dress in a matter-of-fact fashion. The idea was this would be an outreach to the community to evangelize. If you cover a pig in a suit to make him like a man, he is just a pig in a suit.

"How is it that ye do not understand that I spake it not to you concerning bread, that ye should beware of the leaven of the Pharisees and of the Sadducees? Then understood they how that he bade them not beware of the leaven of bread but of the doctrine of the Pharisees and of the Sadducees." (Matthew 16:11-12)

During this era of time, I was convicted of the church's preoccupation with projects which included entertainment, which was and is still called worship.

Worship is a very personal walk with the Lord God. If we love him, we will be an example to others provoking them to jealousy by wanting what we have in that personal relationship with our God. If we look and act as the world does what do we have to offer a lost and dying world? If there is no difference in our lives, then how can we say we have a relationship with the Creator?

"Ye call me (Yeshua) Master and Lord: and ye say well; for so I am. If I then, your Lord and Master, have washed your feet; ye also ought to wash one another's feet. For I have given you an example, that ye should do as I have done to you. Verily, verily, I say unto you, the servant is not greater than his lord; neither he that is sent greater than he that sent him." (John 13:13-16)

"Let no man despise thy youth; but be thou an example of the believers, in the word, in conversation, in charity, in spirit, in faith, in purity." (1 Timothy 4:12)

Many times I have heard it taught at the pulpit that Christmas was not Jesus' (Yeshua's') Birthday and it has its roots in many pagan beliefs and folklore. Like Santa Claus and the Christmas tree. This concerned me deeply from the inconsistency of what was taught then what we are to do. This was an act of hypocrisy that stood out like a fly in a bowl of milk. Yet the church encourages this time as a day of worship. Even as a new believer years ago I observed Christmas as a form of worship to remember the Messiahs Birth.

Then Easter as the death and resurrection of the Messiah Yeshua really puzzled me. Even the Scriptures placed his birth at Passover and the Feast of unleavened bread. The research I undertook into the traditions of the church; can be traced back to the early western church movement that became the Catholic Church.

This subject indeed was a sore spot with my wife and her family who were all raised Catholic. This opened up a pre-verbal can of worms which did lead to the division of thought and practices which became an open conflict between us.

"He answered and said unto them, well hath Esaias prophesied of you hypocrites, as it is written, This people honoureth me with their lips, but their heart is far from me. Howbeit in vain do they worship me, teaching for doctrines the commandments of men." (Mark 7:6-7)

Also, after studying the scriptures and knowing that Easter was not the same as Passover. There is a mathematical error that occurs as a warning a sign to people to day. It is impossible to get three days and three nights from Good Friday to Easter!

"But he (Yeshua) answered and said unto them, An evil and adulterous generation seeketh after a sign; and there shall no sign be given to it, but the sign of the prophet Jonas: For as Jonas was three days and three nights in the whale's belly; so shall the Son of man be three days and three nights in the heart of the earth." (Matthew 12:39-40)

My wife and I were blessed now with two sons, and she was pregnant with the third. I was working as a Clinical Engineer at a hospital in Redlands California. I was talking to my wife on the phone before leaving from work when I began to have terrible chest pains. I told her I was going to the Emergency Room down the hall. When I got there, my friends who were on duty asked me "what's the matter, do you need help?" I said I am having horrible chest pains. They put me in a bed and started the labs and monitored my heart rate and said I had a heart attack. They put me in ICU, and I spent the next three nights there.

My wife and friends from the church came and anointed me with oil and prayed over me. My mother-in-law was having a pacemaker placed in her the same time I was in the hospital, and now my wife was diagnosed with breast cancer.

She had to stop breastfeeding my youngest son, and this crushed her heart. The doctors did a biopsy and confirmed she had cancer, and then she lost the baby during the treatment. My wife's world had gone upside down at this time. Her grief was overwhelming to her. This time she did not recover from the loss. She wanted answers, and I had none, it looked terrible for the both of us. Our children could become orphans' overnight. She told me not to quote scripture, and not to give her that platitude that God will provide. But, I believed that with all my heart and I knew he would. My wife had given up on God and gave it all up to hogwash in her grief and despair. She spent time with me at the hospital then with her mom.

I am not one for sitting on my hands; my staff would come and check on me during my time in the hospital. I would run my office from my hospital bed. The Doctor caught on and knew I would not stop, so they discharged me to go back to work on the condition if I feel bad at any time to return to the E.R. The agreement worked out for the better.

During a follow-up appointment with my cardiologist who is a devout Christian man told me I needed surgery to correct my heart condition after looking over the test results? He told me I needed this done right away or I would die and to go home and get my final arrangements in order.

He said I have a less than 50% chance of recovery and that I might die anyway. On the way home I stopped off at the church and had a talk with my pastor and friend, he gathers serval of the other pastors at the church to pray over me. As they anointed my head with oil and prayed, one of the pastors began to prophesy *"This brother that we love so much he will not die till the Lord returns for all of us."* All Said Amen!

The next day I returned to the Doctors office, and he ran some test before surgery and found the condition was completely gone. I told him what had happened when I went to the church before going home. He said "As a Christian, I know you were healed. I have the proof of your condition in these reports in my hand, and in the other hand God had touched you and made you better than new. Praise God. I asked him if we could call my wife. She didn't say much at first but, was quite relieved I was doing better.

My wife was going through Chemotherapy treatments now, and she was getting very sick and had enough of it, and we looked into alternative medicines. I took some sick leave, and we went to a Natural Health Clinic and their training course that taught healing through Juicing and vegan dieting. We took it all to heart; it appeared to be biblically based Christian organization which was appealing at the time. Their foundation for the diet on the following scriptures:

"And God said, Behold, I have given you every herb bearing seed, which is upon the face of all the earth, and every tree, in which is the fruit of a tree yielding seed; to you, it shall be for meat. And to every beast of the earth, and to every fowl of the air, and to everything that creepeth upon the earth, wherein there is life, I have given every green herb for meat: and it was so." (Genesis 1:29-30)

We completed the course and went home, and within six months we both regained our health entirely. I no longer had a heart condition, and her cancer was gone. Personally, I believe it was due to all the prayer we received, and the diet did help some. I could see hope again in my wife's eyes as her health returned. Also, my mother-in-law regained her health too through this program. We began sharing this with other people.

During this time I shared with my wife we would no longer work on Shabbat to honor God. We would continue to go to church until we found a synagogue or church that accepted the Sabbath. We checked out several churches that did acknowledge the Sabbath but, found there teaching from their so-called prophet was way off from the scriptures. But, I kept looking.

Now our health was doing so well, my wife and I began to spend more time together. She had been going to counseling due to the loss of our third son and now had hopes to have another. I kept this in prayer and did my part.

Day after day she wanted to get pregnant and tried testing her PH and would call me to come home soon so she might conceive. It became an obsession, and she would say give me a child. My reply was the same as Jacobs to Rachel:

"And Jacob's anger was kindled against Rachel: and he said, am I in God's stead, who hath withheld from thee the fruit of the womb?" (Genesis 30:2)

The thought that her dream might have been from God was now dashed to pieces. It was not met with any understanding when I pointed out that God gave her three sons. But, one son is now in heaven. Her heart was broken at this point, and I believe she never recovered from the loss. She grew bitter toward me and God. Asked her to continue counseling at the church and she said" They told me that they agree with you and I am not going back for counseling. From that day forward she was very cold toward me.

The company that hired me at the hospital replaced me and sent me to Pittsburg to prepare them for Y2K. I check with the staff at the hospital in Pittsburg they didn't really want me there. I was sent there to fail and return and be let go. When I returned I confronted the management, and I received 90 days severance pay.

The next week I went to work as an electrician for a year which led to an opportunity as a production manager. It was just a couple of miles from home. God provided an opportunity for me to share my faith and talents at my workplace. After some time our team had upgraded and programmed the robots which increased the productivity from 20% to 60%. Trained new Robotic Technicians to program and updated the robots as needed for production and our productivity gained another 15%. Also, I trained 20 hand welders to be certified to worked on the repairs and manufacturing line which brought us to 123%. Before leaving the department and the company after almost two years, the company was bought out. Now all the repair work and work in progress were on schedule 100% this was an accomplished by using the biblical principles I had taught my supervisors and lead persons.

Our team had a Bible Study during lunch time we covered many subjects which would bless our work and increase production. We use the book of Nehemiah (Nehemiah) as foundational project management and production management as a textbook on how to improve our production professionally. The scripture we all used as our mantra to meditate on is *(Colossians 3:23-24) "And whatsoever ye do, do it heartily, as to the Lord, and not unto men; knowing that of the Lord ye shall receive the reward of the inheritance: for ye serve the Lord Christ (Master Messiah)."*

The new company CEO frond on this practice and ordered the Director over me, who is also a Christian to let me go. The new company CEO Said, "If he did not let me go within the next 30 days, he would let him go too." It was just before Thanksgiving I was given a 30-day notice. My Director said he was leaving too. He had found a new position at another firm. He wished me well, and we prayed for each other. I cashed in my retirement fund to provide for the holidays till I could find some work.

During this time I was convicted on several issues in the church the Sabbath be only one of many. The Idea of three persons in the Godhead or Trinity was not aligned with scriptures. The Sh'ma clearly shows God as One God.

"Hear, O Israel: The LORD our God is one LORD:" (Deuteronomy 6:4)

Yes God had manifested himself as a burning bush, a pillar of Cloud, A pillar of Fire, in dreams and visions. Also as the Creator of all things, Father, Word of God in the flesh (Yeshua), the Son of God and the Son of man. Not limited in how he manifested himself to mankind enabling mankind through His Spirit, or some say the Holy Spirit. I am convinced God is One God (Echad Elohim). The adversary has had a hay day with confusion and false doctrines which divides Gods people from the truth.

"Jesus (Yeshua) saith unto him, have I been so long time with you, and yet hast thou not known me, Philip? He that hath seen me hath seen the Father; and how sayest thou then, Shew us the Father? Believest thou not that I am in the Father, and the Father in me? The words that I speak unto you I speak not of myself: but the Father that dwelled in me, he doeth the works. Believe me that I am in the Father, and the Father in me: or else believe me for the very works' sake.

(John 14:9-11)

My beliefs are now becoming refined as I study and pray over the words of instruction (Torah) God has given his people. Every doctrine of truth can be found in the first five books of the Bible. And Yeshua (The Messiah) during His ministry explained these truths to His Disciples. He established and set the standard for his Disciples so they could carry the message to the world. About half of the New Testament is quoting the Old Testament directly or in principle. I find it hard saying when the church teaches the Law (Torah – Instructions) were done away with, and no longer relevant today? How can this even be possible!

"Then the eleven disciples went away into Galilee, into a mountain where Jesus had appointed them. And when they saw him, they worshipped him: but some doubted. And Jesus (Yeshua) came and spake unto them, saying, All power is given unto me in heaven and in the earth. Go ye therefore, and teach all nations, baptizing them in the name of the Father, and of the Son, and of the Holy Ghost: Teaching them to observe all things whatsoever I have commanded you: and,

lo, I am with you always, even unto the end of the world. Amen." (Matthew 28:16-20)

This was only the tip of the iceberg; the truth is there in the scriptures if anyone wants to know the truth. It seems to me that man has a way of twisting things around to fit his needs. This is backward we need to live our lives to the glory of God. We have only this one life to live then we should live it to the fullest of serving the Creator of all things. We are the creation, and we are subject to Gods instructions on how to live. Yes, he has given us free will, but that too is very limited. God will intervene even on free will. Take the book of Jonah he had to become fish food before he would yield to the plan and purpose that God had for his life. God hardened the heart of Pharaoh to bring the people of Israel out of Egypt. God hardened in pride the heart of Belshazzar to his destruction making way for Cyrus to let Gods people return to Israel. These are just a few examples of God working His will and plan over the free will of men.

"For this cause God gave them up unto vile affections: for even their women did change the natural use into that which is against nature: And likewise also the men, leaving the natural use of the woman, burned in their lust one toward another; men with men working that which is unseemly, and receiving in themselves that recompense of their error which was meet. And even as they did not like to retain God in their knowledge, God gave them over to a reprobate mind, to do those things which are not convenient; Being filled with all unrighteousness, fornication, wickedness, covetousness, maliciousness; full of envy, murder, debate, deceit, malignity; whisperers, Backbiters, haters of God, despiteful, proud, boasters, inventors of evil things, disobedient to parents, Without understanding, covenantbreakers, without natural affection, implacable, unmerciful: Who knowing the judgment of God, that they which commit such things are

worthy of death, not only do the same, but have pleasure in them that do them." (Romans 1:26-32)

Studying the Bible and meditating on the Word of God has changed my life. After being warned at the church I attended that I would never go far in ministry, because of my beliefs, it struck me on how Yeshua must have felt when he too was rejected. Now determined to do what Gods' Word says even if no one else wants to follow, I know God is with me. The warnings in God's Word about changing what is said in the Scriptures, I took this to heart.

"Ye shall not add unto the word which I command you, neither shall ye diminish ought from it, that ye may keep the commandments of the LORD your God which I command you."

(Deuteronomy 4:2)

"And if any man shall take away from the words of the book of this prophecy, God shall take away his part out of the book of life, and out of the holy city, and from the things which are written in this book." (Revelation 22:19)

Abandoned

When my spirit was overwhelmed within me, then thou knewest my path. In the way wherein I walked have they privily laid a snare for me.

(Psalms 142:3)

Starting my own company and worked as an electrical consultant. Local employment was hard to find. Most of the companies were moving from California due to the high taxes and environmental restrictions. Many companies moved to other states, Idaho, Utah, Nevada, Wyoming and overseas.

I remain unemployed for most of a year putting out a resume' after resumes.' Then an Opportunity for me to go to Bakersfield, California to work as an Automation specialist, programming program logic controllers PLCs like the computers I worked on at Disneyland. Working in the oil fields and programming PLCs was right up my alley. It was fun, and I met serval Christians there and began going to church in Bakersfield on the weekends.

The finances and things started to look better. Everything at home began to regain some normalcy. Though I was gone every other weekend; my wife and I decided to renew our vows after twenty-five years of marriage. We invited friends and family and a good friend of mine a pastor at the church performed the ceremony. Our children were there and my second oldest had just got engaged to a very nice young man who she had known since the second grade of school. They met at the church services where we had been attending for over twenty some years.

I would drive from Riverside Sunday nights and home on Fridays every week. It was taking its toll, so I came home every other week and stayed at a hotel on the weekends. I missed my family, and if the job worked out, I planned to move the family to Bakersfield. This was not a popular Idea with my wife or the children. Later I rented a house and asked the family to come to visit me. The idea was not attractive to them. I spent every other week at the house close to my work and then I went home for the weekend every other week.

On the weekend I was away from home I went to church in Bakersfield. I was still looking for a church or synagogue that followed the whole of scriptures and began to think it was as easy as finding chicken lips.

But, I wanted to study the Word of God and did not want to be the lone ranger. Every week I went to church either in, Bakersfield or Riverside. My passion for the Word of God became, even more, a part of me than ever. I was trusting God to provide for all our needs, and I knew I had to do my part. I still listened to the Bible while I drove to and from work or on my travels to Riverside and Bakersfield. It was clear to me that the Bible was a Hebrew Document that was written by the Hebrews who were inspired by God.

"All scripture is given by inspiration of God, and is profitable for doctrine, for reproof, for correction, for instruction in righteousness: That the man of God may be perfect, thoroughly furnished unto all good works."

(2 Timothy 3:16-17)

The money I made paid the bills and helped my children to get a good education, but I was not available as a dad. I wanted to be part of their lives but, had to put food on the table. Taking this to prayer and then an opportunity after opportunity came for me to be interview by several churches in the close proximity of our home in Riverside as a pastor. I was chosen by the church search committees several times after teaching, but the terms of my service were not Biblical, so I turned them all down. Once again the company I was working for was sold, and my services were no longer needed.

The Wyoming Company that purchased the Company I worked for in Bakersfield, California had offered me a position in Wyoming once the project got underway. Meanwhile, I could work from there office in Bakersfield, not much was going on there, so I asked to take my vacation days. They agreed, and I took my wife and two sons on vacation. We went to Canada stayed there for a couple of days my wife had a severe migraine headache, and the boys and I sat outside cooking hot dogs and marshmallow at the fire ring. On the way back I stopped off at the field office to see the progress of the project in Wyoming, and it looked promising.

While we were gone on vacation, disaster has struck the home, my wife's pet dogs she had even before she met me had been stolen while we were on vacation. Grandma and the girls were grief-stricken. Both dogs were gone, and the looks on the faces of the family, it seems as if it was my fault somehow. As if this wasn't enough, I received a call from work.

They had transferred me to Wyoming, and I was to report at the end of the week. I didn't like leaving the family in California, but I had to check things out to see if we could get a place. That week my wife and I put up the house for Sale. I went to Bakersfield, and now the main office wanted me there to assist in a PLC project for the water management system in Bakersfield, California. They put the Wyoming project on hold, and it looked like we could move to Bakersfield after all. I made arrangements to purchase a home with land just outside Temecula.

The another heart wrenching event transpire, I had asked my wife and mother in law to come one weekend to the house I was renting, while getting ready to move to the new home in Temecula. Our pet dog the kids had grown up with died. This traumatic event happened while my oldest daughter and her sisters watch their brother in our absence. Not being there as Dad I was shunned by my oldest son.

After returning, I could see he needed dad more than ever. It was a hot summer and I bought a wading pool. My son was having so much fun in the pool and he would go under the water and up to show me he could swim under water. As he was showing me he came up and a Yellow Jacket was on or near the water and it stung him several times. He started to have hard time breathing; I rushed him to the hospital.

We were in the waiting room and they took their time to see him and he was gasping for air. I went to the desk and said they had better call security because I was going to make a lot of trouble if they do not get a doctor to him right now. They call security and took my son in to see the Doctor. He gave him an injection and said it was a good thing we saw him now. He was going into shock.

As I Look back over the years, there is one thing I know that never changes on this earth; is change. The house in Temecula fell through the seller changed their minds. Already I had moved half of our household items in the home and started repairs. I now had to move out! I moved everything to a storage unit and waited. Our house that we were living in had sold, and we needed to move.

What next! The project for the water management system in Bakersfield was coming to a close. I asked if they had another project in Bakersfield, and they said no. It looks like all our work is going to be in Wyoming and if I still wanted the project, I could move there. That weekend I let my family know I was going to check out the possibilities in Wyoming and I would return and if it looked good, we would move there.

This is when my wife put her foot down. She said "If this does not work out it will be entirely your fault. I will go with you on the condition that we buy a house and have some land free and clear with money we receive from escrow then I will stick with you. If this does not work out, I will leave you."

The plans were made, and we would move to Wyoming once we had purchased a home to her satisfaction. We paid cash for a lovely home; with property in a little town in Wyoming. We had saved a large amount of money in the bank.

My three daughters were all going to college now. They were going to live with grandmother till they could get a place together. I would send the money to them to get their own place, and they could continue to go to school.

My youngest daughter, whom I believe to be the smartest of them all; she was only seventeen at the time. I looked back to when I was her age, and I wanted to stay in Arizona and continue to go to school, but my family was moving back to Idaho, and I had no choice. So I asked my youngest daughter if she really wants to stay or join us in Wyoming, she chose to stay.

Now moving from place to place was not a stranger to me. While I was growing up, we moved from home to home so my dad and mom could find work. We really never set down roots to one place all the time I was growing up. This was the main reason I chose the stay in the same place to raise a family. But, this all was about to backfire. It was when the house we had lived in for twenty-five years was sold the realization set in with the family. I had loaded up a large U-Haul truck with everything we needed. Then for the last time, we all sat on the front lawn holding hands and prayed for one another. We would be reunited again in the spring at my daughter's wedding.

My health was taking its toll; there were times that I had spells of stomach and liver pains which would place me in a shape of a human horseshoe. I would go to bed in terrible, yet horrible pain. My wife gave me little attention and telling me I would do anything for attention. I could see she had grown cold with me. No longer had she asked me to help her get pregnant, but she had little to do with me.

Now living and working in Wyoming and the project did not work out as planned but, there was plenty of work I could do there in the gas and oil fields. After working a year in Wyoming I was offered a job as a project manager for an oil refinery.

As far as work there was always work available for my profession. The gas and oil fields were at boom town epic proportions. I had started to build a garage and shop during the summer and hoped to have it completed by winter. There I planned to make Robotics with the help of my sons who found a great interest in computers and programming. I could retire with money in the bank; I had purchased two lots of land next to our home when we bought the place so each of my sons could build a house for themselves and their future families. These plans all sounded good to me, and I thought this would please my wife and sons too. I believe it did for the short term.

"Order my steps in thy word: and let not any iniquity have dominion over me." (Psalms 119:133)

After the wedding of our oldest, I had offered my youngest daughter to come to visit us in Wyoming, and I would pick her up at the airport in Salt Lake City. She was going to spend the week and see if she wanted to move to Wyoming and go to college. When I picked her up at the airport, it was in early springtime. We talked along the way, and I shared with her I was preparing for my Master Electrician License test so I could work in the gas and oil fields installing PLC and telemetry equipment. Also, I was attending online classes to obtain a Program Management certification which would give me even more opportunities in the future.

As we drove home it began to snow, and we were now in a whiteout, but I was able to make my way home. My youngest daughter was terrified and she wanted to go back to California. When we arrived home, my sons smothered her with love and hugs. My wife showed her to her room we had prepared for her to stay as long as she wanted. Looking she looked outside and saw the two foot of snow on the ground, and the sun started to shine, and it was so clear you could see for a hundred miles. Typical Wyoming weather nice one minute and bad the next. This weather is not agreeable with a California wife and children who had never seen four seasons before.

After the week my youngest daughter spent together she never spoke to me again. This was when things started to go wrong; with hindsight, I can see it now.

My focus was to provide and protect my family. The communication with my daughters was managed through my wife. When she was on the phone talking to them, I asked to speak with them, and there was always an excuse. Later it got worse; she would just hang up and not say a word. The only time I was able to talk to the girls was through their mother, and it was because they needed something. I gave my car to my youngest daughter before we left California and had bought the oldest daughter a car.

Now the middle daughter needed a car, and she was overdrawn in her bank account and needed money. I agreed to send her money if I could talk to her, and I was not going to cosign for her.

But, her mother put her foot down and gave me an ultimatum to send money or she would leave. After some harsh words and later an argument, which she dumped on me all the things from before we were married to the present? She had been carrying this load with her for almost 28 years.

And the fact that I could not give her another son was paramount I signed the papers for my daughter to attend college and later on that month she asked me to take her and the boys to Salt Lake City to rent a car so she could spend the winter with her mom. I requested she go to counseling at the church we had attended for over twenty years. We had already spent two winters there, and the winters were hard so, I agreed, and she left and never came back.

The average week I was conducting a bible study at the community church. The elders at the church had got together and asked me to take the pastors' job. They loved to hear me teach and wanted to me to replace the pastor. I said you have a pastor, and I am not going to take his place. God has placed him here, who am I to do this thing against God and sin. They were in shock. I wrote a letter of resignation as assistant pastor. My wife was distraught that we left the church, and we attended one in the next county. But, we did visit the church until the family left for California.

This led to a bitter divorce, and I was mentally, physically, spiritually damaged and asking God WHY? My health continued to go downhill with all the stress. Mentally I was on autopilot, and spiritually the loss left me with a pain that was so hard to endure. If my family had died in some horrible accident, I think it would have been hard to take, but to be rejected by the very family I had loved and served was more than I could bear. This had haunting regrets which I could hardly wrap my brain around. The wound was deep and I wanted to know why? For days I did not eat and lay on the floor of our home crying out to God asking why?

Fallen

My heart is sorely pained within me: and the terrors of death are fallen upon me. Fearfulness and trembling have come upon me, and horror hath overwhelmed me.

(Psalms 55:4-5)

It is February, and I make arrangements to send flowers to my wife. While I was at work, she left a message thanking me for the flowers and said she loved me and missed me. This looked promising so that weekend I had four days off. I decided to leave early that afternoon from Wyoming, and I would arrive around midnight in California at my mother-in-law's home.

Had the car packed and ready to leave after work, As I was about to enter Las Vegas I made a phone call to let my wife and mother-in-law know that I would be arriving about midnight and not to be alarmed.

My wife told me to stay in Wyoming and never come to California, and it was over between the both of us. And if I came to visit in California, she would call the police and have me arrested. I was dumbfounded by the contrast between the phone messages and this phone call. I was in shock I don't even know how I made it back to my home in Wyoming I definitely was on autopilot, God was watching over me.

"How excellent is thy lovingkindness, O God! therefore the children of men put their trust under the shadow of thy wings." (Psalms 36:7)

Later the next couple of days I called my wife in California to find out what was going on. She said I will not talk to you anymore and you want to find out what's going on called the church and talk to my counselor.

So, I called the church and talked to the pastor who was in charge of the counseling team at one time we were terrific friends. He told me he could not discuss this over the phone I'd have to come to California to talk to him personally. I asked him why is it that you can't speak to me about this over the phone. Things have changed since you have left; I'm not at liberty to speak to you unless you're here in person.

The stress was overwhelming of not knowing what was going on. I continued praying and calling out to God asking him why. The pain I had suffered from time to time came back with a vengeance. My stomach and liver pain now was so severe. I just wanted to die; I needed some relief from this dreadful pain. I laid there on the living room floor for three days. The pain had gone away, and I got dressed and went to work. The project was coming to a close and would be over in the spring in late March. I placed a bid as a project manager's position on the next project coming up at the gas refinery which would take place in mid-April. I know God was listening to me and watching over me at this time. I continue to go to church, and I visited with my pastor for counseling and prayer.

I asked him to call the church in California to find out what is going on. My pastor made the call to California, and they would not talk with him about what was going on. He was informed that I would have to go to California to find out for myself. He too was mystified to why they would want me to go to California to find out what was going on.

I was holding on to my faith in God, but I had to find out for myself what was going on. After the project was completed in Wyoming, I packed a bag and headed to California to talk to the pastor-counselor at the church. I packed up the car with my wife's clothes and the boy's clothes. Also, I packed up the boy's toys and computer so they would have something to do at grandma's house.

When I arrived, I unloaded the boxes into the counseling office so that my wife could pick it up there and had a talk with the counselor. He informed me that my wife was going to counseling there at the church. But he still was not at liberty to tell me why she would call the police. He said if you promise not to visit your wife at your mother-in-law's house we could start counseling.

I said what is really going on here I sent my wife down here to go to counseling and I made sure that she had a car to come down to visit her mom . The plan was she was going to spend the winter here, then come back in the spring.

He said I cannot tell you anything right now. Well, I said you must be a liar! You told me when I come to California you would tell me what is going on. Now you're telling me you're not going to tell me at all unless; I make a promise not to go see my wife. I said this is hogwash and I'm not going to put up with it and you're going to tell me what is going on because you made a promise.

I have known you for over 20 years, and you're really acting strange right now what is going on? He said don't worry about your wife the church is now going to provide for her and take care of her. Well, I said it sounds like you are married to her now. If that is the case, I then handed him the ring off my finger. I'm going to go stay with a friend for a couple of days. Call me if you decide to keep your word and tell me what is going on. None of this makes any sense to me!

Little did I know that he had called my wife and told her that she could go to Wyoming pick up everything she wanted from the house while I was gone? She and her mother went to Wyoming to take everything that they wanted from home. They also took my shotgun and her 22 rifle. While staying at my friend's house in California just before I was ready to leave I received a call from the counselor and asked me to come in he would like to talk to me.

Well when I arrived and got to his office, he showed me a list of items that my wife said I had done. I looked at the list and almost laughed. The details on the list she had dumped on me before she left for California. Over half the things on the list dated back over twenty-eight years ago when we were engaged. The list was almost a page long only a few issues were recent, and they were her complains about Wyoming and my service to the church when I refused to take the pastors position. She felt I had caused a lot of problems and she lost friends and felt isolated because of my choice. She also thought I should not spank the boys and considered this punishment child abuse. Is this what it's all about, punishing my boys is the right thing to do?

"He that spareth his rod hateth his son: but he that loveth him chasteneth him betimes." (Proverbs 13:24)

My supposed friend and pastor counselor asked me are these things true. My response was from her point of view yes. I said these items that are on here most of them happen before we got married. The majority of the other half date back to when we first got married. We went to counseling for these items, and she said she had forgiven me. We both had a list back then, and what was on my list I do not even remember. I mentioned in First Corinthians 13 states that were not supposed to keep a list, and I'm not going to play that game. So if this is all it's about she has no biblical grounds for divorce or separation. So what's the deal?

"Dare any of you, having a matter against another, go to law before the unjust, and not before the saints? Do ye not know that the saints shall judge the world? And if the world shall be judged by you, are ye unworthy to judge the smallest matters?" (1 Corinthians 6:1-2)

His response was straightforward if she believes it's real it's real, and we have to protect her at the church. She feels that you are dangerous and she is scared of you and for her safety. I said could you show me the Scriptures that support that. His response was a shock to me "We are to hold with the laws of California then the bible in that order in this case. He says no longer you will question what I have to say or quote Scripture. You will sit there and listen, and I will tell you what you will have to do. She is under the churches authority right now. You are to obey the church and if you refuse to do that you'll be in violation of the Scriptures. You have a rebellious heart that is considered an act of witchcraft." He then gives me a name of a Christian lawyer and told me to contact him my wife has filed for separation which may lead to a divorce. He also said," If anyone asks I did not give you this information."

I said I know the Scriptures and what you're quoting is out of context, and I'm not going to put up with this. He told me to set down, I tore my shirt, and he said: "why did you do that." My reply "if you know the Scriptures so well you'll understand. In short, if you don't exceed the scribes and Pharisees nowise will you enter the kingdom of heaven.

"And it came to pass, when King Hezekiah heard it, that he rent his clothes, and covered himself with sackcloth, and went into the house of the LORD." (2 Kings 19:1)

The lawyer said "If you do not counter sue, your wife through a divorce she will have you in jail. Your case files which I am unable to gain access to; Leads me to believe the case is considered under the law as an abuse of some sort. I requested he make arrangements for arbitration, to see if we could reconcile, and he contacted the court so I could see my sons. This did not last long. After some time he got it through my head this was not going anywhere.

"But brother goeth to law with brother and that before the unbelievers. Now, therefore, there is utterly a fault among you because ye go to law one with another. Why do ye not rather take wrong? Why do ye not rather suffer yourselves to be defrauded? "(1 Corinthians 6:6-7)

During the arbitration, she agreed to reconcile through counseling. After leaving the court office, she stopped me and said" I see you don't have a house to live in now. You should have stayed in Wyoming. I will make sure that your children will never talk to you again." That was the turning point, which led to a nasty divorce.

The pastor who was counseling me continued, or I should say his interrogations continued for almost 6 months before I left and went back to Wyoming. The last day of his so-called counseling appointment led to a verbal war of scriptures' taken out of context, and I could no longer be silent. He told me to sit down, and if I leave, I could never return. I stood in the doorway and said "So now I am excommunicated from this church, just fine with me!

The house sold in Wyoming and I moved all the items we had to storage in California. I notified the court, and everything went into a trust till the divorce was final. The wife and kids could take whatever they wanted.

Over that course of six months, my lawyer wanted to continue to bleed me for money. The counselor pastor at the church kept calling me and sending me emails of what I considered harassing and threating messages. I contacted my Lawyer, and he had a court order to stop the harassment.

I told my lawyer to give my wife all she wants and keep what you need to pay your bill. I want this to stop and start over. He refused, and I told him he works for me and to get the job done or I would fire him.

"And if any man will sue thee at the law, and take away thy coat, let him have thy cloke also. And whosoever shall compel thee to go a mile, go with him twain. Give to him that asketh thee, and from him that would borrow of thee turn not thou away." (Matthew 5:40-42)

He said" That Lady Judge out there will not give you a fair deal; we have to ask for another court date. I said "No, it stops here and now! We then went into the court, and the Lawyer said to the judge he and I have a disagreement and he can no longer represent me. The Judge asked me is this correct? I said," I fired him; also he said that you being a Lady Judge would not treat me fair and I want to bring this to a close today." The lawyer asked that my statement is stricken from the record. The Judge said this is not the first time I have heard this from you. No, it will remain on the record. Then the Judge asked me are you going to get a new lawyer or represent yourself. I said I will represent myself. The Judge said I will have the bailiff give you the proper forms and we can settle the matter in my court on Monday.

The following Monday my wife's lawyer and I go through the hit list. I gave them everything. But, they overlooked I had about two thousand dollars that were to be returned to me from my lawyer from the trust. Went before the judge and it was all done in less than ten minutes. Later that afternoon as I was on my way to Bakersfield I received a call from my ex-wife's lawyer. She asked if they could have the two thousand dollars too. I said kiss my donkey if you get my meaning and that was the last communication.

"For the lips of a strange woman drop as a honeycomb, and her mouth is smoother than oil: But her end is bitter as wormwood, sharp as a two-edged sword. Her feet go down to death; her steps take hold on hell." (Proverbs 5:3-5)

I had found a new girlfriend. This was less than a wise thing at the time. She gave me a shoulder to lean on and later we got married. Biggest mistake of my life as I looked back if I had been leaning on God more and the world less I would have been better off.

I was making more money now than I had ever in my entire career as a project manager. I became very sick and spent a week in the hospital, the stomach and liver pains were back. The Doctors were baffled and could not find the problem, and they sent me back home and to work.

"He goeth after her straightway, as an ox goeth to the slaughter, or as a fool to the correction of the stocks; Till a dart strike through his liver; as a bird hasteth to the snare, and knoweth not that it is for his life." (Proverbs 7:22-23)

The project lasted a year, and when I was laid off, she kicked me out of the house. A couple weeks later I got a better job the contract was for a year. When that project was over, she kicked me out again and then later on she wanted me to come back. I got very sick again, and she asked me to go to church with her and her two daughters which lived with us. I sat in the back of the church while she sang at choir practice. Her daughters were playing with a ball in the hall and a classroom making a terrible distraction. I scolded them both and had the girls both sit with me in the church pew until their mother was finished with practice.

When we got home I was so sick, I spent most of the next day in bed. Now my wife told me never to correct her daughters again. You are not their dad, and it is not your place. The wife and her friend were sitting at the table in the kitchen, and her friend gave me an ear full. At this present time, I was in pain, and I needed rest. And told them I am sick I want to die, and I don't want to listen to their horse pucky. Left them and sat outside on the front porch.

Her friend called the police and said I was suicidal. The next thing I know the Police hauled me off for a mental evaluation. I was interviewed by a Doctor and told him what the problem was. That night the pains started again, and they sent me to the hospital. The Doctor who saw me said you are from the mental ward I will have nothing to do with you, you want to die, and then die. Nice fellow, sure he has his problems too. I was so sick I could not argue.

Later I was sent back, and I had a second visit from the Doctor on staff. His recommendation is I could get someone to take me home then pick up the things you need and leave. You cannot stay in the house any longer, and you must find a new place to live. If you desire an escort from the police, we can arrange this too. A complaint has been made, and you must agree to these terms. I will interview the person who will accompany you to pick up your belongings. Then you will sign the agreement and be released.

I made arrangements with a friend, and I returned home to find a garage sale going on. I did not say a word to the wife, I got some clothes and a few items from my office and put them in the RV, and I left to find a place to live. I stopped at the bank and took out my savings which were four hundred dollars.

Stayed at an RV Park in Bakersfield for a couple of months till; I had enough money to return to Idaho. It is an Irony that I left for California nearly 30 years ago with a suitcase half full of clothes, in a car with a hundred dollars in my pocket. After returning to Idaho; I had a closet half full of clothes, and old RV, and about hundred dollars left in my pocket?

I visited my daughter and her family. I stayed in an RV park in Nampa, Idaho for a couple of days then moved to Fruitland and found an RV park there. Then I spent time with my Dad. I hired a lawyer the wife told me she would have nothing to do with me ever again. The only thing she would agree with is for me to file for divorce; she didn't have the money to do it herself. I asked her to move to Idaho, and I would find a place for us to live. She told me to file for divorce, and I do not want to hear from you ever again.

While living in California I was active in the church and was teaching bible studies once a week. I was also working as a tent maker with Gideon's ministry. She had caused a lot of problems with the church and the Gideon's, which later was settled on my behalf by the pastor and the board of elders. They reviewed all the complaints which she had presented to the church and the Gideon's and found she had been lying. I received a letter from the Gideon's and the church informing me of their findings, and the record was set straight. They wished me God's speed, and I would always be welcome to return to the ministry if I chose.

My brother let me park my RV at his place so I could save some money. I bought a car and later moved back to Fruitland so I could be closer to my Dad.

"He restoreth my soul: he leadeth me in the paths of righteousness for his name's sake." (Psalms 23:3)

Returning Home

And thou shalt return and obey the voice of the LORD and do all his commandments which I command thee this day. And the LORD thy God will make thee plenteous in every work of thine hand, in the fruit of thy body, and in the fruit of thy cattle, and in the fruit of thy land, for good: for the LORD will again rejoice over thee for good, as he rejoiced over thy fathers: If thou shalt hearken unto the voice of the LORD thy God, to keep his commandments and his statutes which are written in this book of the law, and if thou turn unto the LORD thy God with all thine heart, and with all thy soul.

(Deuteronomy 30:8-10)

Returning to my homeland in Idaho I spent a lot of my time with my dad. He was in ill health, and he was troubled why the Lord has allowed him to live a long life. He was still in morning for my mother who passed away seventeen years earlier. Since this time he had been baptized in the church which he and mom were married just across the street from where he now lived.

Dad asked me why God has allowed me to live such a long time. I thought for a moment and said God must have plans for you.

He said what could that be? I asked my dad how many children and grandchildren and great-grandchildren Dad has. We counted he has four children, 27 grandchildren, and 12 great-grandchildren. Dad asked why?

Well, dad, you are to pray for them, and it seems that could be a full-time job. I pointed out what it says Deuteronomy in the Shema, and we talked about this in some length. I asked Dad you know the secret to everlasting life now as a believer. What better thing is there in this world than to share it with all your children, grandchildren and great-grandchildren and meet them someday in heaven?

"Hear, O Israel: The LORD our God is one LORD: And thou shalt love the LORD thy God with all thine heart, and with all thy soul, and with all thy might. And these words, which I command thee this day, shall be in thine heart: And thou shalt teach them diligently unto thy children, and shalt talk of them when thou sittest in thine house, and when thou walkest by the way, and when thou liest down, and when thou risest up. And thou shalt bind them for a sign upon thine hand, and they shall be as frontlets between thine eyes. And thou shalt write them upon the posts of thy house, and on thy gates." (Deuteronomy 6:4-9 Shema)

Explained the Shema to Dad he was very interested. I told him the first word Shema in Hebrew is a verb, an action word. It means to listen and obey. To Love is a verb too, so to love God we are obedient to his commandments. He is commanding us to place this scripture in our hearts. How we do this is with all our heart or best put with our mind, soul who we are and might with all our strength. We are to do this diligently, without fail 24 hours a day seven days a week. First by our example and then by word and explain to them the Love of God.

Binding them on our hand is to put all we do in our lives to His glory as an example of your love. And to place them in the forefront of our mind that we never forget He is Master and God of our lives. And by this, it will be known that your house and all who visit it know beyond a doubt that you serve the true and living God of Israel.

He then challenged me, so what are your plans now that you have returned to Idaho? Well, I need to go to Boise to the VA and see what kind of help I can get there. In the meanwhile I will be looking for work. I have sent a few resume' out and hope to go to an interview soon. The VFW has asked me if I would be willing to be a chaplain for their post, the other chaplain wants to retire.

Till then, I hope to spend more time with you, and just get caught up with all the things I have missed out on in Idaho while I was away. Dad says" You need to start your own church and teach the Bible, even if it is a small bible study. I believe that is what God has planned for you." We spent a lot of time together visiting and in prayer sharing the word of God.

During this time dad shared with me a few things that were on his heart before he passed. One of his questions was "Do you think I spanked you too much when you were a kid?"

My response was "Dad you should have spanked me more, I did get away with a few things while I was growing up."

Dad had a regret he shared with me "I wished I had taken you kids to church when you were young.'

Over the course of that year with much prayer, God used me to help my brother just younger than myself to reconcile with Dad. The sweetest words to my ears were when Dad said to him he loved him. They asked forgiveness and the joy they had at that moment was a treasure from heaven.

I became very lonely even though I was around family and friends. I have spent most of my life married and had a companion to share the experience with. I was torn from the hurt of the past and the loneliness of the present.

Praying for guidance, I spent a lot of time studying and reading the Word of God. I found that from Adam, Job, Abraham, Jacob, Moses, David, And Solomon; these men of the Bible had there ups and downs with their wife or wives. So I proceeded to do a little research:

(Adam) "And the LORD God said, it is not good that the man should be alone; I will make him a help meet for him." (Genesis 2:18)

(Adam) "And unto Adam he said, Because thou hast hearkened unto the voice of thy wife, and hast eaten of the tree, of which I commanded thee, saying, Thou shalt not eat of it: cursed is the ground for thy sake; in sorrow shalt thou eat of it all the days of thy life; Thorns also and thistles shall it bring forth to thee; and thou shalt eat the herb of the field; In the sweat of thy face shalt thou eat bread, till thou return unto the ground; for out of it wast thou taken: for dust thou art, and unto dust shalt thou return." (Genesis 3:17-19)

(Job) "And the LORD said unto Satan, Hast thou considered my servant Job, that there is none like him in the earth, a perfect and an upright man, one that feareth God, and escheweth evil?"

(Job 1:8)

(Job) "Then said his wife unto him, dost thou still retain thine integrity? Curse God, and die. But he said unto her, Thou speakest as one of the foolish women speaketh. What? Shall we receive good at the hand of God, and shall we not receive evil? In all this did not Job sin with his lips.

(Job 2:9-10)

(Abram - Abraham) "And the scripture was fulfilled which saith, Abraham believed God, and it was imputed unto him for righteousness: and he was called the Friend of God." (James 2:23)

(Abram - Abraham) "And Sarai said unto Abram, Behold now, the LORD hath restrained me from bearing: I pray thee,

go in unto my maid; it may be that I may obtain children by her. And Abram hearkened to the voice of Sarai. And Sarai Abram's wife took Hagar her maid the Egyptian, after Abram had dwelt ten years in the land of Canaan, and gave her to her husband Abram to be his wife." (Genesis 16:2-3)

(Jacob – Israel) "And God said unto him, Thy name is Jacob: thy name shall not be called any more Jacob, but Israel shall be thy name: and he called his name Israel. And God said unto him, I am God Almighty: be fruitful and multiply; a nation and a company of nations shall be of thee, and kings shall come out of thy loins; and the land which I gave Abraham and Isaac, to thee I will give it, and to thy seed after thee will I give the land." (Genesis 35:10-12)

(Jacob – Israel) "And when Rachel saw that she bare Jacob no children, Rachel envied her sister; and said unto Jacob, Give me children, or else I die. And Jacob's anger was kindled against Rachel: and he said, am I in God's stead, who hath withheld from thee the fruit of the womb? (Genesis 30:1-2)

(Moses) "And the LORD said unto Moses, When thou goest to return into Egypt, see that thou do all those wonders before Pharaoh, which I have put in thine hand: but I will harden his heart, that he shall not let the people go. And thou shalt say unto Pharaoh, Thus saith the LORD, Israel is my son, even my firstborn: And I say unto thee, Let my son go, that he may serve me: and if thou refuse to let him go, behold, I will slay thy son, even thy firstborn. And it came to pass by the way in the inn, that the LORD met him, and sought to kill him. Then Zipporah took a sharp stone, and cut off the foreskin of her son, and cast it at his feet, and said, surely a bloody husband art thou to me. So he let him go: then she said, a bloody husband thou art, because of the circumcision." (Exodus 4:21-26)

"Then Jethro, Moses' father in law, took Zipporah, Moses' wife, after he had sent her back, And her two sons; of which the name of the one was Gershom; for he said, I have been an alien in a strange land: And the name of the other was Eliezer; for the God of my father, said he, was my help, and delivered me from the sword of Pharaoh: And Jethro, Moses' father in law, came with his sons and his wife unto Moses into the wilderness, where he encamped at the mount of God: And he said unto Moses, I thy father in law Jethro am come unto thee, and thy wife, and her two sons with her." (Exodus 18:2-6)

(Moses) "And the LORD said unto him, this is the land which I swear unto Abraham, unto Isaac, and unto Jacob, saying, I will give it unto thy seed: I have caused thee to see it with thine eyes, but thou shalt not go over thither. So Moses the servant of the LORD died there in the land of Moab, according to the word of the LORD. And he buried him in a valley in the land of Moab, over against Bethpeor: but no man knoweth of his sepulcher unto this day."

(Deuteronomy 34:4-6)

(David) "But now thy (Saul) kingdom shall not continue: the LORD hath sought him a man after his own heart, and the LORD hath commanded him to be captain over his people, because thou hast not kept that which the LORD commanded thee." (1 Samuel 13:14)

(David) "Wherefore hast thou despised the commandment of the LORD, to do evil in his sight? thou hast killed Uriah the Hittite with the sword, and has taken his wife to be thy wife, and hast slain him with the sword of the children of Ammon. Now therefore the sword shall never depart from thine house; because thou hast despised me, and hast taken the wife of Uriah the Hittite to be thy wife. Thus saith the LORD, Behold, I will raise up evil against thee out of thine own house, and I will take thy wives before thine eyes, and give them unto thy neighbor, and he shall lie with thy wives in the sight of this sun. For thou didst it secretly: but I will do this *thing before all Israel, and before the sun. And David said unto Nathan, I have sinned against the LORD. And Nathan said unto David, The LORD also hath put away thy sin; thou shalt not die. Howbeit, because by this deed thou hast given great occasion to the enemies of the LORD to blaspheme, the child also that is born unto thee shall surely die."(2 Samuel 12:9-14)*

(Solomon) "In Gibeon the LORD appeared to Solomon in a dream by night: and God said, Ask what I shall give thee. And Solomon said, Thou hast shewed unto thy servant David my father great mercy, according as he walked before thee in truth, and in righteousness, and in uprightness of heart with thee; and thou hast kept for him this great kindness, that thou hast given him a son to sit on his throne, as it is this day. And now, O LORD my God, thou hast made thy servant king instead of David, my father: and I am but a little child: I know not how to go out or come in. And thy servant is in the midst of thy people which thou hast chosen, a great people, that cannot be numbered nor counted for multitude. Give therefore thy servant an understanding heart to judge thy people that I may discern between good and bad: for who is able to judge this thy so great a people? And the speech pleased the Lord, that Solomon had asked this thing. And God said unto him, Because thou hast asked this thing, and hast not asked for thyself long life; neither hast asked riches for thyself, nor hast asked the life of thine enemies; but hast asked for thyself understanding to discern judgment; Behold, I have done according to thy words: lo, I have given thee a wise and an understanding heart; so that there was none like thee before thee, neither after thee shall any arise like unto thee. And I have also given thee that which thou hast not asked, both riches, and honor: so that there shall not be any among the kings like unto thee all thy days. And if thou wilt walk in my ways, to keep my statutes and my commandments, as thy father David did walk, then I will lengthen thy days." (1 Kings 3:5-14)

(Solomon) "For it came to pass, when Solomon was old, that his wives turned away his heart after other gods: and his heart was not perfect with the LORD his God, as was the heart of David his father." (1 Kings 11:4)

All these scriptures I have found that having problems with a spouse is not an uncommon thing. If I am to get involved with another relationship, God must be first in both our lives. God first above all else!

Sarah

Who can find a virtuous woman? For her price is far above rubies. The heart of her husband doth safely trust in her so that he shall have no need of spoil. She will do him good and not evil all the days of her life.

(Proverbs 31:10-12)

I joined a so-called Christian online dating service. Found what most of these ladies were looking for was not a godly man. But, a source of income or entertainment, now I was a little discouraged. But, a couple of months later, I made arrangement to meet one for a dinner date. This confirmed my suspicion. When we met, her Bio and picture didn't really match. I believe she was really disappointed with me. The picture she had posted was ten years old, and she was looking for a guy who rode motorcycles, drank beer and watched football. Well, this disqualified me right away, I don't drink, don't have a motorcycle or watch football.

She found me boring because my conversation was directed toward the Word of God. I asked where she was fellowshipping and how long she had been serving the Lord. She was not looking for a believer, and the so-called date ended.

I paid for the bill, and she was upset because I didn't share the cost. She said why are you paying for both of us, is it because I am a lady. I said, "No, it's because I am a gentleman and a believer in God." She stomped off, and I never heard from her again.

When I returned home, I looked up her bio again thinking I might have missed something. Well, her bio wasn't anything like her, it was just a sham. Then I saw I had a message in my inbox. And the message sent me to a profile with no picture. The message went something like this:

Subject: Seeking a godly man who serves the Lord.

A Korean Christian lady, I have read you're Bio and that you have been a missionary.

You're a 99% match for me.

If you are interested, please email me.

Sarah

I returned the email, and I wrote: "God must be first!" We communicated through email for several months, then we exchanged phone numbers, and we would talk to one another for hours and later till the batteries run down on our cell phones. This went on for some time. We shared our lives with one another and the problems we were faced with.

We both have a lot of baggage to deal with. She amazed me how she coped with the problems she was faced with. She was helping her grandmother, her father. Also, she visited her mother who was now in Hospice. She babysat her grandchildren so her daughter could find work and her ex-husband had been living in his car. He was now staying in the living room until he could get a job. He first came to visit her daughter and the grandchildren and now hangs around.

She fixes meals for the ex-husband, daughter, and grandchildren. Then she would go and help her grandmother, visit her dad and help him out and visit her mom while she was in hospice. She seemed to be very selfless with a faithful servant's heart.

Her health was taking its toll. She had been serving in the church for over twenty some years and was active in the Korean church she attended. She sang in the choir while growing up in Korea. Most of her family is active in ministry in the church they attend. She was living in California and had spent most of her twenty years in America in Korean Town in LA and with the Korean community. I spoke some Korean, and she thought that was good. Her English was far better than my Korean.

And for me, I spent time with my dad, my youngest brother, and his family. I was giving my nieces transportation to their workplace dropping them off and picking them up after their shifts.

I was on unemployment and seeking work, this took a lot of my time sending out resumes' and going place to place hoping to get an interview for employment. No one would say it but, being fifty-five years old work was hard to find. I was not what they were looking for. I was living in an 18 foot RV in a trailer park in Fruitland Idaho. I was active in the church I attended and was the chaplain for the VFW.

Sarah was trying to make arrangements to move to Northern California and be with some friends there. She asked if I would be willing to help her move from Southern California to Northern California when the time comes for her to move.

Later on, her move to Northern California fell through she asked me to find a place near where I live. And send her the information so she could make arrangements to pay for a place so she can move closer to me.

Looking for work, sending out resumes' and filling out applications took up a lot of my time. I visited my dad almost every day and told him about Sarah. I spent some time taking pictures and getting information on homes and apartments in the local area and sent them to Sarah. Sarah seemed excited about the idea of moving to Idaho so we can live close to one another.

Couple months later, Sarah sent me some money to come down and help her move to Idaho. When I arrived in California, she had me meet her at her grandmother's. Her grandmother and Sarah had made a wonderful Korean dinner for me, and I spent time visiting with both of them.

I spent the night at her grandmother's living room, and the next day Sarah and I went to her apartment and started to pack up Sarah's' stuff and put it in my RV. Before leaving Sarah's grandmother told me in Korean to take good care of Sarah and put Sarah's hand in mine and says you take good care of her and for her to care for me.

After returning to Fruitland Idaho Sarah and I unloaded the RV into a storage area in Payette. Sarah had followed me to Idaho in her car, and I parked the RV, and we went out looking for a place for her to stay.

Till then she decided it would probably be best if she stayed in the RV with me. That arrangement only lasted for a month, and later we got married. We got married on the first snow October 29, 2009.

We did find a little house in Weiser Idaho it seemed like the perfect small home. We paid for the rent in advance, and they were still fixing it up. The landlord and her mother seem to be very kind; Later Sarah becomes excellent friends with them. We moved in a week after being married and started a home Bible study.

Later we formed of Christian home Fellowship and had services teaching through the Bible. I became very involved with the community and the other pastors in the area. At community projects And I helped at the Community Food Bank. Together Sarah and I did home visitations and ministered to as many people as we could in the area.

Sarah held a birthday party for me and invited my family. She made a lot of traditional Korean food special for me, and most of the family enjoyed the Korean diet. We invited friends and family for Thanksgiving, and we had 17 people join us.

Our Bible studies in the middle of the week and on the weekend averaged about 10 to 12 people.

Sarah's health was going downhill, and I did not realize that the medications she had were not working correctly. She ended up in the hospital several times. During this trying time, we managed. Then we had been in our home for about 10 months, and Sarah and I decided to take a weekend and go on a road trip. I got very sick during a road trip in my stomach, and liver pains come back to where I was in excruciating pain. Sarah managed to get me back to Weiser and take me to the hospital.

While in the hospital they gave me something for the pain in the cramps but it didn't help much. They wanted me to relax to take a CT and see what the problem may be. I insisted that they use contrast to find the problem. After reviewing the CT results, they found something that wasn't right and said that it was beyond their scope to be able to deal with this problem.

The doctor said he had no idea what it was that he saw on the CT, but it appeared to be the problem. So the doctor made arrangements for me to be transported by an ambulance to Boise Veterans Administration hospital.

It was at the hospital in Boise that the doctors who were looking over me suspected a carcinoid tumor behind my small intestines. They schedule me for a biopsy where cancer had metastasized to my liver. The first time they tried I went into a spasm in pain was excruciating. They asked me if I'd be willing to go through the processed again. I say go ahead I'm here we need find out what the problem is. After the doctors took the biopsy in the operating room they identified that it was a carcinoid tumor and I had cancer.

Sarah was due for an MRI in Boise later on, and it confirmed that she had a cyst in her brain and that she would have to have follow-up MRIs every five years to see if it's growing. As long as it doesn't become any more significant in size, she will be out of danger but if it does increase it could be fatal.

We bought another RV and moved out of the house and to New Plymouth, Idaho to move to my cousin's house and to save money we would hook up the RV there. The idea was that is closer to Boise VA so I could get treatments for my cancer and Sarah could get treatments and medication for her medical condition. Later we moved to Emmet and rented an RV spot there because it was even closer to our Doctors. We didn't have to drive so far and we spent the winter there.

So during our first year, we both found out that we had severe medical conditions. On top of all the baggage that we were bringing from our previous relationships; we are now living in a small RV but at sometimes seem to become a small battleground. But we always managed to kiss and make up and work together through the problems because God is our strength. Our most significant challenges were inside each of us. But, we had God to help us to be able to work those things out.

As time passed, Sarah found an opportunity to work as a translator for an acupuncturist. He was going to move his office to northern Idaho and wanted Sarah and I to help. Story short we moved to Post Falls Idaho where the acupuncturists set up his office. Sarah's health issues made it difficult for her to spend long periods of time helping the acupuncturist.

Sarah's daughter came to stay with Sarah and pulls Falls Idaho where the acupuncturists helped us get an apartment. I stayed in the RV in New Plymouth Idaho getting treatments for my cancer and in Boise.

I began to make arrangements to move my medical treatment to Spokane Washington from Boise Idaho. Once I had made the arrangements, then I would also move to the apartment in Post Falls Idaho.

It took some time to get everything transferred from Boise to Spokane, but once it was accomplished, I was reunited with Sarah. Sarah and her daughter had unpacked most everything that we had moved into the apartment.

Over the years Sarah and I have had many setbacks that we always work them out. I believe it because we both put our trust in the Lord. We've learned to put our differences aside to live life together serving a holy and awesome God whom we both trust and put first. Sarah and I have served together in the area at several different churches and places of fellowship trying to find a true friendship that teaches from the whole of God's Scriptures. It's going on four years now that we have been attending Chavurat HaMashiach, a messianic congregation.

When we first attended services we saw that it was true fellowship and all the people there loved and cared and prayed for one another. But the most important thing is that God is first in everything. So now I could share the wonderful blessing of my journey started in darkness, and then later led me to the cross as a believer, then to the star; which is the Star of David.

Now that Sarah and I have placed God first in everything even through all the trials and troubles. So there is joy knowing that God is in control. I believe through it all God has sent me a beautiful lady to live with me on this journey of life. A now we have found a place of fellowship which observes Gods' Instructions (Torah). We will be able to continue this journey of life serving a Mighty and Wonderful God who has seen us through good times and bad.

Lesson Learned:

1. Gods Way is the only way!

2. God is the same today and never changes.

3. We need to follow the whole instruction that God has given us.

4. Life everlasting only comes from the true and living God. Yeshua is the only One Way to Salvation.

Application:

"That thou mightest fear the LORD thy God, to keep all his statutes and his commandments, which I command thee, thou, and thy son, and thy son's son, all the days of thy life; and that thy days may be prolonged." (Deuteronomy 6:2)

"Jesus (Yeshua) saith unto him, I am the way, the truth, and the life: no man cometh unto the Father, but by me. If ye had known me, ye should have known my Father also: and from henceforth ye know him, and have seen him." (John 14:6-7)

"God is faithful, by whom ye were called unto the fellowship of his Son Jesus Christ our Lord (Yeshua the Messiah our Master)." (1 Corinthians 1:9)"

Our journey together is not over, but together one (Echad) in God's service we are on our way to out desired destination, to be with our God forever and ever.

The journey has taken me from the darkness; God removed the chains of slavery of sin with the wisdom, knowledge and understanding that God is my strength. Led me to the Cross to lay down my burdens of life and empowered me with His Holy Spirit (Born-Again). Then opened my eyes to the truth of God's Instructions and teaching so I can live life abundantly. Leaving the hurts, troubles behind and giving me a forgiving heart that has led me to the Star of David – My Lord and God Yeshua.

"I Yeshua have sent mine angel to testify unto you these things in the churches. I am the root and the offspring of David, and the bright and morning star." (Revelation 22:16)

Yeshua said *"Wherefore I say unto thee, her sins, which are many, are forgiven; for she loved much: but to who little is forgiven, the same loveth little."* (Luke 7:47)

The Vision Series:

The Vision Assignment

The Vision Journey

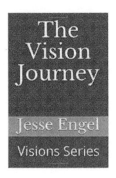

Living the Journey

To be released early

2020

Made in the USA
Lexington, KY
10 November 2019